Dornröschen und andere Kindermärchen

Sleeping Beauty and other Grimm Fairy Tales

[Bilingual Edition]

German – English

by Jacob and Wilhelm Grimm

Translated by Möwenstein

© **2025 Möwenstein Books**
All rights reserved.

ISBN: 979-8-89513-205-0

Original text: *Sleeping Beauty and other Grimm Fairy Tales* (1812) by
Jacob Grimm (1785-1863) and Wilhelm Grimm (1786-1859)

This bilingual edition—including translation, editorial revisions,
formatting, and supplementary content—is produced and edited by
Mowenstein Books LLC, with the original text faithfully reproduced
from public-domain sources.

Cover Art: Inspired by *Hustling Sunlight* by Matthew Bakkom
(www.hustlingsunlight.xyz)

Möwenstein Books™ is a trademark of and imprint published by
Mowenstein Books LLC.

For permissions or inquiries:

Website: mowenstein.com
Email: copyright@mowenstein.com

Mowenstein Books LLC
DE, USA

Contents

Die drei Männlein im Walde

The Three Little Men in the Forest

1.1 Es war einmal ein Mann, dem starb seine Frau, und eine Frau, der starb ihr Mann:

Once upon a time there was a man whose wife died, and a woman whose husband died:

1.2 und der Mann hatte eine Tochter,

and the man had a daughter,

1.3 und die Frau hatte auch eine Tochter.

and the woman also had a daughter.

1.4 Die Mädchen waren miteinander bekannt und gingen zusammen spazieren und kamen hernach zu der Frau ins Haus.

The girls were acquainted with each other and went for a walk together and afterwards came to the woman's house.

1.5 Da sprach sie zu des Mannes Tochter:

Then she said to the man's daughter,

»Hör, sag deinem Vater, ich wollt ihn heiraten, dann sollst du jeden Morgen dich in Milch waschen und Wein trinken, meine Tochter aber soll sich in Wasser waschen und Wasser trinken.«

"Listen, tell your father that I want to marry him, then you should wash yourself in milk and drink wine every morning, but my daughter should wash herself in water and drink water."

1.6

Das Mädchen ging nach Hause und erzählte seinem Vater, was die Frau gesagt hatte.

The girl went home and told her father what the woman had said.

1.7

Der Mann sprach: »Was soll ich thun?

The man said, "What shall I do?

1.8

das Heiraten ist eine Freude und ist auch eine Qual.«

Marriage is a joy and also a torment."

1.9

Endlich, weil er keinen Entschluß fassen konnte, zog er seinen Stiefel aus und sagte:

At last, because he could not make up his mind, he took off his boot and said,

1.10

»Nimm diesen Stiefel, der hat in der Sohle ein Loch, geh damit auf den Boden, häng ihn an den großen Nagel und gieß dann Wasser hinein.

"Take this boot, it has a hole in the sole, put it on the ground, hang it on the big nail and then pour water into it.

1.11

Hält er das Wasser, so will ich wieder eine Frau nehmen, läuft's aber durch, so will ich nicht.«

If it holds the water, I will take another wife, but if it leaks, I will not."

1.12

2

1.13 Das Mädchen that wie ihm geheißen war: aber das Wasser zog das Loch zusammen und der Stiefel ward voll bis obenhin.

The girl did as she was told, but the water drew the hole together and the boot became full to the top.

1.14 Es verkündete seinem Vater wie's ausgefallen war.

She told her father how it had turned out.

1.15 Da stieg er selbst hinauf, und als er sah, daß es seine Richtigkeit hatte, ging er zu der Witwe und freite sie, und die Hochzeit ward gehalten.

Then he went up himself, and when he saw that it was right, he went to the widow and set her free, and the wedding was held.

2.1 Am anderen Morgen, als die beiden Mädchen sich aufmachten, da stand vor des Mannes Tochter Milch zum Waschen und Wein zum Trinken, vor der Frau Tochter aber stand Wasser zum Waschen und Wasser zum Trinken.

The next morning, when the two girls set out, there was milk for washing and wine for drinking in front of the man's daughter, but there was water for washing and water for drinking in front of the woman's daughter.

2.2 Am zweiten Morgen stand Wasser zum Waschen und Wasser zum Trinken so gut vor des Mannes Tochter als vor der Frau Tochter.

On the second morning, water for washing and water for drinking stood before the man's daughter as well as before the woman's daughter.

Und am dritten Morgen stand Wasser zum Waschen und Wasser zum Trinken vor des Mannes Tochter, und Milch zum Waschen und Wein zum Trinken vor der Frau Tochter, und dabei blieb's. 2.3

And on the third morning there was water for washing and water for drinking before the man's daughter, and milk for washing and wine for drinking before the woman's daughter, and so it remained.

Die Frau ward ihrer Stieftochter spinnefeind und wußte nicht wie sie es ihr von einem Tag zum andern schlimmer machen sollte. 2.4

The woman became very hostile to her stepdaughter and did not know how to make it worse for her from one day to the next.

Auch war sie neidisch, weil ihre Stieftochter schön und lieblich war, ihre rechte Tochter aber häßlich und widerlich. 2.5

She was also envious because her stepdaughter was beautiful and lovely, but her real daughter was ugly and disgusting.

Einmal im Winter, als es steinhart gefroren hatte und Berg und Thal vollgeschneit lag, machte die Frau ein Kleid von Papier, rief das Mädchen und sprach, 3.1

Once in winter, when it was freezing hard and the mountains and valleys were covered with snow, the woman made a paper dress, called the girl and said,

»Da zieh das Kleid an, 3.2

"Put on the dress,

geh hinaus in den Wald und hol mir ein Körbchen voll Erdbeeren; 3.3

go out into the forest and fetch me a basket of strawberries;

4

3.4 ich habe Verlangen danach.«
I have a craving for them."

3.5 »Du lieber Gott.« sagte das Mädchen,
"Dear God." said the girl,

3.6 »im Winter wachsen ja keine Erdbeeren, die Erde ist
gefroren, und der Schnee hat auch alles zugedeckt.
"no strawberries grow in winter, the ground is frozen and
the snow has covered everything.

3.7 Und warum soll ich in dem Papierkleide gehen?
And why should I go in this paper dress?

3.8 Es ist draußen so kalt, daß einem der Atem friert;
It is so cold outside that one's breath freezes;

3.9 da weht ja der Wind hindurch und die Dornen reißen
mir's vom Leib.«
the wind blows through it and the thorns tear it off my
body."

3.10 »Willst du mir noch widersprechen?« sagte die
Stiefmutter,
"Will you contradict me?" said the stepmother,

3.11 »mach, daß du fortkommst, und laß dich nicht eher
wieder sehen, als bis du das Körbchen voll Erdbeeren
hast.«
"go away, and don't let me see you again till you have the
basket full of strawberries."

3.12 Dann gab sie ihm noch ein Stückchen hartes Brot und
sprach,
Then she gave him another piece of hard bread, and said,

»Davon kannst du den Tag über essen.« und dachte, 3.13
"You can eat it all day long." and thought,

»draußen wird's erfrieren und verhungern und mir 3.14
nimmermehr wieder vor die Augen kommen.«
"Outside it will freeze and starve, and never come before
my eyes again."

Nun war das Mädchen gehorsam, 4.1
Now the girl was obedient,

that das Papierkleid an und ging mit dem Körbchen 4.2
hinaus.
put on the paper dress and went out with the basket.

Da war nichts als Schnee die Weite und Breite, 4.3
There was nothing but snow for miles and miles,

und war kein grünes Hälmchen zu merken. 4.4
and not a little green stalk to be seen.

Als es in den Wald kam, sah es ein kleines Häuschen, 4.5
daraus guckten drei kleine Haulemännerchen.
When she came into the wood, she saw a little house, and
from it peeped three little haymen.

Es wünschte ihnen die Tageszeit und klopfte 4.6
bescheidentlich an die Thür.
He wished them the time of day and knocked modestly at
the door.

Sie riefen herein und es trat in die Stube und setzte 4.7
sich auf die Bank am Ofen,
They called her in and she came into the parlor and sat
down on the bench by the stove,

4.8 da wollte es sich wärmen und sein Frühstück essen.
where she wanted to warm herself and eat her breakfast.

4.9 Die Haulemännerchen sprachen: »Gieb uns auch etwas davon.«
The little haymen said, "Give us some of that too."

4.10 »Gern.« sprach es,
"Gladly." he said,

4.11 teilte sein Stückchen Brot entzwei und gab ihnen die Hälfte.
cut his piece of bread in two and gave them half.

4.12 Sie fragten:
They asked:

4.13 »Was willst du zur Winterszeit in deinem dünnen Kleidchen hier im Wald.«
"What are you doing here in the forest in your thin little dress in winter."

4.14 »Ach.« antwortete es.
"Oh." she replied.

4.15 »ich soll ein Körbchen voll Erdbeeren suchen und darf nicht eher nach Hause kommen, als bis ich es mitbringe.«
"I have to look for a basket of strawberries and must not come home until I bring them back."

4.16 Als es sein Brot gegessen hatte, gaben sie ihm einen Besen und sprachen,
When he had eaten his bread, they gave him a broom and said,

4.17 »Kehre damit an der Hinterthür den Schnee weg.«
"Sweep away the snow at the back door with it."

Wie es aber draußen war, sprachen die drei
Männerchen unter einander:
4.18

But when he was outside, the three little men said to each
other,

»Was sollen wir ihm schenken, weil es so artig und
gut ist und sein Brot mit uns geteilt hat?«
4.19

"What shall we give him because he is so good and kind and
has shared his bread with us?"

Da sagte der erste,
4.20

The first said,

»Ich schenk ihm, daß es jeden Tag schöner wird.«
4.21

"I'll give him a present that will make him more beautiful
every day."

Der zweite sprach:
4.22

The second said,

»Ich schenk ihm, daß Goldstücke ihm aus dem Mund
fallen, so oft es ein Wort spricht.«
4.23

"I will give him gold pieces to fall out of his mouth as often
as he speaks a word."

Der dritte sprach:
4.24

The third said,

»Ich schenk ihm, daß ein König kommt und es zu
seiner Gemahlin nimmt.«
4.25

"I'll give it a king to come and take it as his wife."

5.1 Das Mädchen aber that wie die Haulemännerchen gesagt hatten, kehrte mit dem Besen den Schnee hinter dem kleinen Hause weg, und was glaubt ihr wohl, daß es gefunden hat?

But the girl did as the little haymen had said, swept away the snow behind the little house with the broom, and what do you think she found?

5.2 Lauter reife Erdbeeren, die ganz dunkelrot aus dem Schnee hervorkamen.

All ripe strawberries, dark red, coming out of the snow.

5.3 Da raffte es in seiner Freude sein Körbchen voll, dankte den kleinen Männern, gab jedem die Hand und lief nach Haus, und wollte der Stiefmutter das Verlangte bringen.

Then, in her joy, she filled her basket, thanked the little men, shook hands with each of them, and ran home to bring her stepmother what she had asked for.

5.4 Wie es eintrat und »guten Abend« sagte,

As he entered and said "Good evening",

5.5 fiel ihm gleich ein Goldstück aus dem Mund.

a piece of gold fell out of his mouth.

5.6 Darauf erzählte es, was ihm im Walde begegnet war, aber bei jedem Worte, das es sprach, fielen ihm die Goldstücke aus dem Mund, sodaß bald die ganze Stube damit bedeckt ward.

Then he told what he had met in the forest, but with every word he spoke, the gold pieces fell out of his mouth, so that soon the whole parlor was covered with them.

5.7 »Nun sehe einer den Übermut.« rief die Stiefschwester,

"Now, look at the mischief." exclaimed the stepsister,

»das Geld so hinzuwerfen.« 5.8
"to throw the money away like that."

aber heimlich war sie neidisch darüber und wollte 5.9
auch hinaus in den Wald und Erdbeeren suchen.
But secretly she was envious of it, and wanted to go out into
the forest and look for strawberries.

Die Mutter aber sprach: 5.10
But her mother said,

»Nein, mein liebes Töchterchen, es ist zu kalt, du 5.11
könntest mir erfrieren.«
"No, my dear little daughter, it's too cold, you could freeze
to death."

Weil sie ihr aber keine Ruhe lieh, gab sie endlich 5.12
nach, nähte ihm einen prächtigen Pelzrock, den
es anziehen mußte, und gab ihm Butterbrot und
Kuchen mit auf den Weg.
But because she wouldn't let her rest, she finally gave in,
sewed him a beautiful fur coat, which he had to wear, and
gave him sandwiches and cake to take with him.

Das Mädchen ging in den Wald und gerade auf das 6.1
kleine Häuschen zu.
The girl walked into the forest and straight towards the
little house.

Die drei kleinen Haulemänner guckten wieder, 6.2
aber es grüßte sie nicht, und ohne sich nach ihnen
umzusehen und ohne sie zu grüßen, stolperte es in
die Stube hinein, setzte sich an den Ofen und fing an
sein Butterbrot und seinen Kuchen zu essen.
The three little haymen looked again, but she did not greet
them, and without looking around for them and without
greeting them, she stumbled into the living room, sat down
by the stove and began to eat her sandwich and cake.

6.3 »Gieb uns etwas davon.« riefen die Kleinen,
"Give us some of that." cried the little ones,

6.4 aber es antwortete: »Es schickt mir selber nicht,
but he replied: "I don't feel like it myself,

6.5 wie kann ich anderen noch davon abgeben?«
how can I give it to others?"

6.6 Als es nun fertig war mit dem Essen, sprachen sie,
When he had finished eating, they said,

6.7 »Da hast du einen Besen,
"Here's a broom,

6.8 kehr uns draußen vor der Hinterthür rein.«
sweep us outside the back door."

6.9 »Ei, kehrt euch selber.« antwortete es,
"Oh, sweep yourselves." she answered,

6.10 »ich bin eure Magd nicht.«
"I am not your maid."

6.11 Wie es sah, daß sie ihm nichts schenken wollten, ging es zur Thür hinaus.
When he saw that they would give him nothing, he went out of the door.

6.12 Da sprachen die kleinen Männer untereinander:
Then the little men said to each other,

6.13 »Was sollen wir ihm schenken, weil es so unartig ist und ein böses, neidisches Herz hat, das niemand etwas gönnt?«
"What shall we give him, because he is so naughty, and has a wicked, envious heart, which does not favor anyone?"

Der erste sprach,

6.14

The first said,

»Ich schenk ihm, daß es jeden Tag häßlicher wird.«

6.15

"I'll give him a present that will make him uglier every day."

Der zweite sprach:

6.16

The second said,

»Ich schenk ihm, daß ihm bei jedem Wort, das es spricht, eine Kröte aus dem Mund springt.«

6.17

"I'll give him a toad jumping out of his mouth every time he speaks."

Der dritte sprach,

6.18

The third said,

»Ich schenk ihm, daß es eines unglücklichen Todes stirbt.«

6.19

"I'll give him an unhappy death."

Das Mädchen suchte draußen nach Erdbeeren, als es aber keine fand, ging es verdrießlich nach Hause.

6.20

The girl went out to look for strawberries, but when she found none, she went home in a bad mood.

Und wie es den Mund aufthat und seiner Mutter erzählen wollte, was ihm im Walde begegnet war, da sprang ihm bei jedem Wort eine Kröte aus dem Mund, sodaß alle einen Abscheu vor ihm bekamen.

6.21

And when she opened her mouth to tell her mother what she had met with in the forest, a toad jumped out of her mouth at every word, so that everybody was disgusted with her.

7.1 Nun ärgerte sich die Stiefmutter noch viel mehr und dachte nur darauf, wie sie der Tochter des Mannes alles Herzeleid anthun wollte, deren Schönheit doch alle Tage größer ward.

Now the stepmother was even more annoyed and only thought about how she wanted to do all the heartache to the man's daughter, whose beauty was growing every day.

7.2 Endlich nahm sie einen Kessel, setzte ihn zum Feuer und sott Garn darin.

At last she took a kettle, put it to the fire, and boiled yarn in it.

7.3 Als es gesotten war, hing sie es dem armen Mädchen auf die Schulter und gab ihm eine Axt dazu, damit sollte es auf den gefrorenen Fluß gehen, ein Eisloch hauen und das Garn schlittern.

When it was boiled, she hung it on the poor girl's shoulder, and gave her an axe, with which she was to go to the frozen river, hew a hole in the ice, and cut the yarn.

7.4 Es war gehorsam, ging hin und hackte ein Loch in das Eis, und als es mitten im Hacken war, kam ein prächtiger Wagen hergefahren, worin der König saß.

She was obedient, went and chopped a hole in the ice, and when she was in the middle of chopping, a splendid carriage came driving up, in which the King was sitting.

7.5 Der Wagen hielt still und der König fragte: »Mein Kind,

The carriage stopped and the king asked, "My child,

7.6 wer bist du und was machst du da?«

who are you and what are you doing?"

7.7 »Ich bin ein armes Mädchen und schlittere Garn.«

"I am a poor girl and I am slithering yarn."

Da fühlte der König Mitleid und als er sah wie es
sogar schön war, 7.8

The king felt sorry for her and when he saw how beautiful
she was,

sprach er: »Willst du mit mir fahren?« 7.9

he said: "Will you ride with me?"

»Ach ja, von Herzen gern.« 7.10

"Oh, yes, with all my heart."

antwortete es, denn es war froh, daß es der Mutter
und Schwester aus den Augen kommen sollte. 7.11

she answered, for she was glad to get out of her mother's
and sister's sight.

Also stieg es in den Wagen und fuhr mit dem König
fort, und als sie auf sein Schloß gekommen waren,
ward die Hochzeit mit großer Pracht gefeiert, wie
es die kleinen Männlein dem Mädchen geschenkt
hatten. 8.1

So she got into the carriage and went away with the King,
and when they had come to his castle, the wedding was
celebrated with great splendor, just as the little men had
given the girl.

Über ein Jahr gebar die junge Königin einen Sohn,
und als die Stiefmutter von dem großen Glücke
gehört hatte, so kam sie mit ihrer Tochter in das
Schloß und that, als wollte sie einen Besuch machen. 8.2

About a year later the young queen gave birth to a son, and
when the stepmother had heard of the great happiness, she
came to the castle with her daughter, and pretended to pay
a visit.

8.3 Als aber der König einmal hinausgegangen und sonst niemand zugegen war, packte das böse Weib die Königin am Kopf, und ihre Tochter packte sie an den Füßen, hoben sie aus dem Bett und warfen sie zum Fenster hinaus in den vorbeifließenden Strom.

But when the King had gone out, and no one else was present, the wicked woman seized the Queen by the head, and her daughter seized her by the feet, lifted her out of bed, and threw her out of the window into the stream that was flowing by.

8.4 Darauf legte sich ihre häßliche Tochter ins Bett und die Alte deckte sie zu bis über den Kopf.

Then her ugly daughter lay down in bed and the old woman covered her up over her head.

8.5 Als der König wieder zurückkam und mit seiner Frau sprechen wollte, rief die Alte:

When the king came back and wanted to speak to his wife, the old woman called out,

8.6 »Still, still, jetzt geht das nicht, sie liegt in starkem Schweiß, Ihr müßt sie heute ruhen lassen.«

"Hush, hush, it won't do now, she is in a heavy sweat, you must let her rest today."

8.7 Der König dachte nichts Böses dabei und kam erst den anderen Morgen wieder, und wie er mit seiner Frau sprach, und sie ihm Antwort gab, sprang bei jedem Wort eine Kröte hervor, während sonst ein Goldstück herausgefallen war.

The King thought no harm of it, and did not return till the next morning, and as he spoke to his wife, and she answered him, a toad sprang out at every word, while otherwise a piece of gold had fallen out.

Da fragte er, was das wäre, aber die Alte sprach, das hätte sie von dem starken Schweiß gekriegt, und würde sich schon wieder verlieren. 8.8

Then he asked what it was, but the old woman said she had got it from the heavy sweat, and would lose it again.

In der Nacht aber sah der Küchenjunge wie eine Ente durch die Gosse geschwommen kam, die sprach: 9.1

In the night, however, the kitchen boy saw a duck come swimming through the gutter and it spoke:

»König, was machst du? | "King, what are you doing?

schläfst du oder wachst du?« | Are you asleep or awake?"

Und als er keine Antwort gab, sprach sie: 11.1

And when he gave no answer, she spoke:

»Was machen meine Gäste?« 12.1

"What are my guests doing?"

Da antwortete der Küchenjunge: 13.1

Then the kitchen boy replied:

»Sie schlafen feste!« 14.1

"You're fast asleep!"

Fragte sie weiter: 15.1

She asked further:

16.1 »Was macht mein Kindelein?«
"What is my little child doing?"

17.1 Antwortete er:
He replied:

18.1 »Es schläft in der Wiege fein.«
"It sleeps well in the cradle."

19.1 Da ging sie in der Königin Gestalt hinauf, gab ihm zu trinken, schüttelte ihm sein Bettchen, deckte es zu und schwamm als Ente wieder durch die Gosse fort.
Then she went up in the queen's shape, gave him a drink, shook his little bed, covered it up, and swam away again through the gutter as a duck.

19.2 So kam sie zwei Nächte, in der dritten sprach sie zu dem Küchenjungen:
Thus she came two nights, and on the third she said to the scullion,

19.3 »Geh und sage dem König, daß er sein Schwert nimmt und auf der Schwelle dreimal über mir schwingt.«
"Go and tell the king to take his sword and swing it three times over me on the threshold."

19.4 Da lief der Küchenjunge und sagte es dem König, der kam mit seinem Schwert und schwang es dreimal über dem Geist, und beim dritten Mal stand seine Gemahlin vor ihm, frisch, lebendig und gesund, wie sie vorher gewesen war.
So the scullion ran and told the King, who came with his sword and swung it three times over the ghost, and the third time his wife stood before him, fresh, alive and well, as she had been before.

Nun war der König in großer Freude, er hielt aber die Königin in einer Kammer verborgen bis auf den Sonntag, wo das Kind getauft werden sollte. 20.1

Now the king was in great joy, but he kept the queen hidden in a chamber until the Sunday when the child was to be baptized.

Und als es getauft war, sprach er: 20.2

And when it was baptized, he said,

»Was gehört einem Menschen, der den andern aus dem Bett trägt und ins Wasser wirft?« 20.3

"What belongs to a man who carries another out of bed and throws him into the water?"

»Nichts Besseres.« antwortete die Alte, 20.4

"Nothing better." answered the old woman,

»als daß man den Bösewicht in ein Faß steckt, das mit Nägeln ausgeschlagen ist, und den Berg hinab ins Wasser rollt.« 20.5

"than to put the wicked man into a barrel that is nailed with nails, and roll him down the hill into the water."

Da sagte der König: »Du hast dein Urteil gesprochen.« 20.6

Then the king said, "You have pronounced your judgment."

ließ ein solches Faß holen und die Alte mit ihrer Tochter hineinstecken, dann ward der Boden zugehämmert und das Faß bergab gekollert, bis es in den Fluß rollte. 20.7

The king had such a barrel fetched and the old woman and her daughter put into it, then the bottom was hammered down and the barrel rolled downhill until it rolled into the river.

Die drei Spinnerinnen

The Three Spinners

1.1 Es war ein Mädchen faul und wollte nicht spinnen, und die Mutter mochte sagen was sie wollte, sie konnte es nicht dazu bringen.

A girl was lazy and did not want to spin, and her mother could say what she liked, she could not make her do it.

1.2 Endlich übernahm die Mutter einmal Zorn und Ungeduld, daß sie ihm Schläge gab, worüber es laut zu weinen anfing.

At last her mother's anger and impatience got the better of her, and she gave her a beating, at which she began to cry aloud.

1.3 Nun fuhr gerade die Königin vorbei, und als sie das Weinen hörte, ließ sie anhalten, trat in das Haus und fragte die Mutter, warum sie ihre Tochter schlüge, daß man draußen auf der Straße das Schreien hörte.

Just then the Queen drove by, and when she heard the crying, she stopped, entered the house, and asked the mother why she was beating her daughter so that the crying could be heard in the street outside.

Da schämte sich die Frau, daß sie die Faulheit ihrer Tochter offenbaren sollte und sprach:

1.4

Then the woman was ashamed that she should reveal her daughter's laziness, and said,

»Ich kann sie nicht vom Spinnen abbringen, sie will immer und ewig spinnen, und ich bin arm und kann den Flachs nicht herbeischaffen.«

1.5

"I cannot make her stop spinning, she wants to spin for ever and ever, and I am poor and cannot get the flax."

Da antwortete die Königin,

1.6

Then the queen replied,

»Ich höre nichts lieber als spinnen,

1.7

"I like nothing better than to hear spinning,

und bin nicht vergnügter als wenn die Räder schnurren:

1.8

and I am not happier than when the wheels are whirring:

gebt mir Eure Tochter mit ins Schloß, ich habe Flachs genug, da soll sie spinnen so viel sie Lust hat.«

1.9

give your daughter to me in the castle, I have enough flax, and she shall spin as much as she likes."

Die Mutter war's von Herzen gern zufrieden und die Königin nahm das Mädchen mit.

1.10

The mother was heartily pleased, and the queen took the girl with her.

Als sie ins Schloß gekommen waren, führte sie es hinauf zu drei Kammern, die lagen von unten bis oben voll vom schönsten Flachs.

1.11

When they had come into the castle, she led her up to three chambers, which were full of the most beautiful flax from bottom to top.

1.12 »Nun spinn mir diesen Flachs.« sprach sie,

"Now spin this flax for me." she said,

1.13 »und wenn du es fertig bringst,

"and if you can do it,

1.14 so sollst du meinen ältesten Sohn zum Gemahl haben;

you shall have my eldest son for your husband;

1.15 bist du gleich arm, so acht ich nicht darauf, dein unverdrossener Fleiß ist Ausstattung genug.«

if you are poor, I will not care, your undaunted diligence is endowment enough."

1.16 Das Mädchen erschrak innerlich, denn es konnte den Flachs nicht spinnen, und wär's dreihundert Jahre alt geworden, und hätte jeden Tag vom Morgen bis Abend dabei gesessen.

The girl was inwardly frightened, for she could not spin flax, and would have been three hundred years old, and would have sat at it every day from morning till night.

1.17 Als es nun allein war, fing es an zu weinen und saß so drei Tage ohne die Hand zu rühren.

When she was alone, she began to weep, and sat thus for three days without lifting a hand.

1.18 Am dritten Tage kam die Königin und als sie sah, daß noch nichts gesponnen war, verwunderte sie sich, aber das Mädchen entschuldigte sich damit, daß es vor großer Betrübnis über die Entfernung aus seiner Mutter Hause noch nicht hätte anfangen können.

On the third day the Queen came, and when she saw that nothing had yet been spun, she was astonished, but the girl excused herself by saying that she had not yet been able to begin because of her great sorrow at being away from her mother's house.

Das ließ sich die Königin gefallen, sagte aber beim
Weggehen,
1.19

The queen put up with this, but said as she went away,

»Morgen mußt du mir anfangen zu arbeiten.«
1.20

"Tomorrow you must begin to work for me."

Als das Mädchen wieder allein war, wußte es sich
nicht mehr zu raten und zu helfen, und trat in seiner
Betrübnis vor das Fenster.
2.1

When the girl was alone again, she did not know what to do
or how to help herself, and in her sorrow stepped outside
the window.

Da sah es drei Weiber herkommen, davon hatte die
erste einen breiten Platschfuß, die zweite hatte
eine so große Unterlippe, daß sie über das Kinn
herunterhing, und die dritte hatte einen breiten
Daumen.
2.2

There she saw three women coming in, the first of whom
had a broad flat foot, the second had a lower lip so large
that it hung down over her chin, and the third had a broad
thumb.

Die blieben vor dem Fenster stehen,
2.3

They stopped in front of the window,

schauten hinauf und fragten das Mädchen was ihm
fehlte.
2.4

looked up and asked the girl what was wrong.

Es klagte ihnen seine Not, da trugen sie ihm ihre
Hilfe an und sprachen:
2.5

She told them of her need, and they offered to help her,
saying,

2.6 »Willst du uns zur Hochzeit einladen, dich unser nicht schämen und uns deine Basen heißen, auch an deinen Tisch setzen, so wollen wir dir den Flachs wegspinnen und das in kurzer Zeit.«
"If thou wilt invite us to the wedding, and not be ashamed of us, and call us thy bases, and sit us at thy table, we will spin the flax for thee, and that in a short time."

2.7 »Von Herzen gern.« antwortete es,
"With all my heart." he replied,

2.8 »kommt nur herein und fangt gleich die Arbeit an.«
"come in and start work straight away."

2.9 Da ließ es die drei seltsamen Weiber herein und machte in der ersten Kammer eine Lücke,
Then she let the three strange women in and made a gap in the first chamber,

2.10 wo sie sich hinsetzten und ihr Spinnen anhuben.
where they sat down and began their spinning.

2.11 Die eine zog den Faden und trat das Rad, die andere netzte den Faden, die dritte drehte ihn und schlug mit dem Finger auf den Tisch, und so oft sie schlug, fiel eine Zahl Garn zur Erde und das war aufs feinste gesponnen.
One pulled the thread and kicked the wheel, the other wove the thread, the third twisted it and struck the table with her finger, and as often as she struck, a quantity of yarn fell to the ground, and it was spun to the finest quality.

Vor der Königin verbarg sie die drei Spinnerinnen und zeigte ihr, so oft sie kam, die Menge des gesponnenen Garns, daß diese des Lobes kein Ende fand.

2.12

She hid the three spinners from the Queen, and showed her, as often as she came, the quantity of yarn spun, so that she could not stop praising them.

Als die erste Kammer leer war, ging's an die zweite, endlich an die dritte, und die war auch bald aufgeräumt.

2.13

When the first chamber was empty, they went on to the second, and at last to the third, which was also soon cleared up.

Nun nahmen die drei Weiber Abschied und sagten zum Mädchen:

2.14

Now the three women took their leave and said to the girl,

»Vergiß nicht, was du uns versprochen hast, es wird dein Glück sein.«

2.15

"Do not forget what you have promised us, it will be your happiness."

Als das Mädchen der Königin die leeren Kammern und den großen Haufen Garn zeigte, richtete sie die Hochzeit aus, und der Bräutigam freute sich, daß er eine so geschickte und fleißige Frau bekäme und lobte sie gewaltig.

3.1

When the maiden showed the queen the empty chambers and the great heap of yarn, she arranged the wedding, and the bridegroom rejoiced that he should have so skillful and industrious a wife, and praised her highly.

»Ich habe drei Basen.« sprach das Mädchen,

3.2

"I have three bases." said the maiden,

24

3.3 »und da sie mir viel Gutes gethan haben,
"and as they have done me much good,

3.4 so wollte ich sie nicht gern in meinem Glück vergessen:
I would not like to forget them in my happiness:

3.5 erlaubt doch,
allow me to invite them to the wedding,

3.6 daß ich sie zu der Hochzeit einlade und daß sie mit an dem Tisch sitzen.«
and that they may sit at the table with me."

3.7 Die Königin und der Bräutigam sprachen,
The queen and the bridegroom said,

3.8 »Warum sollen wir das nicht erlauben?«
"Why should we not allow it?"

3.9 Als nun das Fest anhub, traten die drei Jungfern in wunderlicher Tracht herein, und die Braut sprach,
When the feast began, the three maidens came in in their strange costumes, and the bride said,

3.10 »Seid willkommen, liebe Basen.«
"Welcome, dear Bases."

3.11 »Ach.« sagte der Bräutigam,
"Alas." said the bridegroom,

3.12 »wie kommst du zu der garstigen Freundschaft?«
"how did you come by this nasty friendship?"

3.13 Darauf ging er zu der einen mit dem breiten Platschfuß und fragte,
Then he went to the one with the broad flat foot and asked,

»Wovon habt Ihr einen solchen breiten Fuß?«
"What gave you such a broad foot?"

»Vom Treten.« antwortete sie, »vom Treten.«
"From kicking." she replied, "from kicking."

Da ging der Bräutigam zur zweiten und sprach,
Then the bridegroom went to the second one and said,

»Wovon habt Ihr nur die herunterhängende Lippe?«
"Where did you get the drooping lip from?"

»Vom Lecken.« antwortete sie, »vom Lecken.«
"From licking." she replied, "from licking."

Da fragte er die dritte: »Wovon habt Ihr den breiten
Daumen?«
Then he asked the third, "What gave you that broad
thumb?"

»Vom Faden drehen.« antwortete sie,
"From twisting thread." she replied,

»vom Faden drehen.«
"from twisting thread."

Da erschrak der Königssohn und sprach:
Then the king's son was frightened and said,

»So soll mir nun und nimmermehr meine schöne
Braut ein Spinnrad anrühren.«
"So now and never again shall my beautiful bride touch a
spinning wheel."

Damit war sie das böse Flachsspinnen los.
So she was rid of the evil flax spinner.

De Spielhansl

The Gambler

1.1 Is is emohl e Mon gewön, der Hot ninx us (als) g'spielt, und do hobend'n d'Leut nur in Spielhansl g'hoaßen, und wal (weil) e gor nit afg'hört zen spieln, so hot e san (sein) Haus und ullss (alles) vespielt.
He's won a mon, he didn't play at all, and the people only played with their hands, and because he didn't stop playing, he gambled away (his) house and everything.

1.2 Hietzt (jetzt), nette (eben) in lötzten Tog, eh's iahm (ihm) d' Schuldne schon 's Haus hobend wögnehme willn, is unse Herrgout un de halli Pedrus kemme und hobend g'sogt, er sull's übe d'Nacht g'holte (bei sich behalten).
Now, in the last few days, before he wanted to take the debt away from his house, our master and the half pedrus came and told him to take it away for the night.

1.3 Oft (da) hot de Spielhansl g'sogt:
Often (there) the Spielhansl said:

1.4 »Wögn meine kints do bleibn döi Nocht:
"If my kints stay the night:

ober i kong eng koan Bött und ninx z'össn (zu essen) gebn.«   1.5

but I can't give you any bread and nothing to eat."

Oft hot unse Herrgout g'sogt, er sulls ne (nur) g'holten, und söi willetn ian (ihnen) selbe wos z'össn kaffen;   1.6

Our master often said that he should (only) fetch them, and they wanted to buy them something to eat;

dos is in Spielhansl recht g'wön.   1.7

that was quite right in Spielhansl.

Oft hot iahm de halli Pedrus drei Grouschn gebn,   1.8

Often he was given three large slices of bread by the half-pedrus,

und er sull zen Böcke (Bäcker) gehn und e Brot huhln.   1.9

and he had to go to the bakery and buy some bread.

Hietzt is hullt (halt) de Spielhansl gonge, wie er aber ze den Haus kemme is, wou die onnen Spiellumpn drin g'wön sand, döi iahm ullss ogwunge hobnd, do hobn's n g'ruefft und hobend g'schrien: 1.10

But when he came to the house, where the little playthings were in there, which I had already seen, they called out and shouted:

»Hansl, geh ahne (herein).«   1.11

"Hansl, go in."

»Jo.« hot e g'sogt,   1.12

"Yes." he said,

»willt's me die drei Grouschn a non ogwinge.«   1.13

"don't you want me to take the three big ones."

1.14 **Döi hobnd'n obe (aber) nit ausg'lossn.**
But they didn't let them out.

1.15 **Hietzt is e hullt anhi (hinein) und oft hot e die drei Grouschn a non vespielt.**
Now it's full on (inside) and we often didn't play the three big ones.

1.16 **De halli Pedrus und unse Herrgout hobnd ollewall (immer) g'wort't, und wie er ian z'lang nit kemme is, sand's iahm intgögn gonge.**
The half Pedrus and our master were always talking, and as he didn't come for a long time, he got bored.

1.17 **De Spielhansl obe, wie e kemme is, hot thon us wenn iahm's Geld in ne Locken (Lacken) g'folln war, und hot ollewall drin herumkrobbelt:**
The gambler above, as he came, was there when his money was in his curls and he was crawling around in them:

1.18 **obe unse Herrgout hots schon g'wißt, daß e's vespielt hot.**
our master already knew that he was gambling.

1.19 **Oft hot iahm de halli Pedrus non mohl drei Grouschn gebn.**
She often gave him the half pedrus no more than three big ones.

1.20 **Hietzt hot e sie obe nimme veführn losse und hot ian 's Brot brocht.**
Now he didn't let her go at all and broke her bread.

1.21 **Oft hot'n unse Herrgout g'frogt, wou e koan'n Wein nit hot, do e g'sogt:**
Our master often asked her why she didn't have any wine, saying:

»U, Herr, d'Fasse sand alli laar.« 1.22
"Lord, the barrels are all empty."

Oft hot unse Herrgout g'sogt, er sull ner in Költe 1.23
(Keller) ohi (hinab) gehn,
Our Lord often said that he should go down to the cellar,

»is is non de böst Wein int.« 1.24
"it's not the best wine inside."

Er hots long nit glaubn willn, obe af d'löst hot e 1.25
g'sogt:
He didn't want to believe it for a long time, but then he said:

»I will ohi gehn, ober i woaß's, daß koane int is.« 1.26
"I want to go there, but I know there's no wine inside."

Wie er obe's Fassl onzapft hot, 1.27
As he tapped the top of the barrel,

se is de böst Wein ausse g'runne. 1.28
he ran out of the best wine.

Hietzt hot er ian in Wein brocht, 1.29
Now he had one in wine,

und döi zwoa sand übe d'Nocht do blieb'n. 1.30
and the two of them stayed there for the night.

In onnen Tog, in de Früe, hot unse Herrgout zen 1.31
Spielhansl g'sogt, er sull sie (sich) drei Gnodn
ausbittn.
In one day, in the morning, our master told the Spielhansl
that he should buy them (himself) three glasses.

1.32 Er hot g'moant, er wird sie'n Himmel ausbittn, obe de Spielhansl hot bettn um e Korntn, mit der er ullss g'wingt;

He said that he would give them to heaven, but the Spielhansl begged for a grain, with which he waved it all;

1.33 um Würfl, mit den er a ullss g'wingt, und um en Bam (Baum), wou ullss Oubst draf wochst, und wonn oane (einer) affi steigt, daß e nimme ohe kon (herab kann), bis er iahm's schofft (befiehlt).

for dice, with which he waved it all, and for a tree, which he waved all the way up, and when one climbed up so that he could not get down until he ordered him to do so.

1.34 Hietzt hot iahm unse Herrgout ullss gebn, wos e velangt hot un is mit'n hallin Pedrus wiede fuert (fort).

Now our master has given him all that he has asked for and has left again with his hallin Pedrus.

2.1 Hietzt hot hullt de Spielhansl erst recht zen spieln ongfongt, und hätt bold d' halbeti Welt zomg'wunge.

Now, the Spielhansl had really started to play, and had woken up half the world.

2.2 Oft hat de halli Pedrus zen unse Herrgoutn g'sogt:

The half pedrus often said to our Lord:

2.3 »Herr, dos Ding thuet koan guet, er g'winget af d'löst non (noch) d' ganzi Welt;

"Lord, this thing doesn't do any good, it's not (yet) the whole world;

2.4 me müeßn iahm in (den) Toid schickn.«

we have to send him to (the) death."

31

Hietzt habends iahm in Tod g'schickt. Wie de Tod kemme is,   2.5
Now they have sent me to my death. When death came,

is de Spielhansl nette be'n Spieltisch g'sössn;   2.6
the gambler was sitting nicely at the gaming table;

oft hot de Toid g'sagt: »Hansl, kimme bißl ausse.«   2.7
often the kid said: "Hansl, come out a bit."

De Spielhansl obe hot g'sogt: 2.8
The player above said:

»Wort nur e bißl, bis dos G'spiel aus is und steig dewall e weng afn Bam do affi und brouck uns e wengerl wos o, daß me afn Wog was z'noschn hob'n.«   2.9
"Just say a little while until the game is over and get up a little on the bam and give us a little something to eat on the wagon."

Hietzt is hullt de Toid affi g'stiegn, und wie e wiede hot ohi Wille, hot i nit kinne, und de Spielhansl hot'n sieben Johr droubn lossn, und dewall is koan Mensch, nit g'storbn.   2.10
Now the death has come, and how I have no will again, I don't know, and the game has been going on for seven years, and there's no one left, no one has died.

Oft hot de halli Pedrus zen unsen Herrgoutn g'sogt: 3.1
The eldest Pedrus often said to our Lord:

»Herr, dos Ding thuet koan guet, is sterbet jo koan Mensch mehr;   3.2
"Lord, this thing is not good, no one is dying anymore;

mir müeßn schon selbe kemme.«   3.3
we have to come back."

3.4 Hietzt sand's hullt selbe kemme, und do hot iahm unse Herrgout g'schofft, daß er in Toid ohe lossn sull.

Now the same thing had come, and our Lord was hoping that he would die.

3.5 Oft is er obe glei gonge und hot zen Toid g'sagt:

He often went upstairs and said to the boy:

3.6 »Geh ohe.«

"Go upstairs."

3.7 und der hot'n glei g'numme und hot'n okragelt (erwürgt).

And he just went and strangled him.

3.8 Oft sands mit enonne fuert und fand in d' onnert Welt kemme,

He often ran off with one and found himself in the outside world,

3.9 do is hullt man (mein) Spielhansl zen Himmelthoir gonge und hot onkloupft.

then one (my) playmate went to the Himmelthoir and knocked.

3.10 »Wer is draußt?«

"Who's out there?"

3.11 »De Spielhansl.«

"The playmate."

3.12 »Ach, den brauche me nit, geh ne wiede fuert.«

"Oh, I don't need him, go away again."

3.13 Oft is e zen Fegfuirthoir gonge und hot wiede kloupft.

He often went to the Fegfuirthoir and knocked again.

»Wer is draußt?« 3.14
"Who's out there?"

»De Spielhansl.« 3.15
"The Spielhansl."

»Ach is is e so (ohne daß) Jomme und Noit g'nue be'n 3.16
uns, mir willn nit spieln;
"Oh, it's like this (without that), it's time and night with us,
we don't want to play;

geh ne wiede fuert.« 3.17
go back to playing."

Oft is e zen Hüllnthoir gonge, und do hoben's ne anhi 3.18
lossn, is is obe niamd dehoambt g'wön, us de olti
Luzifar und krumpn Tuifln (die g'rodn hobn af de
Welt z'thoan g'hot), und oft hot e sie glei ine (nieder)
g'sötzt und hot wiede zew spieln ong'fongt.
They often went to the enveloping hall, and there they lost
their heads, there was no one left, from the old Luzifar and
crooked Tuifln (who had gone out into the world to play),
and often they just sat down and played again.

Hietzt hot obe de Luzifar ninx g'hot, 3.19
Now the Lucifer had nothing to do with her,

us sani krumpn Tuifln: 3.20
from her crooked hands:

döi hot iahm de Spielhansl ogwunge, wall e mit sann 3.21
Kortn ullss hot g'winge müeßn.
she had to swing her hand with her basket.

3.22 Hietzt is e mit sann krumpn Tuifln fuert, und oft sand's af Hoihefuert (nach Hohenfuert), und hobnd d' Houpfnstange ausg'rissn und san demit zen Himml affi und hobnd zen wägn ong'fongt;

Now he went with his crooked shoes, and often he went to Hoihefuert (to Hohenfuert), and took off the hump pole and went up to the sky and went on his way;

3.23 und hietzt hot de Himmel schon krocht (gekracht).

and now the sky was already cracking.

3.24 Oft hot de halli Pedrus wiede g'sogt:

The eldest Pedrus often said again:

3.25 »Herr, dos Ding thuet koan guet, mir müeßn ne anhe (herein) lossn, sunst werfet er uns in Himml ohi (hinab).«

"Lord, this thing is not good, we have to let it in, otherwise it will throw us into heaven."

3.26 Hietzt hobnd's 'n hullt anhi lossn.

Now they have 'n hullt anhi losn.

3.27 Obe de Spielhansl hot glei wiede zen spieln ong'fongt, und do is glei e Lärm und e Getös won (worden), daß me san oagns Wort nit vestondn hot.

Then the Spielhansl started playing again, and there was so much noise and commotion that I couldn't hear a single word.

3.28 Oft hat de halli Pedrus wiede g'sogt:

The echoing Pedrus often said again:

3.29 »Herr, dos Ding thuet koan guet, mir müeßn ne ohi werfen, er machet uns sunst in gonzn Himml rewellisch.«

"Lord, this thing is no good, we have to throw it over, it will make us reel in the sky."

Hietzt sands hullt her und hobnd'n one g'worfn, 3.30
und da hot sie san Seel z'thoalt (hat sich seine Seele
zerteilt) und is in d'onnen Spiellumpn g'fohrn, döi
non (noch) bis date lebnd.

Now she came back and said one thing, and then she broke
her soul and went into the inner playpen, where she lived
until today.

Hans im Glück

Hans in Luck

1.1 Hans hatte sieben Jahre bei seinem Herrn gedient, da sprach er zu ihm:

Hans had served his master for seven years when he said to him:

1.2 »Herr, meine Zeit ist herum, nun wollte ich gern wieder heim zu meiner Mutter, gebt mir meinen Lohn.«

"Sir, my time is up, now I would like to go home to my mother, give me my wages."

1.3 Der Herr antwortete:

The master replied,

1.4 »Du hast mir treu und ehrlich gedient, wie der Dienst war, so soll der Lohn sein.«

"You have served me faithfully and honestly, as your service has been, so shall your reward be."

1.5 und gab ihm ein Stück Gold, das so groß als Hansens Kopf war.

and gave him a piece of gold as big as Hans' head.

Hans zog sein Tüchlein aus der Tasche, wickelte den Klumpen hinein, setzte ihn auf die Schulter und machte sich auf den Weg nach Haus.

1.6

Hans pulled his handkerchief out of his pocket, wrapped the lump in it, put it on his shoulder and set off for home.

Wie er so dahin ging und immer ein Bein vor das andere setzte, kam ihm ein Reiter in die Augen, der frisch und fröhlich auf einem munteren Pferd vorbeitrabte.

1.7

As he walked along, always putting one leg in front of the other, a rider came into his sight, trotting along fresh and cheerful on a lively horse.

»Ach.« sprach Hans ganz laut,

1.8

"Oh." said Hans aloud,

»was ist das Reiten ein schönes Ding!

1.9

"what a fine thing riding is!

da sitzt einer wie auf einem Stuhl, stößt sich an keinen Stein, spart die Schuh, und kommt fort, er weiß nicht wie.«

1.10

There is a fellow sitting as if on a chair, not bumping into a stone, saving his shoes, and getting away, he does not know how."

Der Reiter der das gehört hatte, hielt an und rief:

1.11

The horseman who had heard this stopped and cried:

»Ei, Hans, warum laufst du auch zu Fuß?«

1.12

"Why, Hans, why do you walk too?"

»Ich muß ja wohl.« antwortete er,

1.13

"I must." he answered,

»da habe ich einen Klumpen heimzutragen;

1.14

"I have a lump to carry home;

1.15 es ist zwar Gold, aber ich kann den Kopf dabei nicht gerad halten, auch drückt mir's auf die Schulter.«
it is gold, but I cannot keep my head straight, and it presses on my shoulder."

1.16 »Weißt du was.« sagte der Reiter, »wir wollen tauschen:
"You know what." said the rider, "we'll swap:

1.17 ich gebe dir mein Pferd, und du giebst mir deinen Klumpen.«
I'll give you my horse, and you give me your lump."

1.18 »Von Herzen gern.« sprach Hans, »aber ich sage Euch,
"With all my heart." said Hans, "but I tell you,

1.19 Ihr müßt Euch damit schleppen.«
you'll have to drag yourself with it."

1.20 Der Reiter stieg ab, nahm das Gold und half dem Hans hinauf, gab ihm die Zügel fest in die Hände und sprach: »Wenn's nun recht geschwind soll gehen, so mußt du mit der Zunge schnalzen und hopp hopp rufen.«
The horseman dismounted, took the gold and helped Hans up, gave him the reins firmly in his hands and said, "If you want to go quickly, you must click your tongue and shout 'hopp hopp'."

2.1 Hans war seelenfroh, als er auf dem Pferde saß und so frank und frei dahin ritt.
Hans was so happy when he sat on the horse and rode along so freely.

Über ein Weilchen fiel's ihm ein, es sollte noch schneller gehen, und fing an mit der Zunge zu schnalzen und hopp hopp zu rufen.

2.2

After a while, it occurred to him that he should go even faster, and he began to click his tongue and shout "hopp hopp".

Das Pferd setzte sich in starken Trab, und ehe sich's Hans versah, war er abgeworfen und lag in einem Graben, der die Äcker von der Landstraße trennte.

2.3

The horse set off at a strong trot, and before Hans knew it, he was thrown off and lying in a ditch that separated the fields from the country road.

Das Pferd wäre auch durchgegangen, wenn es nicht ein Bauer aufgehalten hätte, der des Weges kam und eine Kuh vor sich her trieb.

2.4

The horse would have gone through if it had not been stopped by a farmer who came along the road driving a cow in front of him.

Hans suchte seine Glieder zusammen und machte sich wieder auf die Beine.

2.5

Hans gathered his limbs and got back on his feet.

Er war aber verdrießlich und sprach zu dem Bauer:

2.6

But he was vexed, and said to the farmer,

»Es ist ein schlechter Spaß, das Reiten, zumal, wenn man auf so eine Mähre gerät wie diese, die stößt und einen herabwirft, daß man den Hals brechen kann;

2.7

"It is bad fun to ride, especially when one gets on such a cow as this, which knocks and throws one down so that one may break one's neck;

ich setze mich nun und nimmermehr wieder auf.

2.8

I will not sit up again now or ever.

2.9 Da lob ich mir Eure Kuh, da kann einer mit Gemächlichkeit hinterher gehen, und hat obendrein seine Milch, Butter und Käse jeden Tag gewiß.

I praise your cow, someone can walk behind it with ease, and on top of that he is sure of his milk, butter and cheese every day.

2.10 Was gäb ich darum, wenn ich so eine Kuh hätte!«

What I would give to have a cow like that!"

2.11 »Nun.« sprach der Bauer,

"Well." said the farmer,

2.12 »geschieht Euch so ein großer Gefallen,

"if you will do me such a great favor,

2.13 so will ich Euch wohl die Kuh für das Pferd vertauschen.«

I will trade you the cow for the horse."

2.14 Hans willigte mit tausend Freuden ein:

Hans agreed with a thousand joys:

2.15 der Bauer schwang sich aufs Pferd und ritt eilig davon.

the farmer swung himself on his horse and rode off hurriedly.

3.1 Hans trieb seine Kuh ruhig vor sich her und bedachte den glücklichen Handel.

Hans calmly drove his cow along and contemplated the happy deal.

»Hab ich nur ein Stück Brot, und daran wird mir's doch nicht fehlen, so kann ich, so oft mir's beliebt, Butter und Käse dazu essen;

3.2

"If I only have a piece of bread, and I won't be short of that, I can eat butter and cheese with it as often as I like;

hab ich Durst, so melk ich meine Kuh und trinke Milch. Herz,

3.3

if I'm thirsty, I'll milk my cow and drink milk. Heart,

was verlangst du mehr?«

3.4

what more do you want?"

Als er zu einem Wirtshaus kam, machte er Halt, aß in der großen Freude alles, was er bei sich hatte, sein Mittags - und Abendbrot, rein auf und ließ sich für seine letzten paar Heller ein halbes Glas Bier einschenken.

3.5

When he came to an inn, he stopped, ate everything he had with him, his lunch and dinner, and had half a glass of beer poured for his last few pennies.

Dann trieb er seine Kuh weiter, immer nach dem Dorfe seiner Mutter zu.

3.6

Then he drove his cow on towards his mother's village.

Die Hitze ward drückender, je näher der Mittag kam, und Hans befand sich in einer Heide, die wohl noch eine Stunde dauerte.

3.7

The heat became more oppressive as midday approached, and Hans found himself in a heath that probably lasted another hour.

Da ward es ihm ganz heiß, sodaß ihm vor Durst die Zunge am Gaumen klebte.

3.8

He became so hot that his tongue stuck to the roof of his mouth from thirst.

42

3.9 »Dem Ding ist zu helfen.« dachte Hans,

"That thing can be helped." thought Hans,

3.10 »jetzt will ich meine Kuh melken und mich an der Milch laben.«

"now I will milk my cow and feast on the milk."

3.11 Er band sie an einen dürren Baum und da er keinen Eimer hatte, so stellte er seine Ledermütze unter, aber wie er sich auch bemühte, es kam kein Tropfen Milch zum Vorschein.

He tied her to a dry tree and, as he had no bucket, he put his leather cap underneath, but no matter how hard he tried, not a drop of milk came out.

3.12 Und weil er sich ungeschickt dabei anstellte, so gab ihm das ungeduldige Tier endlich mit einem der Hinterfüße einen solchen Schlag vor den Kopf, daß er zu Boden taumelte und eine Zeitlang sich gar nicht besinnen konnte wo er war.

And because he was so clumsy, the impatient animal finally gave him such a blow on the head with one of its hind feet that he staggered to the ground and for a while could not remember where he was.

3.13 Glücklicherweise kam gerade ein Metzger des Weges,

Fortunately,

3.14 der auf einem Schubkarren ein junges Schwein liegen hatte.

a butcher had just come along the road with a young pig lying on a wheelbarrow.

3.15 »Was sind das für Streiche!«

"What kind of pranks are these!"

3.16 rief er und half dem guten Hans auf.

he shouted and helped good Hans up.

Hans erzählte, was vorgefallen war. 3.17
Hans told him what had happened.

Der Metzger reichte ihm seine Flasche und sprach: 3.18
The butcher handed him his bottle and said:

»Da trinkt einmal und erholt Euch. 3.19
"Have a drink and recover.

Die Kuh will wohl keine Milch geben, das ist ein altes 3.20
Tier, das höchstens noch zum Ziehen taugt oder zum
Schlachten.«
The cow probably doesn't want to give milk, it's an old
animal that's only good for pulling or slaughtering."

»Ei, ei.« sprach Hans, und strich sich die Haare über 3.21
den Kopf,
"Well, well." said Hans, stroking his hair over his head,

»wer hätte das gedacht! 3.22
"who would have thought it!

es ist freilich gut, wenn man so ein Tier ins Haus 3.23
abschlachten kann, was giebt's für Fleisch!
Of course, it's good to be able to slaughter such an animal in
the house, what meat there is!

Aber ich mache mir aus dem Kuhfleisch nicht viel, 3.24
But I don't care much for cow meat,

es ist mir nicht saftig genug. Ja, 3.25
it's not juicy enough for me. Yes,

wer so ein junges Schwein hätte! das schmeckt 3.26
anders,
who would have such a young pig! It tastes different,

44

3.27 dabei noch die Würste.«

and the sausages too."

3.28 »Hört, Hans.« sprach da der Metzger,

"Listen, Hans." said the butcher,

3.29 »Euch zuliebe will ich tauschen und will Euch das Schwein für die Kuh lassen.«

"for your sake I will swap and let you have the pig for the cow."

3.30 »Gott lohn Euch Eure Freundschaft.«

"God reward you for your friendship."

3.31 sprach Hans, übergab ihm die Kuh, ließ sich das Schweinchen vom Karren losmachen und den Strick, woran es gebunden war, in die Hand geben.

said Hans, handed him the cow, and had the piggy untied from the cart and the rope to which it was tied put into his hand.

4.1 Hans zog weiter und überdachte, wie ihm doch alles nach Wunsch ginge, begegnete ihm ja eine Verdrießlichkeit, so würde sie doch gleich wieder gut gemacht.

Hans moved on and thought about how everything would go as he wished; if he encountered any annoyance, it would be made up to him straight away.

4.2 Es gesellte sich danach ein Bursch zu ihm, der trug eine schöne weiße Gans unter dem Arm.

Afterwards he was joined by a lad who carried a beautiful white goose under his arm.

Sie boten einander die Zeit, und Hans fing an von seinem Glück zu erzählen und wie er immer so vorteilhaft getauscht hätte:

4.3

They offered each other their time, and Hans began to tell of his good fortune, and how he had always bartered so advantageously:

Der Bursch erzählte ihm, daß er die Gans zu einem Kindtaufschmaus brächte.

4.4

the lad told him that he was bringing the goose to a children's feast.

»Hebt einmal.«

4.5

"Lift it once."

fuhr er fort, und packte sie bei den Flügeln,

4.6

he went on, and took it by the wings,

»wie schwer sie ist;

4.7

"how heavy it is;

die ist aber auch acht Wochen lang genudelt worden.

4.8

but it has been noodled for eight weeks.

Wer in den Braten beißt, muß sich das Fett von beiden Seiten abwischen.«

4.9

Whoever bites into the roast must wipe off the fat from both sides."

»Ja.« sprach Hans, und wog sie mit der einen Hand,

4.10

"Yes." said Hans, weighing it with one hand,

»die hat ihr Gewicht, aber mein Schwein ist auch keine Sau.«

4.11

"it has its weight, but my pig is no sow either."

4.12   Indessen sah sich der Bursche nach allen Seiten ganz bedenklich um,

In the meantime the lad looked round in all directions,

4.13   schüttelte auch wohl mit dem Kopfe. »Hört.«

and shook his head. "Listen."

4.14   fing er darauf an,

he began,

4.15   »mit Eurem Schweine mag's nicht ganz richtig sein.

"it may not be quite right with your pig.

4.16   In dem Dorfe, durch das ich gekommen bin, ist eben dem Schulzen eins aus dem Stall gestohlen worden.

In the village through which I have passed, one has just been stolen from the schoolmaster's sty.

4.17   Ich fürchte, ich fürchte, Ihr habt's da in der Hand.

I'm afraid, I'm afraid you've got it in your hands.

4.18   Sie haben Leute ausgeschickt, und es wäre ein schlimmer Handel, wenn sie Euch mit dem Schweine erwischten:

They have sent out men, and it would be a bad bargain if they caught you with the pig:

4.19   das geringste ist, daß ihr ins finstere Loch gesteckt werdet.«

the least they could do is to put you in a dark hole."

4.20   Dem guten Hans ward bange. »Ach Gott.« sprach er,

Good Hans was afraid. "Oh, God." he said,

»helft mir aus der Not, Ihr wißt hier herum besseren
Bescheid, nehmt mein Schwein da und laßt mir Eure
Gans.«
"help me out of this trouble, you know better here, take my
pig there and leave me your goose."

4.21

»Ich muß schon etwas aufs Spiel setzen.«
"I must risk something."

4.22

antwortete der Bursche,
replied the lad,

4.23

»aber ich will doch nicht schuld sein, daß Ihr ins
Unglück geratet.«
"but I don't want to be responsible for your misfortune."

4.24

Er nahm also das Seil in die Hand und trieb das
Schwein schnell auf einem Seitenwege fort;
So he took the rope in his hand, and quickly drove the pig
away by a by-path;

4.25

der gute Hans aber ging, seiner Sorgen entledigt, mit
der Gans unter dem Arme der Heimat zu.
but good Hans, relieved of his cares, went home with the
goose under his arm.

4.26

»Wenn ich's recht überlege.« sprach er mit sich selbst,
"When I come to think of it." he said to himself,

4.27

»habe ich noch Vorteil bei dem Tausch:
"I have still an advantage in the exchange:

4.28

4.29 erstlich den guten Braten, hernach die Menge von Fett, die herausträufeln wird, das giebt Gänsefettbrot auf ein Vierteljahr, und endlich die schönen weißen Federn, die laß ich mir in mein Kopfkissen stopfen, und darauf will ich wohl ungewiegt einschlafen.

first of all the good roast, then the quantity of fat that will drip out, which will give me goose fat bread for a quarter of a year, and finally the beautiful white feathers, which I will have stuffed into my pillow, and I shall sleep on them without being weighed.

4.30 Was wird meine Mutter eine Freude haben!«

What joy my mother will have!"

5.1 Als er durch das letzte Dorf gekommen war, stand da ein Scherenschleifer mit seinem Karren, sein Rad schnurrte, und er sang dazu:

When he had passed through the last village, there was a scissor grinder with his cart, his wheel purring, and he was singing along:

»Ich schleife die Schere und drehe geschwind,

"I grind the scissors and turn quickly,

und hänge mein Mäntelchen nach dem Wind.«

and hang my cloak in the wind."

7.1 Hans blieb stehen und sah ihm zu:

Hans stood still and watched him:

7.2 endlich redete er ihn an und sprach:

at last he spoke to him and said:

»Euch geht's wohl, weil Ihr so lustig bei Eurem
Schleifen seid.«

"You're doing well because you're so funny with your
grinding."

7.3

»Ja.« antwortete der Scherenschleifer,

"Yes." replied the scissors-grinder,

7.4

»das Handwerk hat einen güldenen Boden.

"the craft has a golden bottom.

7.5

Ein rechter Schleifer ist ein Mann, der, so oft er in die
Tasche greift, auch Geld darin findet.

A real grinder is a man who, as often as he reaches into his
pocket, finds money in it.

7.6

Aber wo habt Ihr die schöne Gans gekauft?«

But where did you buy that beautiful goose?"

7.7

»Die hab ich nicht gekauft,

"I didn't buy it,

7.8

sondern für mein Schwein eingetauscht.«

I traded it for my pig."

7.9

»Und das Schwein?«

"And the pig?"

7.10

»Das hab ich für eine Kuh gekriegt.«

"I got that for a cow."

7.11

»Und die Kuh?«

"And the cow?"

7.12

»Die hab ich für ein Pferd bekommen.«

"I got it for a horse."

7.13

7.14 »Und das Pferd?«

"And the horse?"

7.15 »Dafür hab ich einen Klumpen Gold, so groß als mein Kopf, gegeben.«

"I gave you a lump of gold as big as my head."

7.16 »Und das Gold?«

"And the gold?"

7.17 »Ei, das war mein Lohn für sieben Jahre Dienst.«

"Egg, that was my reward for seven years of service."

7.18 »Ihr habt Euch jederzeit zu helfen gewußt.«

"You have always known how to help yourself."

7.19 sprach der Schleifer,

said the grinder,

7.20 »könnt Jhr's nun dahin bringen, daß Ihr das Geld in der Tasche springen hört, wenn Ihr aufsteht, so habt Ihr Euer Glück gemacht.«

"and if you can make it so that you hear the money jump in your pocket when you get up, you have made your fortune."

7.21 »Wie soll ich das anfangen?« sprach Hans.

"How shall I begin?" said Hans.

7.22 »Ihr müßt ein Schleifer werden wie ich;

"You must become a grinder like me;

7.23 dazu gehört eigentlich nichts als ein Wetzstein,

all you really need is a whetstone,

7.24 das andere findet sich schon von selbst.

the rest will come by itself.

Da hab ich einen, der ist zwar ein wenig schadhaft, dafür sollt Ihr mir aber auch weiter nichts als Eure Gans geben:

7.25

I have one, but it's a bit damaged, but you'll give me nothing but your goose in return:

wollt Ihr das?«

7.26

is that what you want?"

»Wie könnt Ihr noch fragen.« antwortete Hans;

7.27

"How can you ask." replied Hans;

»ich werde ja zum glücklichsten Menschen auf Erden:

7.28

"I am becoming the happiest man on earth:

habe ich Geld, so oft ich in die Tasche greife, was brauche ich da länger zu sorgen?«

7.29

I have money to spend as often as I reach into my pocket, what need have I to worry any longer?"

reichte ihm die Gans hin und nahm den Wetzstein in Empfang.

7.30

and he handed him the goose and took the whetstone.

»Nun.«

7.31

"Well."

sprach der Schleifer, und hob einen gewöhnlichen schweren Feldstein, der neben ihm lag, auf,

7.32

said the grinder, picking up an ordinary heavy field-stone that lay beside him,

»da habt Ihr noch einen tüchtigen Stein dazu, auf dem sich's gut schlagen läßt, und Ihr Eure alten Nägel gerade klopfen könnt.

7.33

"you have another good stone to beat on, and you can hammer your old nails straight.

7.34 Nehmt ihn und hebt ihn ordentlich auf.«

Take it and pick it up properly."

8.1 Hans lud den Stein auf und ging mit vergnügtem Herzen weiter:

Hans picked up the stone and walked on with a happy heart:

8.2 seine Augen leuchteten vor Freude.

his eyes shone with joy.

8.3 »Ich muß in einer Glückshaut geboren sein.« rief er aus,

"I must have been born in a lucky skin." he exclaimed,

8.4 »alles, was ich wünsche, trifft mir ein wie einem Sonntagskind.«

"everything I wish for comes to me like a Sunday child."

8.5 Indessen, weil er seit Tagesanbruch auf den Beinen gewesen war, begann er müde zu werden;

Meanwhile, as he had been on his feet since daybreak, he began to feel tired;

8.6 auch plagte ihn der Hunger,

he was also hungry,

8.7 da er allen Vorrat auf einmal in der Freude über die erhandelte Kuh aufgezehrt hatte.

as he had consumed all his food at once in his joy over the cow he had bought.

8.8 Er konnte endlich nur mit Mühe weiter gehen und mußte jeden Augenblick Halt machen;

At last he could only go on with difficulty and had to stop at every moment;

dabei drückten ihn die Steine ganz erbärmlich.

8.9

the stones weighed him down miserably.

Da konnte er sich des Gedankens nicht erwehren, wie gut es wäre, wenn er sie gerade jetzt nicht zu tragen brauchte.

8.10

Then he could not help thinking how good it would be if he did not have to carry them just then.

Wie eine Schnecke kam er zu einem Feldbrunnen geschlichen,

8.11

He crept like a snail to a well in the field,

wollte da ruhen und sich mit einem frischen Trunk laben;

8.12

where he wanted to rest and refresh himself with a drink;

damit er aber die Steine im Niedersitzen nicht beschädigte,

8.13

but to avoid damaging the stones as he sat down,

legte er sie bedächtig neben sich auf den Rand des Brunnens.

8.14

he carefully placed them beside him on the edge of the well.

Darauf setzte er sich nieder und wollte sich zum Trinken bücken, da versah er's, stieß ein klein wenig an, und beide Steine plumpten hinab.

8.15

Then he sat down and was about to bend over to drink, when he made a mistake, bumped them a little, and both stones plopped down.

8.16 Hans, als er sie mit seinen Augen in die Tiefe hatte versinken sehen, sprang vor Freuden auf, kniete dann nieder und dankte Gott mit Thränen in den Augen, daß er ihm auch diese Gnade noch erwiesen und ihn auf eine so gute Art und ohne daß er sich einen Vorwurf zu machen brauchte, von den schweren Steinen befreit hätte, die ihm allein noch hinderlich gewesen wären.

Hans, when he had seen them sink into the depths with his own eyes, jumped up for joy, then knelt down and thanked God with tears in his eyes that he had shown him this mercy, and had freed him in such a good way, and without his having to reproach himself, from the heavy stones, which alone would have been a hindrance to him.

8.17 So glücklich wie ich.« rief er aus,

As happy as I am." he exclaimed,

8.18 »giebt es keinen Menschen unter der Sonne.«

"there is no man under the sun."

8.19 Mit leichtem Herzen und frei von aller Last sprang er nun fort,

With a light heart and free from all burdens,

8.20 bis er daheim bei seiner Mutter war.

he skipped away until he reached his mother's house.

Hans heiratet

Hans Marries

1.1 **Es war einmal ein junger Bauer, der hieß Hans, dem wollte sein Vetter gern eine reiche Frau werben.**
Once upon a time there was a young farmer called Hans whose cousin wanted to woo a rich wife.

1.2 **Da setzte er den Hans hinter den Ofen und ließ gut einheizen.**
So he put Hans behind the stove and gave it a good heating.

1.3 **Dann holte er einen Topf Milch und eine gute Menge Weißbrot, gab ihm einen neugemünzten glänzenden Heller in die Hand und sprach:**
Then he fetched a pot of milk and a good quantity of white bread, put a newly minted, shiny penny in his hand and said:

1.4 **»Hans, den Heller da halt fest und das Weißbrot das brocke in die Milch, und bleib da sitzen, und geh mir nicht von der Stelle, bis ich wiederkomme.«**
"Hans, hold on to that penny and the white bread and dip it in the milk, and stay there and don't leave my side until I come back."

»Ja.« sprach der Hans, »das will ich alles ausrichten.«　　1.5
"Yes." said Hans, "I will do all that."

Nun zog der Werber ein Paar alte verplackte
Hosen an, ging ins andere Dorf zu einer reichen
Bauerntochter und sprach,　　1.6
Now the wooer put on a pair of old, ratty pants, went to the
other village to a rich farmer's daughter and said,

»Wollt Ihr nicht meinen Vetter Hans heiraten?　　1.7
"Won't you marry my cousin Hans?

Ihr kriegt einen wackeren und gescheiten Mann, der
Euch gefallen wird.«　　1.8
You will get a brave and clever man who will please you."

Fragte der geizige Vater:　　1.9
The stingy father asked:

»Wie sieht's aus mit seinem Vermögen?　　1.10
"What about his fortune?

Hat cr auch was einzubrocken?«　　1.11
Does he have anything to bring in?"

»Lieber Freund.« antwortete der Werber,　　1.12
"My dear friend." replied the advertiser,

»mein junger Vetter sitzt warm, hat einen guten
schönen Pfennig in der Hand und, hat wohl
einzubrocken.　　1.13
"my young cousin is sitting warmly, has a good penny in his
hand and has probably got a lot to lose.

1.14 Er sollte auch nicht weniger Placken (wie man die
Güter nannte) zählen als ich.«

He shouldn't count any less placken (as the goods were
called) than I do."

1.15 und schlug sich dabei auf seine geplackte Hose.

and he slapped his trousers.

1.16 »Wollt Ihr Euch die Mühe nehmen mit mir
hinzugehen, soll Euch zur Stunde gezeigt werden,
daß alles so ist wie ich sage.«

"If you will take the trouble to go with me, you shall be
shown by the hour that everything is as I say."

1.17 Da wollte der Geizhals die gute Gelegenheit nicht
fahren lassen und sprach:

Then the miser would not let the good opportunity pass,
and said,

1.18 »Wenn dem so ist, so habe ich weiter nichts gegen die
Heirat.«

"If so, I have no further objection to the marriage."

2.1 Nun ward die Hochzeit an dem bestimmten Tag
gefeiert, und als die junge Frau ins Feld gehen und
die Güter des Bräutigams sehen wollte, zog Hans erst
sein sonntägliches Kleid aus und seinen verplackten
Kittel an und sprach,

Now the wedding was celebrated on the appointed day, and
when the young wife wished to go into the field and see the
bridegroom's goods, Hans first took off his Sunday dress
and put on his puddled smock, and said,

2.2 »Ich könnte mir das gute Kleid verunehren.«

"I might disgrace my good dress."

Da gingen sie zusammen ins Feld, und wo sich auf   2.3
dem Weg der Weinstock abzeichnete, oder Äcker
und Wiesen abgeteilt waren, deutete Hans mit dem
Finger und schlug dann an einen großen oder kleinen
Placken seines Kittels und sprach:

Then they went into the field together, and where the vine
was visible on the path, or where fields and meadows were
divided, Hans pointed with his finger and then struck a
large or small patch of his smock and said,

»Der Placken ist mein und jener auch, mein Schatz,   2.4
schauet nur danach.«

"This patch is mine and that one too, my darling, just look
at it."

und wollte damit sagen, die Frau sollte nicht in das   2.5
weite Feld gaffen, sondern auf sein Kleid schauen, das
wäre sein eigen.

He meant to say that the woman should not look at the
wide field, but at his dress, which was his own.

»Bist du auch auf der Hochzeit gewesen?«   3.1

"Did you go to the wedding too?"

»Ja wohl, bin ich darauf gewesen, und in vollem   3.2
Staat.

"Yes, I was there, and in full state.

Mein Kopfputz war von Schnee, da kam die Sonne,   3.3
und er ist mir abgeschmolzen;

My headdress was of snow, and the sun came and melted it
off;

mein Kleid war von Spinneweb, da kam ich durch   3.4
Dornen, die rissen mir es ab;

my dress was of spider's web, and when I came through
thorns, they tore it off;

3.5 meine Pantoffel waren von Glas, da stieß ich an einen Stein, da sagten sie klink!

my slippers were of glass, and when I struck a stone, they said clink!

3.6 und sprangen entzwei.«

and burst asunder."

Die Goldkinder
The Golden Children

1.1 Es war ein armer Mann und eine arme Frau, die hatten nichts als eine kleine Hütte, und nährten sich vom Fischfang, und es ging bei ihnen von Hand zu Mund.

There was a poor man and a poor woman, who had nothing but a little hut, and they lived by fishing, and they had from hand to mouth.

1.2 Es geschah aber, als der Mann eines Tages beim Wasser saß und sein Netz auswarf, daß er einen Fisch herauszog, der ganz golden war.

But it happened one day, as the man was sitting by the water and casting his net, that he pulled out a fish that was quite golden.

1.3 Und als er den Fisch voll Verwunderung betrachtete, hub dieser an zu reden und sprach:

And as he looked at the fish in amazement, it began to talk and said,

»Hör, Fischer, wirfst du mich wieder hinab ins Wasser, so mach ich deine kleine Hütte zu einem prächtigen Schloß.«

1.4

"Listen, fisherman, if you throw me back into the water, I will make your little hut into a magnificent castle."

Da antwortete der Fischer:

1.5

The fisherman replied:

»Was hilft mir ein Schloß, wenn ich nichts zu essen habe?«

1.6

"What good is a castle if I have nothing to eat?"

Sprach der Goldfisch weiter:

1.7

The goldfish continued:

»Auch dafür soll gesorgt sein, es wird ein Schrank im Schloß sein, wenn du den aufschließest, so stehen Schüsseln darin mit den schönsten Speisen, so viel du dir wünschest.«

1.8

"That will also be taken care of, there will be a cupboard in the castle, when you open it, there will be bowls with the most beautiful food, as much as you want."

»Wenn das ist.« sprach der Mann,

1.9

"If that is the case." said the man,

»so kann ich dir wohl den Gefallen thun.«

1.10

"I can do you the favor."

»Ja.« sagte der Fisch,

1.11

"Yes." said the fish,

1.12 »es ist aber die Bedingung dabei, daß du keinem Menschen auf der Welt, wer es auch immer sein mag, entdeckst, woher dein Glück gekommen ist;

"but it is on condition that you do not reveal to anyone in the world, whoever it may be, where your happiness has come from;

1.13 sprichst du ein einziges Wort, so ist alles vorbei.«

if you speak a single word, it is all over."

2.1 Nun warf der Mann den wunderbaren Fisch wieder ins Wasser und ging heim.

Then the man threw the miraculous fish back into the water and went home.

2.2 Wo aber sonst seine Hütte gestanden hatte,

But where his hut used to stand,

2.3 da stand jetzt ein großes Schloß.

there was now a large castle.

2.4 Da machte er ein paar Augen, trat hinein und sah seine Frau, mit schönen Kleidern geputzt, in einer prächtigen Stube sitzen.

Then he opened his eyes, stepped inside and saw his wife, dressed in beautiful clothes, sitting in a splendid parlor.

2.5 Sie war ganz vergnügt und sprach: »Mann,

She was quite delighted, and said, "Man,

2.6 wie ist das auf einmal gekommen? das gefällt mir wohl.«

how did this come about all at once? I like it."

2.7 »Ja.« sagte der Mann,

"Yes." said the man,

»es gefällt mir auch, aber es hungert mich auch gewaltig, gieb mir erst was zu essen.« 2.8
"I like it too, but I am very hungry, first give me something to eat."

Sprach die Frau: 2.9
Said the woman,

»Ich habe nichts und weiß in dem neuen Haus nichts zu finden.« 2.10
"I have nothing, and I know nothing to find in the new house."

»Das hat keine Not.« sagte der Mann, 2.11
"There's no need." said the man,

»dort sehe ich einen großen Schrank, den schließ einmal auf.« 2.12
"I see a big cupboard there, open it."

Wie sie den Schrank aufschloß, stand da Kuchen, Fleisch, Obst, Wein, und lachte einen ordentlich an. 2.13
When she opened the cupboard, there were cakes, meat, fruit, wine, and a good laugh.

Da rief die Frau voll Freude: »Herz, 2.14
Then the woman called out joyfully, "Heart,

was begehrst du nun?« und sie setzten sich nieder, 2.15
what do you want now?" and they sat down,

aßen und tranken zusammen. Wie sie satt waren, fragte die Frau: 2.16
ate and drank together. When they were full, the woman asked:

»Aber Mann, wo kommt all dieser Reichtum her?« 2.17
"But man, where did all this wealth come from?"

2.18 »Ach.« antwortete er,

"Oh." he replied,

2.19 »frage mich nicht darum, ich darf dir's nicht sagen, wenn ich's jemand entdecke, so ist unser Glück wieder dahin.«

"don't ask me about it, I mustn't tell you, if I find out, our happiness will be gone again."

2.20 »Gut.« sprach sie,

"Very well." she said,

2.21 »wenn ich's, nicht wissen soll, so begehr ich's auch nicht zu wissen.«

"if I am not to know, I do not wish to know."

2.22 Das war aber ihr Ernst nicht, es ließ ihr keine Ruhe Tag und Nacht, und sie quälte und stachelte den Mann so lange, bis er in der Ungeduld heraussagte, es käme alles von einem wunderbaren goldenen Fisch, den er gefangen und dafür wieder in Freiheit gelassen hätte.

But she was not in earnest; it left her no peace day and night, and she pestered and goaded the man until he said impatiently that it all came from a wonderful golden fish which he had caught and set free again.

2.23 Und wie's heraus war, da verschwand alsbald das schöne Schloß mit dem Schrank, und sie saßen wieder in der alten Fischerhütte.

And as soon as it was out, the beautiful castle with the wardrobe disappeared, and they were back in the old fisherman's hut.

3.1 Der Mann mußte von vorn anfangen,

The man had to start all over again,

seinem Gewerbe nachgehen und fischen. 3.2
pursue his trade and go fishing.

Das Glück wollte es aber, daß er den goldenen Fisch 3.3
noch einmal herauszog.
As luck would have it, however, he pulled out the golden
fish once more.

»Hör.« sprach der Fisch, 3.4
"Listen." said the fish,

»wenn du mich wieder ins Wasser wirfst, 3.5
"if you throw me back into the water,

so will ich dir noch einmal das Schloß mit dem 3.6
Schrank voll Gesottenem und Gebratenem
zurückgeben;
I will give you back the lock with the cupboard full of
boiled and fried fish;

nur halt dich fest und verrat beileibe nicht, von wem 3.7
du's hast, sonst geht's wieder verloren.«
just hold on tight and don't tell me who gave it to you,
otherwise it will be lost again."

»Ich will mich schon hüten.« 3.8
"I'll be careful."

antwortete der Fischer und warf den Fisch in sein 3.9
Wasser hinab.
replied the fisherman and threw the fish down into the
water.

Daheim war nun alles wieder in voriger Herrlichkeit, 3.10
At home everything was again in its former splendor,

und die Frau war in einer Freude über das Glück; 3.11
and the woman was delighted with her good fortune;

3.12 aber die Neugierde ließ ihr doch keine Ruhe, daß sie nach ein paar Tagen wieder zu fragen anhub, wie es zugegangen wäre und wie er es angefangen habe.

but her curiosity left her no peace, so that after a few days she began to ask again how it had happened, and how he had begun it.

3.13 Der Mann schwieg eine Zeitlang still dazu, endlich aber machte sie ihn so ärgerlich, daß er herausplatzte und das Geheimnis verriet.

The man was silent for some time, but at last she made him so angry that he blurted out the secret.

3.14 In dem Augenblick verschwand das Schloß und sie saßen wieder in der alten Hütte.

At that moment the castle disappeared and they were sitting in the old hut again.

3.15 »Nun hast du's.« sagte der Mann,

"Now you've got it." said the man,

3.16 »jetzt können wir wieder am Hungertuch nagen.«

"now we can go back to gnawing on our hunger pangs."

3.17 »Ach.« sprach die Frau,

"Oh." said the woman,

3.18 »ich will den Reichtum lieber nicht, wenn ich nicht weiß von wem er kommt;

"I'd rather not have the wealth if I don't know where it comes from;

3.19 sonst habe ich doch keine Ruhe.«

otherwise I'll have no peace of mind."

Der Mann ging wieder fischen, und über eine Zeit
so war's nicht anders, er holte den Goldfisch zum
drittenmal heraus.

4.1

The man went fishing again, and after a time he brought
out the goldfish for the third time.

»Hör.« sprach der Fisch,

4.2

"Listen." said the fish,

»ich sehe wohl, ich soll immer wieder in deine Hände
fallen, nimm mich mit nach Hause und zerschneid
mich in sechs Stücke, zwei davon gieb deiner Frau zu
essen, zwei deinem Pferd und zwei leg in die Erde, so
wirst du Segen davon haben.«

4.3

"I see that I shall fall into your hands again and again, take
me home with you and cut me into six pieces, give two of
them to your wife to eat, two to your horse and two to the
ground, and you will be blessed."

Der Mann nahm den Fisch mit nach Hause und that
wie er ihm gesagt hatte.

4.4

The man took the fish home and did as he had told him.

Es geschah aber, daß aus den zwei Stücken, die in die
Erde gelegt waren, zwei goldene Lilien aufwuchsen,
und daß das Pferd zwei goldene Füllen bekam, und
des Fischers Frau zwei Kinder gebar, die ganz golden
waren.

4.5

And it came to pass that out of the two pieces which were
laid in the ground two golden lilies grew up, and the horse
had two golden fillings, and the fisherman's wife bore two
children who were all golden.

Die Kinder wuchsen heran, wurden groß und schön,
und die Lilien und Pferde wuchsen mit ihnen.

5.1

The children grew up, became tall and beautiful, and the
lilies and horses grew with them.

70

5.2 **Da sprachen sie: »Vater,**
Then they said: "Father,

5.3 **wir wollen uns auf unsere goldenen Rosse setzen und in die Welt ausziehen.«**
we want to get on our golden horses and go out into the world."

5.4 **Er aber antwortete betrübt:**
But he answered sadly:

5.5 **»Wie will ich's aushalten, wenn ihr fortzieht und ich nicht weiß wie's euch geht?«**
"How will I bear it if you go away and I don't know how you are?"

5.6 **Da sagten sie:**
Then they said,

5.7 **»Die zwei goldenen Lilien bleiben hier, daran könnt Ihr sehen, wie's uns geht;**
"The two golden lilies will stay here, so you can see how we are;

5.8 **sind sie frisch, so sind wir gesund; sind sie welk,**
if they are fresh, we are healthy; if they are withered,

5.9 **so sind wir krank; fallen sie um, so sind wir tot.«**
we are sick; if they fall over, we are dead."

5.10 **Sie ritten fort und kamen in ein Wirtshaus, darin waren viele Leute, und als sie die zwei Goldkinder erblickten, fingen sie an zu lachen und zu spotten.**
They rode away and came to an inn, where there were many people, and when they saw the two golden children, they began to laugh and mock.

Wie der eine das Gespött hörte, so schämte er sich, wollte nicht in die Welt, kehrte um und kam wieder heim zu seinem Vater.

5.11

When one of them heard the mockery, he was ashamed, did not want to go into the world, turned back and returned home to his father.

Der andere aber ritt fort und gelangte zu einem großen Wald.

5.12

But the other rode away and came to a great forest.

Und als er hineinreiten wollte, sprachen die Leute:

5.13

And when he wanted to ride in, the people said,

»Es geht nicht, daß Ihr durchreitet, der Wald ist voll Räuber, die werden übel mit Euch umgehen, und gar, wenn sie sehen, daß Ihr golden seid und Euer Pferd auch, so werden sie Euch tot schlagen.«

5.14

"You cannot ride through, the forest is full of robbers, they will deal with you badly, and even if they see that you are golden and your horse too, they will beat you to death."

Er aber ließ sich nicht schrecken und sprach,

5.15

But he was not frightened, and said,

»Ich muß und soll hindurch.«

5.16

"I must and shall pass through."

Da nahm er Bärenfelle und überzog sich und sein Pferd damit, daß nichts mehr vom Gold zu sehen war und ritt getrost in den Wald hinein.

5.17

So he took bearskins and covered himself and his horse with them, so that nothing of the gold was to be seen, and rode confidently into the forest.

5.18 Als er ein wenig fortgeritten war, so hörte er es in den Gebüschen rauschen und vernahm Stimmen, die miteinander sprachen.

When he had ridden a little way, he heard a rustling in the bushes, and heard voices talking together.

5.19 Von der einen Seite rief's: »Da ist einer.«

From one side he cried, "There is one."

5.20 von der anderen aber:

but from the other,

5.21 »Laß ihn laufen, das ist ein Bärenhäuter, und arm und kahl wie eine Kirchenmaus, was sollen wir mit ihm anfangen!«

"Let him go, he is a bear-skinned man, and as poor and bald as a church mouse, what shall we do with him!"

5.22 So ritt das Goldkind glücklich durch den Wald und geschah ihm kein Leid.

So the golden child rode happily through the forest, and no harm came to him.

6.1 Eines Tages kam er in ein Dorf, darin sah er ein Mädchen, das war so schön, daß er nicht glaubte, es könnte ein schöneres auf der Welt sein.

One day he came to a village and saw a girl who was so beautiful that he did not believe there could be a more beautiful girl in the world.

6.2 Und weil er eine so große Liebe zu ihm empfand, so ging er zu ihm und sagte,

And because he felt such great love for her, he went to her and said,

6.3 »Ich habe dich von ganzem Herzen lieb,

"I love you with all my heart,

willst du meine Frau werden?« 6.4

will you be my wife?"

Er gefiel aber auch dem Mädchen so sehr, daß es 6.5
einwilligte und sprach:

And he pleased the girl so much that she consented and
said:

»Ja, 6.6

"Yes,

ich will deine Frau werden und dir treu sein mein 6.7
Lebelang.«

I will be your wife and be faithful to you all my life."

Nun hielten sie Hochzeit zusammen, und als sie 6.8
eben in der größten Freude waren, kam der Vater
der Braut heim, und als er sah, daß seine Tochter
Hochzeit machte, verwunderte er sich und sprach:

Now they held the wedding together, and just as they were
in the greatest joy, the bride's father came home, and
when he saw that his daughter was getting married, he was
astonished, and said,

»Wo ist der Bräutigam?« Sie zeigten ihm das 6.9
Goldkind,

"Where is the bridegroom?" They showed him the golden
child,

das hatte aber noch seine Bärenfelle um. 6.10

but he still had his bearskins on.

Da sprach der Vater zornig: 6.11

Then the father said angrily,

»Nimmermehr soll ein Bärenhäuter meine Tochter 6.12
haben.«

"Never again shall a bear-skinner have my daughter."

6.13 und wollte ihn ermorden.
and wanted to murder him.

6.14 Da bat ihn die Braut, was sie konnte, und sprach:
Then the bride begged him as much as she could, and said,

6.15 »Er ist einmal mein Mann, und ich habe ihn von Herzen lieb.«
"He is my husband for once, and I love him dearly."

6.16 bis er sich endlich besänftigen ließ.
until at last he was appeased.

6.17 Doch aber kam's ihm nicht aus den Gedanken, sodaß er am anderen Morgen früh aufstand und seiner Tochter Mann sehen wollte, ob er ein gemeiner und verlumpter Bettler wäre.
But he could not get it out of his mind, so that he got up early the next morning, and went to see his daughter's husband to see if he was a mean and lousy beggar.

6.18 Wie er aber hinblickte, sah er einen herrlichen, goldenen Mann im Bette, und die abgeworfenen Bärenfelle lagen auf der Erde.
But when he looked, he saw a splendid golden man in bed, and the bearskins he had thrown off were lying on the ground.

6.19 Da ging er zurück und dachte:
Then he went back and thought,

6.20 »Wie gut ist's, daß ich meinen Zorn bändigte, ich hätte eine große Missethat begangen.«
"How good it is that I restrained my anger, for I had committed a great misdeed."

Dem Goldkind aber träumte, er zöge hinaus auf die Jagd mach einem prächtigen Hirsch, und als er am Morgen erwachte, sprach er zu seiner Braut, 7.1

But the golden child dreamed that he was going out to hunt a magnificent stag, and when he awoke in the morning, he said to his bride,

»Ich will hinaus auf die Jagd.« 7.2

"I want to go out hunting."

Ihr ward angst und sie bat ihn dazubleiben und sagte, 7.3

She was afraid, and begged him to stay, saying,

»Leicht kann dir ein großes Unglück begegnen.« 7.4

"A great misfortune may easily befall you."

aber er antwortete: »Ich soll und muß fort.« 7.5

but he answered, "I must and must go."

Da stand er auf und zog Hinaus in den Wald, und gar nicht lange, so hielt, auch ein stolzer Hirsch vor ihm, ganz nach seinem. 7.6

So he got up and went out into the forest, and not long afterward a proud stag stopped before him, just as he had dreamed.

Traume. Er legte an und wollte ihn schießen, 7.7

dream. He set about shooting it,

aber der Hirsch sprang fort. 7.8

but the stag sprang away.

Da jagte er ihm nach, über Graben und durch Gebüsche, und ward nicht müde den ganzen Tag; 7.9

So he chased after it, over ditch and through bushes, and never tired all day;

7.10 am Abend aber verschwand der Hirsch vor seinen Augen.

but in the evening the stag disappeared before his eyes.

7.11 Und als das Goldkind sich umsah, so stand er vor einem kleinen Haus, darin saß eine Hexe.

And when the golden child looked around, he stood in front of a small house where a witch was sitting.

7.12 Er klopfte an und ein Mütterchen kam heraus und fragte:

He knocked and a little mother came out and asked:

7.13 »Was wollt Ihr so spät noch mitten in dem großen Wald?«

"Why are you out so late in the middle of the big forest?"

7.14 Er sprach: »Habt Ihr keinen Hirsch gesehen?«

He said, "Have you not seen a deer?"

7.15 »Ja.« antwortete sie, »den Hirsch kenn' ich wohl.«

"Yes." she answered, "I know the stag."

7.16 und ein Hündlein, das mit ihr aus dem Haus gekommen war, bellte dabei den Mann heftig an.

and a little dog that had come out of the house with her barked fiercely at the man.

7.17 »Willst du schweigen, du böse Kröte.« sprach er,

"Will you be quiet, you wicked toad." he said,

7.18 »sonst schieß ich dich tot.« Da rief die Hexe zornig: »Was,

"or I'll shoot you dead." Then the witch cried angrily, "What,

mein Hündchen willst du töten!«

7.19

you want to kill my little dog!"

und verwandelte ihn alsbald, daß er dalag wie ein Stein, und seine Braut erwartete ihn umsonst und dachte:

7.20

and immediately turned him so that he lay there like a stone, and his bride waited for him in vain, thinking,

»Es ist gewiß eingetroffen, was mir so angst machte und so schwer auf dem Herzen lag.«

7.21

"What I was so afraid of and so heavy on my heart has certainly come true."

Daheim aber stand der andere Bruder bei den Goldlilien, als plötzlich eine davon umfiel.

8.1

But at home the other brother was standing by the golden lilies when suddenly one of them fell over.

»Ach Gott.« sprach er,

8.2

"Oh God." he said,

»meinem Bruder ist ein großes Unglück zugestoßen, ich muß fort, ob ich ihn vielleicht errette.«

8.3

"a great misfortune has befallen my brother, I must go away to see if I can save him."

Da sagte der Vater,

8.4

Then the father said,

»Bleib hier, wenn ich auch dich verliere, was soll ich anfangen?«

8.5

"Stay here, if I lose you too, what shall I do?"

Er aber antwortete: »Ich soll und muß fort.«

8.6

But he answered, "I must and must go away."

8.7 Da setzte er sich auf sein goldenes Pferd und ritt fort und kam in den großen Wald,

So he mounted his golden horse and rode away,

8.8 wo sein Bruder lag und Stein war.

and came to the great forest where his brother lay and was stone.

8.9 Die alte Hexe kam aus ihrem Haus, rief ihn an und wollte ihn auch berücken, aber er näherte sich nicht, sondern sprach:

The old witch came out of her house, called to him and wanted to touch him, but he did not approach, but said,

8.10 »Ich schieße dich nieder, wenn du meinen Bruder nicht wieder lebendig machst.«

"I will shoot you down if you do not bring my brother back to life."

8.11 Sie rührte, so ungern sie's auch that, den Stein mit dem Finger an, und alsbald erhielt er sein menschliches Leben zurück.

She touched the stone with her finger, however reluctantly, and he was soon restored to human life.

8.12 Die beiden Goldkinder aber freuten sich, als sie sich wiedersahen, küßten und herzten sich und ritten zusammen fort aus dem Wald, der eine zu seiner Braut, der andere heim zu seinem Vater.

The two golden children rejoiced when they saw each other again, kissed and hugged each other and rode away together from the forest, one to his bride, the other home to his father.

8.13 Da sprach der Vater:

Then the father said,

»Ich wußte wohl, daß du deinen Bruder erlöst hattest, denn die goldene Lilie ist auf einmal wieder aufgestanden und hat fortgeblüht.«

8.14

"I knew well that you had redeemed your brother, for the golden lily has suddenly risen again and blossomed."

Nun lebten sie vergnügt und es ging ihnen wohl bis an ihr Ende.

8.15

Now they lived happily ever after.

Der Fuchs und die Gänse

The Fox and the Geese

1.1 Der Fuchs kam einmal auf eine Wiese, wo eine Herde
schöner fetter Gänse saß, da lachte er und sprach:
The fox once came across a meadow where a flock of
beautiful, fat geese were sitting, and he laughed and said:

1.2 »Ich komme ja, wie gerufen, ihr sitzt hübsch
beisammen, so kann ich eine nach der anderen
auffressen.«
"I've come as called, you're sitting together nicely, so I can
eat them up one by one."

1.3 Die Gänse gackerten vor Schrecken, sprangen auf,
fingen an zu jammern und kläglich um ihr Leben zu
bitten.
The geese cackled in horror, jumped up, began to wail and
beg miserably for their lives.

1.4 Der Fuchs aber wollte auf nichts hören und sprach:
But the fox would listen to nothing and said:

1.5 »Da ist keine Gnade, ihr müßt sterben.«
"There is no mercy, you must die."

Endlich nahm sich eine das Herz und sagte: 1.6

At last one of them took heart, and said,

»Sollen wir armen Gänse doch einmal unser jung 1.7
frisch Leben lassen, so erzeige uns die einzige Gnade
und erlaub uns noch ein Gebet, damit wir nicht in
unseren Sünden sterben;

"If we poor geese are to live our young lives, show us the
only mercy, and allow us one more prayer, that we may not
die in our sins;

hernach wollen wir uns auch in eine Reihe stellen, 1.8

and then we will line ourselves up,

damit du dir immer die fetteste aussuchen kannst.« 1.9

so that you may always choose the fattest."

»Ja.« sagte der Fuchs, 1.10

"Yes." said the fox,

»das ist billig und ist eine fromme, Bitte; betet, 1.11

"that is a fair and pious request; pray,

ich will solange warten.« 1.12

I will wait till then."

Also fing die erste ein recht langes Gebet an, immer 1.13
»ga! ga!«

So the first one began a very long prayer, always "ga! ga!"

und weil sie gar nicht aufhören wollte, wartete die 1.14
zweite nicht, bis die Reihe an sie kam, sondern fing
auch an

and because she didn't want to stop, the second one didn't
wait until it was her turn, but also began

»ga! ga!« Die dritte und vierte folgten ihr, 1.15

"ga! ga!" The third and fourth followed her,

1.16 **und bald gackerten sie alle zusammen.**

and soon they were all cackling together.

1.17 **(Und wenn sie ausgebetet haben, soll das Märchen weiter erzählt werden, sie beten aber alleweil noch immer fort.)**

(And when they had finished praying, the fairy tale would continue to be told, but they still continued to pray.)

Dornröschen

Sleeping Beauty

1.1 Vor Zeiten war ein König und eine Königin, die sprachen jeden Tag:

Once upon a time there was a king and a queen who said every day:

1.2 »Ach, wenn wir doch ein Kind hätten!«

"Oh, if only we had a child!"

1.3 und kriegten immer keins.

and they never had one.

1.4 Da trug sich zu, als die Königin einmal im Bade saß, daß ein Frosch aus dem Wasser ans Land kroch und zu ihr sprach,

Then it happened once, when the queen was in the bath, that a frog crept out of the water on to the land and said to her,

1.5 »Dein Wunsch wird erfüllt werden;

"Your wish will be fulfilled;

1.6 ehe ein Jahr vergeht, wirst du eine Tochter zur Welt bringen.«

before a year passes you will give birth to a daughter."

Was der Frosch gesagt hatte, das geschah, und die Königin gebar ein Mädchen, das war so schön, daß der König vor Freude sich nicht zu lassen wußte und ein großes Fest anstellte.

1.7

What the frog had said came true, and the queen gave birth to a girl, who was so beautiful that the king could not contain his joy and made a great feast.

Er ladete nicht bloß seine Verwandten, Freunde und Bekannten, sondern auch die weisen Frauen dazu ein, damit sie dem Kind hold und gewogen wären.

1.8

He invited not only his relatives, friends, and acquaintances, but also the wise women, that they might be kind and favorable to the child.

Es waren ihrer dreizehn in seinem Reiche, weil er aber nur zwölf goldene Teller hatte, von welchen sie essen sollten, so mußte eine von ihnen daheim bleiben.

1.9

There were thirteen of them in his kingdom, but because he only had twelve golden plates for them to eat from, one of them had to stay at home.

Das Fest ward mit aller Pracht gefeiert, und als es zu Ende war, beschenkten die weisen Frauen das Kind mit ihren Wundergaben:

1.10

The feast was celebrated with great splendor, and when it was over, the wise women presented the child with their miraculous gifts:

die eine mit Tugend, die andere mit Schönheit, die dritte mit Reichtum, und so mit allem, was auf der Welt zu wünschen ist.

1.11

one with virtue, the other with beauty, the third with riches, and so with everything that could be desired in the world.

1.12 Als elfe ihre Sprüche eben gethan hatten,

When the eleven had just finished their spells,

1.13 trat plötzlich die dreizehnte herein.

the thirteenth suddenly entered.

1.14 Sie wollte sich dafür rächen, daß sie nicht eingeladen war, und ohne jemand zu grüßen oder nur anzusehen, rief sie mit lauter Stimme:

She wanted revenge for not having been invited, and without greeting or even looking at anyone, she cried out in a loud voice,

1.15 »Die Königstochter soll sich in ihrem fünfzehnten Jahre an einer Spindel stechen und tot hinfallen.«

"The King's daughter shall prick herself on a spindle in her fifteenth year, and fall down dead."

1.16 Und ohne ein Wort weiter zu sprechen,

And without saying another word,

1.17 kehrte sie sich um und verließ den Saal.

she turned and left the hall.

1.18 Alle waren erschrocken;

All were frightened;

1.19 da trat die zwölfte hervor, die ihren Wunsch noch übrig hatte und weil sie den bösen Spruch nicht aufheben, sondern nur ihn mildern konnte, so sagte sie: »Es soll aber kein Tod sein, sondern ein hundertjähriger tiefer Schlaf, in welchen die Königstochter fällt.«

then the twelfth came forward, who still had her wish left, and because she could not cancel the evil sentence, but only soften it, she said, "But it shall not be death, but a hundred years' deep sleep into which the king's daughter shall fall."

Der König, der sein liebes Kind vor dem Unglück gern 2.1
bewahren wollte, ließ den Befehl ausgehen, daß alle
Spindeln im ganzen Königreiche sollten verbrannt
werden.

The king, who wished to save his dear child from
misfortune, gave orders that all the spindles in the whole
kingdom should be burnt.

An dem Mädchen aber würden die Gaben der 2.2
weisen Frauen sämtlich erfüllt, denn es war so
schön, sittsam, freundlich und verständig, daß es
jedermann, der es ansah, lieb haben mußte.

But the gifts of the wise women were all fulfilled in the girl,
for she was so beautiful, modest, kind and intelligent that
everyone who looked at her must have loved her.

Es geschah, daß an dem Tage, wo es gerade fünfzehn 2.3
Jahre alt ward, der König und die Königin nicht
zu Hause waren, und das Mädchen ganz allein im
Schloß zurückblieb.

It happened that on the day when she was just fifteen years
old, the King and Queen were not at home, and the maiden
was left all alone in the castle.

Da ging es allerorten herum, besah Stuben und 2.4
Kammern, wie es Lust hatte, und kam endlich auch
an einen alten Turm.

So she went about everywhere, visiting parlors and
chambers as she pleased, and at last came to an old tower.

Es stieg die enge Wendeltreppe hinauf und gelangte 2.5
zu einer kleinen Thür.

She climbed the narrow spiral staircase and came to a small
door.

2.6 In dem Schloß steckte ein verrosteter Schlüssel, und als es umdrehte, sprang die Thür auf, und saß da in einem kleinen Stübchen eine alte Frau mit einer Spindel und spann emsig ihren Flachs.

There was a rusty key in the lock, and when he turned it, the door burst open, and there in a little room sat an old woman with a spindle, busily spinning her flax.

2.7 »Guten Tag, du altes Mütterchen.« sprach die Königstochter,

"Good day, you old mother." said the king's daughter,

2.8 »was machst du da?«

"what are you doing?"

2.9 »Ich spinne.« sagte die Alte und nickte mit dem Kopf.

"I'm spinning." said the old woman, nodding her head.

2.10 »Was ist das für ein Ding, das so lustig herumspringt?«

"What is that thing that is jumping around so merrily?"

2.11 sprach das Mädchen, nahm die Spindel und wollte auch spinnen.

said the girl, taking the spindle and wanting to spin too.

2.12 Kaum hatte sie aber die Spindel angerührt, so ging der Zauberspruch in Erfüllung, und sie stach sich damit in den Finger.

But no sooner had she touched the spindle than the spell came true and she pricked her finger with it.

3.1 In dem Augenblick aber, wo sie den Stich empfand, fiel sie auf das Bett nieder, das da stand, und lag in einem tiefen Schlaf.

But the moment she felt the sting, she fell down on the bed that stood there and lay in a deep sleep.

Und dieser Schlaf verbreitete sich über das ganze Schloß:

3.2

And this sleep spread over the whole castle:

der König und die Königin, die eben heimgekommen waren und in den Saal getreten waren, fingen an einzuschlafen und der ganze Hofstaat mit ihnen.

3.3

the king and queen, who had just come home and entered the hall, began to fall asleep, and the whole court with them.

Da schliefen auch die Pferde im Stall, die Hunde im Hofe, die Tauben auf dem Dache, die Fliegen an der Wand, ja, das Feuer, das auf dem Herde flackerte, ward still und schlief ein, und der Braten hörte auf zu brutzeln, und der Koch, der den Küchenjungen, weil er etwas versehen hatte, in den Haaren ziehen wollte, ließ ihn los und schlief.

3.4

Then the horses in the stable, the dogs in the courtyard, the pigeons on the roof, the flies on the wall, and even the fire that flickered on the hearth became quiet and fell asleep, and the roast meat ceased to sizzle, and the cook, who wanted to pull the scullion's hair because he had made a mistake, let him go and slept.

Und der Wind legte sich,

3.5

And the wind died down,

und auf den Bäumen vor dem Schloß regte sich kein Blättchen mehr.

3.6

and not a leaf stirred on the trees in front of the castle.

4.1 Rings um das Schloß aber begann eine Dornenhecke zu wachsen, die jedes Jahr höher ward, und endlich das ganze Schloß umzog, und darüber hinaus wuchs, daß gar nichts mehr davon zu sehen war, selbst nicht die Fahne auf dem Dach.

Around the castle, however, a hedge of thorns began to grow, which grew higher every year, and at last encircled the whole castle, and grew beyond it, so that nothing could be seen of it, not even the banner on the roof.

4.2 Es ging aber die Sage in dem Land von dem schönen schlafenden Dornröschen, denn so ward die Königstochter genannt, also daß von Zeit zu Zeit Königssöhne kamen und durch die Hecke in das Schloß dringen wollten.

But there was a legend in the country about the beautiful sleeping Sleeping Beauty, for that was what the king's daughter was called, so that from time to time the king's sons came and tried to get into the castle through the hedge.

4.3 Es war ihnen aber nicht möglich, denn die Dornen, als hätten sie Hände, hielten fest zusammen, und die Jünglinge blieben darin hängen, konnten sich nicht wieder los machen und starben eines jämmerlichen Todes.

But they could not do so, for the thorns, as if they had hands, held fast together, and the youths got caught in them, could not free themselves, and died a miserable death.

Nach langen langen Jahren kam wieder einmal ein Königssohn in das Land und hörte wie ein alter Mann von der Dornenhecke erzählte, es sollte ein Schloß dahinter stehen, in welchem eine wunderschöne Königstochter, Dornröschen genannt, schon seit hundert Jahren schliefe, und mit ihr schliefe der König und die Königin und der ganze Hofstaat.

4.4

After many long years, a king's son once again came to the country and heard an old man talking about the thorn hedge, saying that there was a castle behind it, in which a beautiful princess, called Sleeping Beauty, had been sleeping for a hundred years, and that the king and queen and the whole court slept with her.

Er wußte auch von seinem Großväter, daß schon viele Königssöhne gekommen wären und versucht hätten durch die Dornenhecke zu dringen, aber sie wären darin hängen geblieben und eines traurigen Todes gestorben.

4.5

He also knew from his grandfather that many of the king's sons had already come and tried to get through the thorn hedge, but they had got stuck in it and died a sad death.

Da sprach der Jüngling: »Ich fürchte mich nicht,

4.6

Then the youth said, "I am not afraid,

ich will hinaus und das schöne Dornröschen sehen.«

4.7

I will go out and see the beautiful Sleeping Beauty."

Der gute Alte mochte ihm abraten wie er wollte,

4.8

The good old man could advise him against it,

er hörte nicht auf seine Worte.

4.9

but he did not listen to his words.

5.1 Nun waren aber gerade die hundert Jahre verflossen und der Tag war gekommen, wo Dornröschen wieder erwachen sollte.

But now the hundred years had just passed and the day had come when Sleeping Beauty was to awake again.

5.2 Als der Königssohn sich der Dornenhecke näherte, waren es lauter schöne große Blumen, die thaten sich von selbst auseinander und ließen ihn unbeschädigt hindurch, und hinter ihm thaten sie sich wieder als eine Hecke zusammen.

As the king's son approached the hedge of thorns, it was full of beautiful large flowers, which parted of their own accord and let him pass through unharmed, and behind him they gathered together again as a hedge.

5.3 Im Schloßhof sah er die Pferde und scheckigen Jagdhunde liegen und schlafen,

In the courtyard he saw the horses and piebald hounds lying and sleeping,

5.4 auf dem Dache saßen die Tauben und hatten das Köpfchen unter den Flügel gesteckt.

and the pigeons sitting on the roof with their heads tucked under their wings.

5.5 Und als er ins Haus kam, schliefen die Fliegen an der Wand, der Koch, in der Küche hielt noch die Hand, als wollte er den Jungen anpacken, und die Magd saß vor dem schwarzen Huhn, das sollte gerupft werden.

And when he came into the house, the flies were sleeping on the wall, the cook in the kitchen was still holding his hand as if he wanted to take hold of the boy, and the maid was sitting in front of the black chicken that was to be plucked.

Da ging er weiter und sah im Saale den ganzen Hofstaat liegen und schlafen, und oben bei dem Throne lag der König und die Königin.

5.6

Then he went on, and saw the whole court lying asleep in the hall, and the king and queen up by the throne.

Da ging er noch weiter, und alles war so still, daß einer seinen Atem hören konnte, und endlich kam er zu dem Turm und öffnete die Thür zu der kleinen Stube, in welcher Dornröschen schlief.

5.7

Then he went still farther, and all was so still that some one could hear his breathing, and at last he came to the tower, and opened the door to the little room where Sleeping Beauty was sleeping.

Da lag es und war so schön, daß er die Augen nicht abwenden konnte, und er bückte sich und gab ihm einen Kuß.

5.8

There she lay, and was so beautiful that he could not take his eyes off her, and he stooped down and gave her a kiss.

Wie er es mit dem Kuß berührt hatte, schlug Dornröschen die Augen auf, erwachte und blickte ihn ganz freundlich an.

5.9

As soon as he had touched her with the kiss, Sleeping Beauty opened her eyes, awoke, and looked at him very kindly.

Da gingen sie zusammen herab, und der König erwachte und die Königin, und der ganze Hofstaat, und sahen einander mit großen Augen an.

5.10

Then they went down together, and the King awoke, and the Queen, and all the court, and looked at each other with wide eyes.

5.11 Und die Pferde im Hof standen auf und rüttelten sich; die Jagdhunde sprangen und wedelten; die Tauben auf dem Dache zogen das Köpfchen unterm Flügel hervor, sahen umher und flogen ins Feld; die Fliegen an den Wänden krochen weiter: das Feuer in der Küche erhob sich, flackerte und kochte das Essen; der Braten fing wieder an zu brutzeln; und der Koch gab dem Jungen eine Ohrfeige, daß er schrie; und die Magd rupfte das Huhn fertig.

And the horses in the courtyard stood up and shook themselves; the hounds jumped and wagged; the pigeons on the roof pulled their heads out from under their wings, looked about, and flew into the field; the flies on the walls crawled on; the fire in the kitchen rose, flickered, and cooked the food; the roast began to sizzle again; and the cook slapped the boy so that he screamed; and the maid finished plucking the chicken.

5.12 Und da wurde die Hochzeit des Königssohns mit dem Dornröschen in aller Pracht gefeiert,

And then the wedding of the King's son and the Sleeping Beauty was celebrated in all its splendor,

5.13 und sie lebten vergnügt bis an ihr Ende.

and they lived happily ever after.

Der Arme und der Reiche

The Rich and the Poor

1.1 Vor alten Zeiten, als der liebe Gott noch selber auf Erden unter den Menschen wandelte, trug es sich zu, daß er eines Abends müde war und ihn die Nacht überfiel, bevor er zu einer Herberge kommen konnte.

In ancient times, when the good Lord himself still walked among men on earth, it happened that one evening he was tired and the night overtook him before he could reach an inn.

1.2 Nun standen auf dem Weg vor ihm zwei Häuser einander gegenüber, das eine groß und schön, das andere klein und ärmlich anzusehen, und gehörte das große einem reichen, das kleine einem armen Manne.

Now on the road before him stood two houses opposite each other, one large and beautiful, the other small and poor to look at, and the large one belonged to a rich man, the small one to a poor man.

1.3 Da dachte unser Herrgott:

Then our Lord thought:

1.4 »Dem Reichen werde ich nicht beschwerlich fallen:

"I will not be a burden to the rich man:

bei ihm will ich übernachten.« 1.5

I will spend the night with him."

Der Reiche, als er an seine Thür klopfen hörte, 1.6
machte das Fenster auf und fragte den Fremdling
was er suche?

The rich man, when he heard a knock at his door, opened
the window and asked the stranger what he was looking
for?

Der Herr antwortete: 1.7

The gentleman replied:

»Ich bitte um ein Nachtlager.« 1.8

"I ask for a place to stay for the night."

Der Reiche guckte den Wandersmann von Haupt bis 1.9
zu den Füßen an, und weil der liebe Gott schlichte
Kleider trug und nicht aussah wie einer, der viel Geld
in der Tasche hat, schüttelte er mit dem Kopf und
sprach:

The rich man looked at the wanderer from head to toe, and
because the gentleman wore simple clothes and did not
look like someone with a lot of money in his pocket, he
shook his head and said,

»Ich kann Euch nicht aufnehmen, meine Kammern 1.10
liegen voll Kräuter und Samen, und sollte ich einen
jeden beherbergen, der an meine Thür klopft, so
könnte ich selber den Bettelstab in die Hand nehmen.

"I cannot take you in, my chambers are full of herbs and
seeds, and if I were to accommodate anyone who knocks at
my door, I could take up the begging stick myself.

Sucht Euch anderswo ein Unterkommen.« 1.11

Find lodgings elsewhere."

1.12 Schlug damit sein Fenster zu und ließ den lieben Gott stehen.

With that he closed his window and left the good Lord standing there.

1.13 Also kehrte ihm der liebe Gott den Rücken und ging hinüber zu dem kleinen Haus.

So the good Lord turned his back on him and went over to the little house.

1.14 Kaum hatte er angeklopft, so klinkte der Arme schon sein Thürchen auf und bat den Wandersmann einzutreten.

No sooner had he knocked than the poor man opened his little door and asked the wanderer to come in.

1.15 »Bleibt die Nacht über bei mir.« sagte er

"Stay with me for the night." he said,

1.16 »es ist schon finster und heute könnt Ihr doch nicht weiterkommen.«

"it's already dark and you can't get any further today."

1.17 Das gefiel dem lieben Gott und er trat zu ihm ein.

This pleased the good Lord and he entered.

1.18 Die Frau des Armen reichte ihm die Hand, hieß ihn willkommen und sagte, er möchte sich's bequem machen und vorlieb nehmen, sie hätten nicht viel, aber was es wäre, gäben sie von Herzen gern.

The poor man's wife shook his hand, welcomed him and said that he should make himself comfortable and make do, they didn't have much, but what they did have, they would gladly give.

Dann setzte sie Kartoffeln ans Feuer, und derweil sie 1.19
kochten, melkte sie ihre Ziege, damit sie ein wenig
Milch dazu hätten.

Then she put potatoes on the fire, and while they were
cooking, she milked her goat, so that they might have a
little milk with them.

Und als der Tisch gedeckt war, setzte sich der liebe 1.20
Gott nieder und aß mit ihnen, und schmeckte ihm
die schlechte Kost gut, denn es waren vergnügte
Gesichter dabei.

And when the table was laid, the good Lord sat down and
ate with them, and he liked the bad food, for there were
happy faces among them.

Nachdem sie gegessen hatten und Schlafenszeit war, 1.21
rief die Frau heimlich ihren Mann und sprach:

After they had eaten and it was bedtime, the wife secretly
called her husband and said,

»Hör, lieber Mann, wir wollen uns heute nacht eine 1.22
Streu machen, damit der arme Wanderer sich in
unser Bett legen und ausruhen kann;

"Listen, dear husband, we want to make ourselves a
bedding tonight, so that the poor wanderer can lie down in
our bed and rest;

er ist den ganzen Tag über gegangen, da wird einer 1.23
müde.«

he has been walking all day, so one gets tired."

»Von Herzen gern.« antwortete er, 1.24

"With all my heart." he replied,

»ich will's ihm anbieten.« 1.25

"I will offer it to him."

100

1.26 ging zu dem lieben Gott und bat ihn, wenn's ihm recht wäre, möchte er sich in ihr Bett legen und seine Glieder ordentlich ausruhen.

The old man went to the good Lord and asked him, if it was all right with him, if he would lie down in her bed and rest his limbs properly.

1.27 Der liebe Gott wollte den beiden Alten ihr Lager nicht nehmen, aber sie ließen nicht ab, bis er es endlich that und sich in ihr Bett legte;

The dear God would not take away the two old men's bed, but they would not let him go until he finally did so and lay down in their bed;

1.28 sich selbst aber machten sie eine Streu auf der Erde.

but they made themselves a litter on the ground.

1.29 Am anderen Morgen standen sie vor Tag schon auf und kochten dem Gast ein Frühstück, so gut sie es hatten.

The next morning they got up before daylight and cooked their guest as good a breakfast as they had.

1.30 Als nun die Sonne durchs Fensterlein schien und der liebe Gott aufgestanden war,

When the sun shone through the little window and the good Lord had risen,

1.31 aß er wieder mit ihnen und wollte dann seines Weges ziehen.

he ate with them again and then wanted to go on his way.

1.32 Als er in der Thür stand, kehrte er sich um und sprach:

As he stood at the door, he turned back and said,

»Weil ihr so mitleidig und fromm seid, so wünscht 1.33
euch dreierlei, das will ich euch erfüllen.«
"Because you are so compassionate and pious, I will grant
you three wishes."

Da sagte der Arme: 1.34
Then the poor man said,

»Was soll ich mir sonst noch wünschen als die 1.35
ewige Seligkeit, und daß wir zwei, solange wir
leben, gesund dabei bleiben und unser notdürftiges
tägliches Brot haben;
"What else can I wish for but eternal happiness, and that
we two may remain healthy as long as we live, and have our
daily bread;

fürs dritte weiß ich mir nichts zu wünschen.« 1.36
for the third I know nothing to wish for."

Der liebe Gott sprach: 1.37
The good God said,

»Willst du dir nicht ein neues Haus für das alte 1.38
wünschen?«
"Will you not wish for a new house for the old one?"

»O ja.« sagte der Mann, 1.39
"Oh yes." said the man,

»wenn ich das auch noch erhalten kann, so wär mir's 1.40
wohl lieb.«
"if I can get that too, I'd like that."

1.41 Da erfüllte der Herr ihre Wünsche, verwandelte ihr altes Haus in ein neues, gab ihnen nochmals seinen Segen und zog weiter.

So the Lord fulfilled their wishes, transformed their old house into a new one, gave them his blessing once again and moved on.

2.1 Es war schon voller Tag, als der Reiche aufstand.

It was already full day when the rich man got up.

2.2 Er legte sich ins Fenster und sah gegenüber ein neues reinliches Haus mit roten Ziegeln,

He lay down in the window and saw a new,

2.3 wo sonst eine alte Hütte gestanden hatte.

clean house with red bricks opposite where an old hut used to stand.

2.4 Da machte er große Augen, rief seine Frau herbei und sprach,

His eyes widened, he called his wife over and said,

2.5 »Sag mir, was ist geschehen?

"Tell me, what has happened?

2.6 Gestern abend stand noch die alte elende Hütte,

Yesterday evening there was still the old miserable hut,

2.7 und heute steht da ein schönes neues Haus.

and today there is a beautiful new house.

2.8 Lauf hinüber und höre wie das gekommen ist.«

Run over and hear how it came to be."

2.9 Die Frau ging und fragte den Armen aus; er erzählte ihr:

The woman went and questioned the poor man; he told her:

»Gestern abend kam ein Wanderer, der suchte
Nachtherberge, und heute morgen beim Abschied
hat er uns drei Wünsche gewährt, die ewige Seligkeit,
Gesundheit in diesem Leben und das notdürftige
tägliche Brot dazu und zuletzt noch statt unserer
alten Hütte ein schönes neues Haus.«

2.10

"Yesterday evening a wanderer came looking for shelter
for the night, and this morning when we said goodbye he
granted us three wishes: eternal bliss, health in this life
and the bare necessities of life, and finally a beautiful new
house instead of our old hut."

Die Frau des Reichen lief eilig zurück und erzählte
ihrem Manne wie alles gekommen war.

2.11

The rich man's wife hurried back and told her husband how
everything had come about.

Der Mann sprach,

2.12

The man said,

»Ich möchte mich zerreißen und zerschlagen;

2.13

"I want to tear myself to pieces and smash myself;

hätte ich das nur gewußt!

2.14

if only I had known!

der Fremde ist zuvor hier gewesen und hat bei uns
übernachten wollen,

2.15

The stranger had been here before and wanted to spend the
night with us,

ich habe ihn aber abgewiesen.«

2.16

but I refused him."

»Eil dich.« sprach die Frau,

2.17

"Make haste." said the woman,

104

2.18 »und setze dich auf dein Pferd, so kannst du den Mann noch einholen, und dann mußt du dir auch drei Wünsche gewähren lassen.«

"and get on your horse, so that you can still catch up with the man, and then you must allow yourself three wishes."

3.1 Der Reiche befolgte den guten Rat, jagte mit seinem Pferde davon und holte den lieben Gott noch ein.

The rich man followed the good advice, chased off on his horse, and caught up with the good Lord.

3.2 Er redete fein und lieblich und bat, er möcht's nicht übel nehmen, daß er nicht gleich wäre eingelassen worden, er hätte den Schlüssel zur Hausthür gesucht, derweil wäre er weggegangen: wenn er des Weges zurückkäme, müßte er bei ihm einkehren.

He spoke sweetly and sweetly, and begged him not to take it amiss that he had not been admitted at once; he had been looking for the key to the door of the house, and in the meantime had gone away, and when he came back he would have to stop at his house.

3.3 »Ja.« sprach der liebe Gott,

"Yes." said the good Lord,

3.4 »wenn ich einmal zurückkomme, will ich es thun.«

"when I come back, I will do so."

3.5 Da fragte der Reiche, ob er nicht auch drei Wünsche thun dürfte wie sein Nachbar?

Then the rich man asked if he might not make three wishes like his neighbor?

Ja, sagte der liebe Gott, das dürfte er wohl, es wäre aber nicht gut für ihn, und er sollte sich lieber nichts wünschen.

3.6

Yes, said the good God, he could, but it would not be good for him, and he had better not wish for anything.

Der Reiche meinte, er wollte sich schon etwas aussuchen, das zu seinem Glück gereiche, wenn er nur wüßte, daß es erfüllt würde.

3.7

The rich man said that he would choose something that would bring him happiness if he only knew that it would be fulfilled.

Sprach der liebe Gott:

3.8

Said the good God,

»Reit heim und drei Wünsche, die du thust, die sollen in Erfüllung gehen.«

3.9

"Go home, and three wishes that you make shall come true."

Nun hatte der Reiche, was er verlangte, ritt heimwärts und fing an nachzusinnen, was er sich wünschen sollte.

4.1

Now the rich man had what he wanted, rode home and began to think about what he should wish for.

Wie er sich so bedachte und die Zügel fallen ließ, fing das Pferd an zu springen, sodaß er immerfort in seinen Gedanken gestört wurde und sie gar nicht zusammenbringen konnte.

4.2

As he pondered and dropped the reins, the horse began to jump, so that he was constantly disturbed in his thoughts and could not bring them together.

4.3 Er klopfte ihm an den Hals und sagte: »Sei ruhig, Liese.«

He patted him on the neck and said, "Be quiet, Liese."

4.4 aber das Pferd machte aufs neue Männchen.

but the horse kept jumping.

4.5 Da ward er zuletzt ärgerlich und rief ganz ungeduldig,

Then at last he became angry, and called out impatiently,

4.6 »So wollt ich, daß du den Hals zerbrächst!«

"I want you to break your neck!"

4.7 Wie er das Wort ausgesprochen hatte, plump, fiel er auf die Erde, und lag das Pferd tot und regte sich nicht mehr;

As soon as he had uttered the word, clumsily, he fell to the ground, and the horse lay dead, and moved no more;

4.8 damit war der erste Wunsch erfüllt.

so the first wish was fulfilled.

4.9 Weil er aber von Natur geizig war, wollte er das Sattelzeug nicht im Stich lassen, schnitt's ab, hing's auf seinen Rücken und mußte nun zu Fuß gehen.

But because he was stingy by nature, he did not want to abandon the saddlery, so he cut it off, hung it on his back and had to walk.

4.10 »Du hast noch zwei Wünsche übrig.«

"You still have two wishes left."

4.11 dachte er und tröstete sich damit.

he thought and comforted himself.

Wie er nun langsam durch den Sand dahin ging, und 4.12
zu Mittag die Sonne heiß brannte, ward's ihm so
warm und verdrießlich zu Mute;

As he walked slowly along through the sand, and at noon
the sun was burning hot, he felt so warm and morose;

der Sattel drückte ihn auf den Rücken, auch war ihm 4.13
noch immer nicht eingefallen, was er sich wünschen
sollte.

the saddle pressed down on his back, and he still could not
think of what he should wish for.

»Wenn ich mir auch alle Reiche und Schätze der Welt 4.14
wünsche.«

"Even if I wish for all the riches and treasures in the
world."

sprach er zu sich selbst, 4.15

he said to himself,

»so fällt mir hernach noch allerlei ein, dieses und 4.16
jenes, das weiß ich im voraus;

"I can think of all sorts of things afterwards, this and that, I
know that in advance;

ich will's aber so einrichten, daß mir gar nichts mehr 4.17
übrig zu wünschen bleibt.«

but I will arrange it so that I have nothing left to wish for."

Dann seufzte er und sprach: 4.18

Then he sighed and said:

4.19 »Ja, wenn ich der bayrische Bauer wäre, der auch drei Wünsche frei hatte, der wußte sich zu helfen, der wünschte sich zuerst recht viel Bier, und zweitens so viel Bier als er trinken könnte, und drittens noch ein Faß Bier dazu.«

"Yes, if I were the Bavarian farmer who also had three wishes, he would know how to help himself, he would first wish for a lot of beer, and secondly as much beer as he could drink, and thirdly a barrel of beer on top."

4.20 Manchmal meinte er, jetzt hätte er es gefunden, aber hernach schien's ihm doch noch zu wenig.

Sometimes he thought he had found it now, but afterwards it still seemed too little.

4.21 Da kam ihm so in die Gedanken, was es seine Frau jetzt gut hätte, die säße daheim in einer kühlen Stube und ließe sich's wohl schmecken.

Then it occurred to him that his wife would have a good time now, sitting at home in a cool room and enjoying herself.

4.22 Das ärgerte ihn ordentlich und ohne daß er's wußte, sprach er so hin:

That really annoyed him, and without knowing it, he said:

4.23 »Ich wollte, die säße daheim auf dem Sattel, und könnte nicht herunter, statt daß ich ihn da auf meinem Rücken schleppe.«

"I wish she were sitting on the saddle at home, and could not get down, instead of me dragging him on my back."

Und wie das letzte Wort aus seinem Munde kam, so war der Sattel von seinem Rücken verschwunden, und er merkte, daß sein zweiter Wunsch auch in Erfüllung gegangen war.

4.24

And as the last word came out of his mouth, the saddle had disappeared from his back, and he realized that his second wish had also come true.

Da ward ihm erst recht heiß, er fing an zu laufen und wollte sich daheim ganz einsam in seine Kammer hinsetzen und auf etwas Großes für den letzten Wunsch sinnen.

4.25

Then he was really hot, and began to run, and wanted to sit down in his chamber at home all alone, and think of something great for his last wish.

Wie er aber ankommt und die Stubenthür aufmacht, sitzt da seine Frau mittendrin auf dem Sattel und kann nicht herunter, jammert und schreit.

4.26

But when he arrived and opened the parlor door, his wife was sitting in the middle of it on the saddle and could not get down, wailing and screaming.

Da sprach er:

4.27

Then he said:

»Gieb dich zufrieden, ich will dir alle Reichtümer der Welt herbeiwünschen, nur bleib da sitzen.«

4.28

"Be content, I will wish you all the riches in the world, just sit there."

Sie schalt ihn aber einen Schafskopf und sprach:

4.29

But she called him a blockhead and said,

»Was helfen mir alle Reichtümer der Welt, wenn ich auf dem Sattel sitze;

4.30

"All the riches in the world won't help me if I sit on the saddle;

4.31 du hast mich darauf gewünscht,

you have wished me up,

4.32 du mußt mir auch wieder herunter helfen.«

you must help me down again."

4.33 Er mochte wollen oder nicht, er mußte den dritten
Wunsch thun, daß sie vom Sattel ledig wäre und
heruntersteigen könnte;

Whether he liked it or not, he had to make the third wish,
that she might get off the saddle and get down again;

4.34 und der Wunsch ward alsbald erfüllt.

and the wish was immediately granted.

4.35 Also hatte er nichts davon als Ärger, Mühe,
Scheltworte und ein verlorenes Pferd;

So he got nothing out of it but trouble, toil, bad words, and
a lost horse;

4.36 die Armen aber lebten vergnügt, still und fromm bis
an ihr seliges Ende.

but the poor woman lived happily, quietly, and piously to
her blessed end.

Das singende springende Löweneckerchen

The Singing Leaping Lion Eagle

1.1 Es war einmal ein Mann, der hatte eine große Reise vor, und beim Abschied fragte er seine drei Töchter, was er ihnen mitbringen sollte.

Once upon a time there was a man who was going on a long journey, and when he left he asked his three daughters what he should bring them.

1.2 Da wollte die älteste Perlen, die zweite wollte Diamanten, die dritte aber sprach:

The eldest wanted pearls, the second wanted diamonds, but the third said:

1.3 »Lieber Vater, ich wünsche mir ein singendes springendes Löweneckerchen (Lerche).«

"Dear father, I would like a singing, leaping lion lark."

1.4 Der Vater sagte,

The father said,

1.5 »Ja, wenn ich es kriegen kann, sollst du es haben.«

"Yes, if I can get it, you shall have it."

küßte alle drei und zog fort. 1.6
He kissed all three and went away.

Als nun die Zeit kam, daß er wieder auf dem 1.7
Heimwege war, so hatte er Perlen und Diamanten
für die zwei ältesten gekauft, aber das singende
springende Löweneckerchen für die jüngste hatte
er umsonst allerorten gesucht, und das that ihm leid,
denn sie war sein liebstes Kind.
When the time came that he was on his way home again,
he had bought pearls and diamonds for the two eldest, but
he had looked everywhere in vain for the singing, leaping
lion-croissant for the youngest, and he was sorry for that,
for she was his dearest child.

Da führte ihn der Weg durch einen Wald, und mitten 1.8
darin war ein prächtiges Schloß, und nahe am
Schloß stand ein Baum, ganz oben auf der Spitze
des Baumes aber sah er ein Löweneckerchen singen
und springen.
Then the path led him through a forest, and in the middle
of it was a magnificent castle, and near the castle stood
a tree, but at the very top of the tree he saw a little lion
singing and jumping.

»Ei, du kommst mir gerade recht.« 1.9
"Oh, you're just in time for me."

sagte er ganz vergnügt und rief seinem Diener, 1.10
he said with great amusement,

er sollte hinaufsteigen und das Tierchen fangen. 1.11
and called to his servant to climb up and catch the little
animal.

1.12 Wie er aber zu dem Baum trat, sprang eine Löwe darunter auf, schüttelte sich und brüllte, daß das Laub an den Bäumen zitterte.

But as he stepped up to the tree, a lion jumped up from under it, shook himself and roared so that the leaves on the trees shook.

1.13 »Wer mir mein singendes springendes Löweneckerchen stehlen will.«

"Whoever wants to steal my singing, leaping lion's eagle."

1.14 rief er, »den fresse ich auf.« Da sagte der Mann,

he shouted, "I'll eat him." Then the man said,

1.15 »Ich habe nicht gewußt, daß der Vogel dir gehört;

"I did not know that the bird belonged to you;

1.16 ich will mein Unrecht wieder gut machen, und mich mit schwerem Golde loskaufen, laß mir nur das Leben.«

I will make amends for my wrong, and buy myself off with heavy gold, only let me live."

1.17 Der Löwe sprach:

The lion said,

1.18 »Dich kann nichts retten, als wenn du mir zu eigen versprichst, was dir daheim zuerst begegnet;

"Nothing can save thee but if thou wilt promise me to own what thou findest at home first;

1.19 willst du das aber thun, so schenke ich dir das Leben und den Vogel für deine Tochter obendrein.«

but if thou wilt do that, I will give thee thy life, and the bird for thy daughter besides."

1.20 Der Mann aber weigerte sich und sprach:

But the man refused and said,

»Das könnte meine jüngste Tochter sein, die hat mich am liebsten und läuft mir immer entgegen, wenn ich nach Haus komme.«   1.21

"That could be my youngest daughter, she loves me best and always runs to meet me when I come home."

Dem Diener aber war angst und er sagte,   1.22

But the servant was afraid and said,

»Muß Euch denn gerade Eure Tochter begegnen,   1.23

"Must you meet your daughter,

es könnte ja auch eine Katze oder ein Hund sein.«   1.24

it could be a cat or a dog."

Da ließ sich der Mann überreden, nahm das singende springende Löweneckerchen und versprach dem Löwen zu eigen, was ihm daheim zuerst begegnen würde.   1.25

So the man allowed himself to be persuaded, took the singing, jumping lion and promised to give the lion what he would meet at home first.

Wie er daheim anlangte und in sein Haus eintrat, war das erste, was ihm begegnete, niemand anders als seine jüngste, liebste Tochter;   2.1

When he arrived home and entered his house, the first thing he met was none other than his youngest, dearest daughter;

die kam gelaufen, küßte und herzte ihn, und als sie sah, daß er ein singendes springendes Löweneckerchen mitgebracht hatte war sie außer sich vor Freude.   2.2

she came running, kissed and hugged him, and when she saw that he had brought a singing, leaping lion bird with him, she was beside herself with joy.

2.3 Der Vater aber konnte sich nicht freuen, sondern fing an zu weinen und sagte:

The father, however, could not rejoice, but began to weep, and said,

2.4 »Mein liebstes Kind, den kleinen Vogel habe ich teuer gekauft, ich habe dich dafür einem wilden Löwen versprechen müssen, und wenn er dich hat, wird er dich zerreißen und fressen.«

"My dearest child, I have bought the little bird at a great price, I have had to promise you to a wild lion for it, and when he has you he will tear you to pieces and eat you."

2.5 und erzählte ihr da alles, wie es zugegangen war, und bat sie nicht hinzugehen, es möchte auch kommen was da wollte.

and then he told her all that had happened, and begged her not to go, and let whatever might come.

2.6 Sie tröstete ihn aber und sprach:

But she comforted him, and said,

2.7 »Liebster Vater, was Ihr versprochen habt, muß auch gehalten werden;

"Dearest father, what you have promised must be kept;

2.8 ich will hingehen und will den Löwen schon besänftigen,

I will go and appease the lion,

2.9 daß ich wieder gesund zu Euch komme.«

so that I may come to you again in good health."

2.10 Am anderen Morgen ließ sie sich den Weg zeigen,

The next morning she asked to be shown the way,

nahm Abschied und ging getrost in den Wald hinein.   2.11

took her leave and went confidently into the forest.

Der Löwe aber war ein verzauberter Königssohn,   2.12
und war bei Tage ein Löwe, und mit ihm wurden alle
seine Leute Löwen, in der Nacht aber hatten sie ihre
natürliche menschliche Gestalt.

But the lion was an enchanted son of the king, and was a
lion by day, and with him all his people became lions, but at
night they had their natural human form.

Bei ihrer Ankunft ward sie freundlich empfangen   2.13
und in das Schloß geführt.

On her arrival she was kindly received and led into the
castle.

Als die Nacht kam,   2.14

When night came,

war er ein schöner Mann und die Hochzeit ward mit   2.15
Pracht gefeiert.

he was a handsome man and the wedding was celebrated
with splendor.

Sie lebten vergnügt miteinander,   2.16

They lived happily together,

wachten in der Nacht und schliefen am Tage.   2.17

waking at night and sleeping during the day.

Zu einer Zeit kam er und sagte: 2.18

At one time he came and said,

2.19 »Morgen ist ein Fest in deines Vaters Haus, weil deine älteste Schwester sich verheiratet und wenn du Lust hast hinzugehen, so sollen dich meine Löwen hinführen.«

"Tomorrow there is a feast at your father's house, because your eldest sister is getting married, and if you feel like going, my lions shall take you there."

2.20 Da sagte sie: »Ja, ich möchte gern meinen Vater wiedersehen.«

Then she said, "Yes, I would like to see my father again."

2.21 fuhr hin und ward von den Löwen begleitet.

She went and was accompanied by the lions.

2.22 Da war große Freude, als sie ankam, denn sie hatten alle geglaubt, sie wäre von dem Löwen zerrissen worden und schon lange nicht mehr am Leben.

There was great joy when she arrived, for they had all believed that she had been torn to pieces by the lion and had not been alive for a long time.

2.23 Sie erzählte aber, was sie für einen schönen Mann hätte und wie gut es ihr ginge, und blieb bei ihnen so lange die Hochzeit dauerte, dann fuhr sie wieder in den Wald.

But she told them what a handsome husband she had and how well off she was, and stayed with them as long as the wedding lasted, then she went back into the forest.

2.24 Wie die zweite Tochter heiratete und sie wieder zur Hochzeit eingeladen war, sprach sie zum Löwen:

When the second daughter got married and she was invited to the wedding again, she said to the lion,

2.25 »Diesmal will ich nicht allein sein, du mußt mitgehen.«

"I don't want to be alone this time, you must go with me."

Der Löwe aber sagte, das wäre zu gefährlich für ihn, denn wenn dort der Strahl eines brennenden Lichts ihn berührte, so würde er in eine Taube verwandelt, und müßte sieben Jahre lang mit den Tauben fliegen. 2.26

But the lion said it would be too dangerous for him, for if the ray of a burning light touched him there, he would be turned into a dove, and would have to fly with the doves for seven years.

»Ach.« sagte sie, »geh nur mit mir; 2.27

"Oh." she said, "go with me;

ich will dich schon hüten und vor allem Licht bewahren.« 2.28

I will guard you and keep you from all light."

Also zogen sie zusammen und nahmen auch ihr kleines Kind mit. 2.29

So they went together and took their little child with them.

Sie ließ dort einen Saal mauern, so stark und dick, daß kein Strahl durchdringen konnte, darin sollte er sitzen, wenn die Hochzeitslichter angesteckt würden. 2.30

She had a hall built there, so strong and thick that no ray could penetrate it, in which he was to sit when the wedding lights were lighted.

Die Thür aber war von frischem Holz gemacht, das sprang und bekam einen kleinen Ritz, den kein Mensch bemerkte. 2.31

The door, however, was made of fresh wood, which cracked and got a small crack that no one noticed.

2.32 Nun ward die Hochzeit mit Pracht gefeiert, wie aber der Zug aus der Kirche zurückkam mit den vielen Fackeln und Lichtern an dem Saal vorbei, da fiel ein haarbreiter Strahl auf den Königssohn, und wie dieser Strahl ihn berührt hatte, in dem Augenblick war er auch verwandelt, und als sie hineinkam und ihn suchte, sah sie ihn nicht, aber es saß da eine weiße Taube.

Now the wedding was celebrated with splendor, but as the procession came back from the church with the many torches and lights past the hall, a ray as wide as a hair fell on the King's son, and as soon as this ray had touched him, he was changed, and when she went in and looked for him, she did not see him, but there was a white dove sitting there.

2.33 Die Taube sprach zu ihr,

The dove said to her,

2.34 »Sieben Jahre muß ich in die Welt fortfliegen;

"Seven years must I fly away into the world;

2.35 alle sieben Schritt aber will ich einen roten Blutstropfen und eine weiße Feder fallen lassen, die sollen dir den Weg zeigen, und wenn du der Spur folgst, kannst du mich erlösen.«

but every seven steps I will let fall a drop of red blood and a white feather, which shall show thee the way, and if thou wilt follow the track, thou canst deliver me."

3.1 Da flog die Taube zur Thür hinaus, und sie folgte ihr auch, und alle sieben Schritt fiel ein rotes Blutströpfchen und ein weißes Federchen herab und zeigte ihr den Weg.

Then the dove flew out of the door, and she also followed her, and every seven steps a drop of red blood and a white feather fell down and showed her the way.

So ging sie immer zu in die weite Welt hinein, und schaute nicht um sich und ruhten sich nicht, und waren fast die sieben Jahre herum; da freute sie sich und meinte, sie wären bald erlöst, und war noch so weit davon.

3.2

Thus she went on and on into the wide world, and did not look about her, and did not rest, and when the seven years were nearly over, she rejoiced, and thought they would soon be delivered, and she was still so far from it.

Einmal, als sie so fortging, fiel kein Federchen mehr und auch kein rotes Blutströpfchen, und als sie die Augen aufschlug, so war die Taube verschwunden.

3.3

Once, when she was thus gone, not a feather fell, nor a drop of red blood, and when she opened her eyes, the dove was gone.

Und weil sie dachte, Menschen könnten ihr da nicht helfen, so stieg sie zur Sonne hinauf und sagte zu ihr,

3.4

And because she thought that people could not help her, she went up to the sun and said to it,

»Du scheinst in Ritzen und über alle Spitzen,

3.5

"You shine in cracks and over all the peaks,

hast du keine weiße Taube fliegen sehen?«

3.6

have you not seen a white dove fly?"

»Nein.« sagte die Sonne,

3.7

"No." said the sun,

»ich habe keine gesehen, aber da schenk ich dir ein Kästchen, das mach auf, wenn du in großer Not bist.«

3.8

"I have not seen one, but I will give you a little box to open when you are in great need."

3.9 Da dankte sie der Sonne und ging weiter, bis es Abend war, und der Mond schien, da fragte sie ihn:

Then she thanked the sun and went on until it was evening and the moon was shining, when she asked him,

3.10 »Du scheinst ja die ganze Nacht und durch alle Felder und Wälder,

"You have been shining all night and through all the fields and woods,

3.11 hast du keine weiße Taube fliegen sehen?«

have you not seen a white dove fly?"

3.12 »Nein.« sagte der Mond,

"No." said the moon,

3.13 »ich habe keine gesehen, aber da schenk ich dir ein Ei, das zerbrich, wenn du in großer Not bist.«

"I have not seen one, but I will give you an egg to break when you are in great distress."

3.14 Da dankte sie dem Mond, und ging weiter, bis der Nachtwind herankam und sie anblies;

Then she thanked the moon, and went on until the night wind came and blew at her;

3.15 da sprach sie zu ihm:

then she said to him,

3.16 »Du wehst ja über alle Bäume und unter allen Blättern weg,

"You are blowing away over all the trees and under all the leaves,

3.17 hast du keine weiße Taube fliegen sehen?«

have you not seen a white dove fly?"

»Nein.« sagte der Nachtwind,   3.18
"No." said the night wind,

»ich habe keine gesehen, aber ich will die drei   3.19
anderen Winde fragen, die haben sie vielleicht
gesehen.«
"I have not seen one, but I will ask the three other winds,
they may have seen it."

Der Ostwind und der Westwind kamen und hatten   3.20
nichts gesehen, der Südwind aber sprach:
The east wind and the west wind came and had seen
nothing, but the south wind said,

»Die weiße Taube habe ich gesehen, sie ist zum roten   3.21
Meer geflogen, da ist sie wieder ein Löwe geworden,
denn die sieben Jahre sind herum, und der Löwe
steht dort im Kampf mit einem Lindwurm, der
Lindwurm aber ist eine verzauberte Königstochter.«
"I have seen the white dove, it has flown to the Red Sea,
where it has become a lion again, for the seven years have
passed, and the lion is there in battle with a lindworm, but
the lindworm is an enchanted king's daughter."

Da sagte der Nachtwind zu ihr: 3.22
Then the night wind said to her:

»Ich will dir Rat geben, geh zum roten Meer, am   3.23
rechten Ufer da stehen große Ruten, die zähle, und
die elfte schneid dir ab, und schlag den Lindwurm
damit, dann kann ihn der Löwe bezwingen, und
beide bekommen auch ihren menschlichen Leib
wieder.
"I will give you advice, go to the Red Sea, on the right bank
there are large rods, count them, and cut off the eleventh,
and beat the lindworm with it, then the lion can defeat him,
and both will also get their human bodies back.

3.24 **Hernach schau dich um, und du wirst den Vogel Greif sehen, der am roten Meer sitzt, schwing dich mit deinem Liebsten auf seinen Rücken;**
Then look around you, and you will see the griffin bird sitting on the Red Sea, swing yourself and your loved one onto its back;

3.25 **der Vogel wird euch übers Meer nach Haus tragen.**
the bird will carry you home across the sea.

3.26 **Da hast du auch eine Nuß, wenn du mitten über dem Meere bist, laß sie herabfallen, alsbald wird sie aufgehen und ein großer Nußbaum wird aus dem Wasser hervorwachsen, auf dem sich der Greif ausruht, und könnte er nicht ruhen, so wäre er nicht stark genug, euch hinüber zu tragen;**
There you have a nut, when you are in the middle of the sea, let it fall, it will soon rise and a great walnut tree will grow out of the water, on which the griffin will rest, and if it could not rest, it would not be strong enough to carry you across;

3.27 **und wenn du vergißt die Nuß herab zu werfen,**
and if you forget to throw down the nut,

3.28 **so läßt er euch ins Meer fallen.«**
it will let you fall into the sea."

4.1 **Da ging sie hin und fand alles wie der Nachtwind gesagt hatte.**
So she went and found everything as the night wind had said.

Sie zählte die Ruten am Meer und schnitt die
elfte ab, damit schlug sie den Lindwurm, und der
Löwe bezwang ihn; alsbald hatten beide ihren
menschlichen Leib wieder.

4.2

She counted the rods by the sea, and cut off the eleventh,
with which she struck the lindworm, and the lion
vanquished him, and at once both had their human bodies
again.

Aber wie die Königstochter, die vorher ein
Lindwurm gewesen war, vom Zauber frei war, nahm
sie den Jüngling in den Arm, setzte sich auf den Vogel
Greif und führte ihn mit sich fort.

4.3

But when the king's daughter, who had previously been a
lindworm, was free from the spell, she took the youth in
her arms, sat on the bird griffin and carried him away with
her.

Da stand die arme Weitgewanderte, und war wieder
verlassen, und setzte sich nieder und weinte.

4.4

There stood the poor far-wanderer, and was again forsaken,
and sat down and wept.

Endlich aber ermutigte sie sich und sprach:

4.5

But at last she encouraged herself, and said,

»Ich will noch so weit gehen als der Wind weht und
so lange als der Hahn kräht, bis ich ihn finde.«

4.6

"I will go as far as the wind blows, and as long as the cock
crows, till I find him."

Und ging fort, lange, lange Wege, bis sie endlich zu
dem Schloß kam, wo beide zusammen lebten;

4.7

And away she went, long, long ways, until at last she came
to the castle where they both lived together;

4.8 da hörte sie, daß bald ein Fest wäre, wo sie Hochzeit miteinander machen wollten.

then she heard that there was soon to be a feast where they were to be married.

4.9 Sie sprach aber: »Gott hilft mir noch.«

But she said, "God help me yet."

4.10 und öffnete das Kästchen, das ihr die Sonne gegeben hatte, da lag ein Kleid darin, so glänzend wie die Sonne selber.

and opened the little box which the sun had given her, and there was a dress in it as brilliant as the sun itself.

4.11 Da nahm sie es heraus und zog es an und ging hinauf in das Schloß, und alle Leute und die Braut selber sahen sie mit Verwunderung an;

So she took it out and put it on, and went up to the castle, and all the people and the bride herself looked at her with astonishment;

4.12 und das Kleid gefiel der Braut so gut, daß sie dachte, es könnte ihr Hochzeitskleid geben, und fragte, ob es nicht feil wäre?

and the dress pleased the bride so much that she thought it might be her wedding-dress, and asked if it were not for sale?

4.13 »Nicht für Geld und Gut.« antwortete sie,

"Not for money and goods." she answered,

4.14 »aber für Fleisch und Blut.«

"but for flesh and blood."

4.15 Die Braut fragte, was sie damit meinte. Da sagte sie:

The bride asked what she meant. Then she said,

»Laßt mich eine Nacht in der Kammer schlafen, wo der Bräutigam schläft.«
4.16

"Let me sleep one night in the chamber where the bridegroom sleeps."

Die Braut wollte nicht, und wollte doch gern das Kleid haben, endlich willigte sie ein, aber der Kammerdiener mußte dem Königssohn einen Schlaftrunk geben.
4.17

The bride did not want to, and yet she wanted to have the dress; at last she consented, but the valet had to give the king's son a nightcap.

Als es nun Nacht war und der Jüngling schon schlief,
4.18

When it was now night and the young man was already asleep,

ward sie in die Kammer geführt.
4.19

she was led into the chamber.

Da setzte sie sich ans Bett und sagte:
4.20

Then she sat down to bed and said,

»Ich bin dir nachgefolgt sieben Jahre, bin bei Sonne und Mond und bei den vier Winden gewesen, und habe nach dir gefragt, und habe dir geholfen gegen den Lindwurm, willst du mich denn ganz verlassen?«
4.21

"I have followed you seven years, I have been by the sun and moon and the four winds, and have asked after you, and helped you against the lindworm, will you leave me altogether?"

Der Königssohn aber schlief so hart, daß es ihm nur vorkam, als rauschte der Wind draußen in den Tannenbäumen.
4.22

But the king's son slept so soundly that it seemed to him as if the wind were rustling in the fir-trees outside.

4.23 Wie nun der Morgen anbrach, da ward sie wieder hinausgeführt und mußte das goldene Kleid hingeben.

When morning came, she was led out again, and had to give up her golden dress.

4.24 Und als auch das nichts geholfen hatte, ward sie traurig, ging hinaus auf eine Wiese, setzte sich und weinte.

And when that did not help either, she became sad, went out into a meadow, sat down and wept.

4.25 Und wie sie so saß, da fiel ihr das Ei noch ein, das ihr der Mond gegeben hatte, sie schlug es auf, da kam eine Glucke heraus mit zwölf Küchlein ganz von Gold, die liefen herum und piepten und krochen der Alten wieder unter die Flügel, sodaß nichts Schöneres auf der Welt zu sehen war.

And as she sat thus, she remembered the egg which the moon had given her, she cracked it open, and out came a mother hen with twelve little chicks all of gold, which ran about and peeped and crawled under the old woman's wings again, so that there was nothing more beautiful to be seen in the world.

4.26 Da stand sie auf, trieb sie auf der Wiese vor sich her, so lange, bis die Braut aus dem Fenster sah, und da gefielen ihr die kleinen Küchlein so gut, daß sie gleich herabkam und fragte, ob sie nicht feil wären?

Then she got up and drove them along the meadow until the bride looked out of the window, and she liked the little chicks so much that she came down at once and asked if they were not for sale?

4.27 »Nicht für Geld und Gut, aber für Fleisch und Blut;

"Not for money and goods, but for flesh and blood;

laßt mich noch eine Nacht in der Kammer schlafen, wo der Bräutigam schläft.« 4.28

let me sleep another night in the chamber where the bridegroom sleeps."

Die Braut sagte: »Ja.« 4.29

The bride said, "Yes."

und wollte sie betrügen wie am vorigen Abend. 4.30

and wanted to deceive them as she had done the night before.

Als aber der Königssohn zu Bett ging, fragte er seinen Kammerdiener, was das Murmeln und Rauschen in der Nacht gewesen sei. 4.31

But when the king's son went to bed, he asked his valet what the murmuring and rustling had been during the night.

Da erzählte der Kammerdiener alles, daß er ihm einen Schlaftrunk hätte geben müssen, weil ein armes Mädchen heimlich in der Kammer geschlafen hätte, und heute nacht sollte er ihm wieder einen geben. 4.32

Then the valet told him everything, that he had had to give him a nightcap because a poor girl had slept secretly in the chamber, and tonight he was to give him another.

Sagte der Königssohn: »Gieß den Trank neben das Bett aus.« 4.33

Said the king's son, "Pour out the drink beside the bed."

4.34 Zur Nacht wurde sie wieder hereingeführt, und als sie anfing zu erzählen wie es ihr traurig ergangen wäre, da erkannte er gleich an der Stimme seine liebe Gemahlin, sprang auf und rief:

At night she was brought in again, and when she began to tell him how sadly she had fared, he at once recognized his dear wife by her voice, jumped up, and cried,

4.35 »Jetzt bin ich erst recht erlöst, mir ist gewesen wie in einem Traum, denn die fremde Königstochter hatte mich bezaubert, daß ich dich vergessen mußte, aber Gott hat noch zu rechter Stunde die Bethörung von mir genommen.«

"Now I am more than ever delivered; it was as if I had been in a dream, for the strange king's daughter had bewitched me, so that I had to forget you, but God took away the pity from me at the right hour."

4.36 Da gingen sie beide in der Nacht heimlich aus dem Schloß, denn sie fürchteten sich vor dem Vater der Königstochter, der ein Zauberer war, und setzten sich auf den Vogel Greif, der trug sie über das rote Meer, und als sie in der Mitte waren, ließ sie die Nuß fallen.

So they both went secretly out of the castle in the night, for they were afraid of the king's daughter's father, who was a magician, and sat on the bird of prey, which carried them over the Red Sea, and when they were in the middle, she dropped the nut.

Alsbald wuchs ein großer Nußbaum, darauf ruhte   4.37
sich der Vogel, und dann führte er sie nach Haus,
wo sie ihr Kind fanden, das war groß und schön
geworden, und sie lebten von nun an vergnügt bis an
ihr Ende.

Soon a great walnut-tree grew up, and the bird rested on it,
and then it led them home, where they found their child,
who had grown great and beautiful, and they lived happily
ever after.

Die Gänsemagd

The Goose Girl

1.1 Es lebte einmal eine alte Königin, der war ihr Gemahl schon lange Jahre gestorben, und sie hatten eine schöne Tochter.

Once upon a time there lived an old queen whose husband had been dead for many years, and they had a beautiful daughter.

1.2 Wie die erwuchs,

As she grew up,

1.3 wurde sie weit über Feld an einen Königssohn versprochen.

she was promised to a king's son far across the field.

Als nun die Zeit kam, wo sie vermählt werden sollten und das Kind in das fremde Reich abreisen mußte, packte ihr die Alte gar viel köstliches Gerät und Geschmeide ein, Gold und Silber, Becher und Kleinode, kurz alles, was nur zu einem königlichen Brautschatz gehörte, denn sie hatte ihr Kind von Herzen lieb.

1.4

When the time came for them to be married and the child had to leave for a foreign kingdom, the old woman packed her a great deal of precious things and jewels, gold and silver, cups and jewels, in short everything that belonged to a royal bride's treasure, for she loved her child dearly.

Auch gab sie ihr eine Kammerjungfer bei, welche mitreiten und die Braut in die Hände des Bräutigams überliefern sollte, und jede bekam ein Pferd zur Reise, aber das Pferd der Königstöchter hieß Falada und konnte sprechen.

1.5

She also gave her a chambermaid, who was to ride with her and deliver the bride into the hands of the bridegroom, and each was given a horse for the journey, but the king's daughters' horse was called Falada and could speak.

Wie nun die Abschiedsstunde da war, begab sich die alte Mutter in ihre Schlafkammer, nahm ein Messerlein und schnitt damit in ihre Finger, daß sie bluteten;

1.6

When the hour for parting came, the old mother went into her bedchamber, took a little knife, and cut her fingers with it, so that they bled;

darauf hielt sie ein weißes Läppchen unter und ließ drei Tropfen Blut hineinfallen, gab sie der Tochter und sprach:

1.7

then she put a little white cloth under it, and let three drops of blood fall into it, and gave it to her daughter, saying,

1.8 »Liebes Kind, verwahre sie wohl, sie werden dir unterwegs not thun.«

"Dear child, keep them well, they will be of need to you on the way."

2.1 Also nahmen sie beide voneinander betrübten Abschied;

So they both bade each other a sad farewell;

2.2 das Läppchen steckte die Königstochter in ihren Busen vor sich, setzte sich aufs Pferd und zog nun fort zu ihrem Bräutigam.

the king's daughter put the lappet in her bosom before her, mounted her horse, and went away to her bridegroom.

2.3 Da sie eine Stunde geritten waren, empfand sie heißen Durst und sprach zu ihrer Kammerjungfer:

After they had ridden for an hour, she felt very thirsty and said to her chambermaid,

2.4 »Steig ab, und schöpfe mir mit meinem Becher, den du für mich mitgenommen hast, Wasser aus dem Bache, ich möchte gern einmal trinken.«

"Dismount, and draw me some water from the stream with the cup you have brought for me, I would like a drink."

2.5 »Wenn Ihr Durst habt.« sprach die Kammerjungfer,

"If you are thirsty." said the chambermaid,

2.6 »so steigt selber ab, legt Euch ans Wasser und trinkt, ich mag Eure Magd nicht sein.«

"get down yourself, lie down by the water and drink, I don't want to be your maid."

Da stieg die Königstochter vor großem Durst
herunter, neigte sich über das Wasser im Bach und
trank, und durfte nicht aus dem goldenen Becher
trinken.
2.7

Then the King's daughter descended from great thirst,
bent over the water in the stream and drank, and was not
allowed to drink from the golden cup.

Da sprach sie: »Ach Gott!«
2.8

Then she said, "Oh God!"

da antworteten die drei Blutstropfen,
2.9

and the three drops of blood replied,

»Wenn das deine Mutter wüßte,
2.10

"If your mother knew that,

das Herz im Leibe thät ihr zerspringen.«
2.11

her heart would burst within her."

Aber die Königsbraut war demütig, sagte nichts, und
stieg wieder zu Pferde.
2.12

But the king's bride was humble, said nothing, and
mounted her horse again.

So ritten sie etliche Meilen weiter fort;
2.13

So they rode on for several miles;

aber der Tag war warm, die Sonne, stach und sie
durstete bald von neuem.
2.14

but the day was warm, the sun was burning, and she was
soon thirsty again.

Da sie nun an einen Wasserfluß kamen, rief sie noch
einmal ihrer Kammerjungfer,
2.15

When they came to a stream of water, she called once more
to her chambermaid,

2.16 »Steig ab und gieb mir aus meinem Goldbecher zu trinken.«
"Dismount, and give me a drink from my gold cup."

2.17 denn sie hatte alle bösen Worte längst vergessen.
for she had long forgotten all her evil words.

2.18 Die Kammerjungfer sprach aber noch hochmütiger:
But the chambermaid said even more haughtily,

2.19 »Wollt Ihr trinken, so trinkt allein, ich mag nicht Eure Magd sein.«
"If you want to drink, drink alone, I don't want to be your maid."

2.20 Da stieg die Königstochter hernieder vor großem Durst, legte sich über das fließende Wasser, weinte und sprach,
Then the king's daughter went down with great thirst, lay down over the flowing water, wept, and said,

2.21 »Ach Gott!« und die Blutstropfen antworteten wiederum,
"Oh, God!" and the drops of blood answered again,

2.22 »Wenn das deine Mutter wüßte,
"If your mother knew that,

2.23 das Herz im Leibe thät ihr zerspringen.«
her heart would burst in her womb."

Und wie sie so trank und sich recht überlehnte, fiel 2.24
ihr das Läppchen, worin die drei Tropfen waren, aus
dem Busen und floß mit dem Wasser fort, ohne daß
sie es in ihrer großen Angst bemerkte.
And as she drank thus, and leaned quite over herself, the
little flap in which the three drops were fell from her
bosom, and flowed away with the water, without her
noticing it in her great anxiety.

Die Kammerjungfer hatte aber zugesehen und freute 2.25
sich, daß sie Gewalt über die Braut bekäme; denn
damit, daß diese die Blutstropfen verloren hatte, war
sie schwach und machtlos geworden.
The chambermaid, however, had been looking on, and
was glad that she would have power over the bride, for she
had become weak and powerless now that she had lost the
drops of blood.

Als sie nun wieder auf ihr Pferd steigen wollte, das da 2.26
hieß Falada, sagte die Kammerfrau,
Now when she wanted to mount her horse again, whose
name was Falada, the chambermaid said,

»Auf Falada gehör ich, und auf meinen Gaul gehörst 2.27
du.«
"I belong on Falada, and you belong on my horse."

und das mußte sie sich gefallen lassen. 2.28
and she had to put up with that.

2.29 Dann befahl ihr die Kammerfrau mit harten Worten, die königlichen Kleider auszuziehen und ihre schlechten anzulegen, und endlich mußte sie sich unter freiem Himmel verschwören, daß sie am königlichen Hofe keinem Menschen etwas davon sprechen wollte;

Then the chambermaid ordered her with harsh words to take off her royal clothes and put on her bad ones, and finally she had to swear in the open air that she would not speak of this to anyone at the royal court;

2.30 und wenn sie diesen Eid nicht abgelegt hätte,

and if she had not taken this oath,

2.31 wäre sie auf der Stelle umgebracht worden.

she would have been killed on the spot.

2.32 Aber Falada sah das alles an und nahm's wohl in acht.

But Falada saw all this and took it well.

3.1 Die Kammerfrau stieg nun auf Falada und die wahre Braut auf das schlechte Roß, und so zogen sie weiter, bis sie endlich in dem königlichen Schloß eintrafen.

The chambermaid now mounted Falada, and the true bride mounted the bad horse, and so they went on till at last they arrived at the royal palace.

3.2 Da war große Freude über ihre Ankunft, und der Königssohn sprang ihnen entgegen, hob die Kammerfrau vom Pferde und meinte, sie wäre seine Gemahlin;

There was great joy at their arrival, and the king's son sprang to meet them, lifted the chambermaid off her horse, and said she was his wife;

3.3 sie ward die Treppe hinaufgeführt,

she was led up the stairs,

die wahre Königstochter aber mußte unten stehen bleiben.   3.4

but the true king's daughter had to remain below.

Da schaute der alte König am Fenster, und sah sie im Hof halten und sah wie sie fein war, zart und gar schön;   3.5

Then the old King looked at the window, and saw her standing in the court, and saw how fine she was, delicate and very beautiful;

ging alsbald hin ins königliche Gemach und fragte die Braut nach der, die sie bei sich hätte und da unten im Hof stände, und wer sie wäre?   3.6

he went at once into the royal chamber, and asked the bride who she had with her, and was standing down there in the court, and who she was?

»Die hab ich mir unterwegs mitgenommen zur Gesellschaft;   3.7

"I took her with me for company on the way;

gebt der Magd was zu arbeiten, daß sie nicht müßig steht.«   3.8

give the maid something to do, that she may not stand idle."

Aber der alte König hatte keine Arbeit für sie und wußte nichts, als daß er sagte: 3.9

But the old king had no work for her, and knew nothing but to say,

»Da hab ich so einen kleinen Jungen, der hütet die Gänse, dem mag sie helfen.«   3.10

"I have a little boy who looks after the geese, and she may help him."

3.11 **Der Junge hieß Kürdchen (Konrädchen),**
The boy's name was Kürdchen (Konrädchen),

3.12 **dem mußte die wahre Braut helfen Gänse hüten.**
and the true bride had to help him herd the geese.

4.1 **Bald aber sprach die falsche Braut zu dem jungen König:**
But soon the false bride said to the young king:

4.2 **»Liebster Gemahl, ich bitte Euch, thut mir einen Gefallen.«**
"Dearest husband, I beg you to do me a favor."

4.3 **Er antwortete: »Das will ich gern thun.«**
He answered, "I will gladly do it."

4.4 **»Nun so laßt den Schinder rufen und da dem Pferde, worauf ich hergeritten bin, den Hals abhauen, weil es mich unterwegs geärgert hat.«**
"Now, then, let the drudge be called and cut off the neck of the horse on which I rode, because it has annoyed me on the way."

4.5 **Eigentlich aber fürchtete sie, daß das Pferd sprechen möchte, wie sie mit der Königstochter umgegangen war.**
But she was actually afraid that the horse would speak of how she had treated the King's daughter.

Nun war das so weit geraten, daß es geschehen und der treue Falada sterben sollte, da kam es auch der rechten Königstochter zu Ohr, und sie versprach dem Schinder heimlich ein Stück Geld, das sie ihm bezahlen wollte, wenn er ihr einen kleinen Dienst erwiese. 4.6

Now this had come to such a pass that it was to happen, and the faithful Falada was to die, and then it reached the ears of the right king's daughter, and she secretly promised to pay the knave a piece of money if he would do her a little service.

In der Stadt war ein großes finsteres Thor, 4.7

There was a great dark gate in the town,

wo sie abends und morgens mit den Gänsen durch mußte; 4.8

through which she had to pass in the evening and morning with the geese;

unter das finstere Thor möchte er dem Falada seinen Kopf hinnageln, 4.9

under the dark gate he would nail Falada's head,

daß sie ihn doch noch mehr als einmal sehen könnte. 4.10

so that she might see him more than once.

Also versprach das der Schindersknecht zu thun, hieb den Kopf ab und nagelte ihn unter das finstere Thor fest. 4.11

And so the servant promised to do so, cut off his head, and nailed it under the dark gate.

Des Morgens früh, da sie und Kürdchen unterm Thor hinaustrieben, sprach sie im Vorbeigehen: 5.1

Early one morning, as she and Kürdchen were driving out from under the gate, she spoke as they passed:

6.1 »O du Falada, der du hangest.«
"O Falada, you who hang."

7.1 da antwortete der Kopf:
the head answered:

»O du Jungfer Königin, da du gangest,
"O maiden queen, since you walked,

wenn das deine Mutter wüßte,
if your mother knew that,

ihr Herz thät ihr zerspringen.«
Her heart would burst."

9.1 Da zogen sie still weiter zur Stadt hinaus,
So they went quietly on out of the town,

9.2 und sie trieben die Gänse aufs Feld.
and drove the geese into the field.

9.3 Und wenn sie auf der Wiese angekommen war, saß sie nieder und machte ihre Haare auf, die waren eitel Gold, und Kürdchen sah sie und freute sich wie sie glänzten, und wollte ihr ein paar ausraufen.
And when she had arrived in the meadow, she sat down and undid her hair, which was like gold, and Kürdchen saw it and rejoiced at how it shone, and wanted to pluck some out for her.

9.4 Da sprach sie:
Then she said:

»Weh, weh, Windchen,
"Woe, woe, little wind,

nimm Kürdchen sein Hütchen,	take Kürdchen's little hat,
und laß'n sich mit jagen,	and let themselves be hunted,
bis ich mich geflochten und geschnatzt	until I am braided and cut
und wieder aufgesatzt.«	and put it back on again."

Und da kam ein so starker Wind, daß er dem   11.1
Kürdchen sein Hütchen weg wehte über alle Lande,
und es mußte ihm nachlaufen.
And then there came such a strong wind that it blew the
little cowl's hat away over all the land, and she had to run
after it.

Bis es wieder kam war sie mit dem Kämmen und   11.2
Aufsetzen fertig,
By the time she came back she had finished combing and
putting on her hat,

und er konnte keine Haare kriegen.   11.3
and he could not get any hair.

Da war Kürdchen bös und sprach nicht mit ihr;   11.4
Then Kürdchen was angry, and would not speak to her;

und so hüteten sie die Gänse, bis daß es Abend ward,   11.5
dann gingen sie nach Haus.
and so they tended the geese till evening, and then they
went home.

12.1 Den anderen Morgen, wie sie unter dem finsteren Thor hinaustrieben, sprach die Jungfrau:
The next morning, as they drove out under the dark gate, the maiden spoke:

13.1 »O du Falada, da du hangest.«
"O Falada, since you are hanging."

14.1 Falada antwortete:
Falada replied:

»O du Jungfer Königin; da du gangest,	"O maiden queen, since you went,
wenn das deine Mutter wüßte,	if your mother knew that,
das Herz thät ihr zerspringen.«	her heart would burst."

16.1 Und in dem Felde setzte sie sich wieder auf die Wiese und fing an ihr Haar auszukämmen, und Kürdchen lief und wollte danach greifen, da sprach sie schnell:
And in the field she sat down again in the meadow and began to comb out her hair, and Kürdchen ran and wanted to reach for it, but she spoke quickly:

»Weh, weh, Windchen,	"Woe, woe, little wind,
nimm Kürdchen sein Hütchen,	take Kürdchen's little hat,
und laß'n sich mit jagen,	and let themselves be hunted,

145

bis ich mich geflochten und geschnatzt

until I am braided and cut

und wieder aufgesatzt.«

and put it back on again."

Da wehte der Wind und wehte ihm das Hütchen vom Kopf weit weg,

18.1

Then the wind blew and blew the little hat far away from his head,

daß Kürdchen nachlaufen mußte;

18.2

so that Kürdchen had to run after it;

und als es wieder kam, hatte sie längst ihr Haar zurecht, und es konnte keins davon erwischen;

18.3

and when it came again, she had long since got her hair in order, and it could not catch any of it;

und so hüteten sie die Gänse, bis es Abend ward.

18.4

and so they tended the geese until evening came.

Abends aber, nachdem sie heimgekommen waren, ging Kürdchen vor den alten König und sagte:

19.1

But in the evening, after they had come home, Kürdchen went before the old king and said,

»Mit dem Mädchen will ich nicht länger Gänse hüten.«

19.2

"I don't want to herd geese with that girl any longer."

»Warum denn?« fragte der alte König. »Ei,

19.3

"Why is that?" asked the old king. "Well,

das ärgert mich den ganzen Tag.«

19.4

it's been annoying me all day."

19.5 Da befahl ihm der alte König zu erzählen, wie's ihm denn mit ihr ginge.

Then the old king ordered him to tell him how he was doing with her.

19.6 Da sagte Kürdchen:

Then Kürdchen said:

19.7 »Morgens, wenn wir unter dem finsteren Thor mit der Herde durchkommen, so ist da ein Gaulskopf an der Wand, zu dem redet sie:

"In the morning, when we pass under the dark gate with the herd, there is a horse's head on the wall and she talks to it:

20.1 ›Falada, da du hangest,‹

'Falada, since you are hanging,'

21.1 da antwortet der Kopf:

the head answers:

›O du Königsjungfer, da du gangest,

'O you royal maiden, since you walked,

wenn das deine Mutter wüßte,

if your mother knew that,

das Herz thät ihr zerspringen. «

her heart would burst. "'

23.1 Und so erzählte Kürdchen weiter, was auf der Gänsewiese geschähe, und wie es da dem Hut im Winde nachlaufen müßte.

And so Kürdchen went on talking about what was happening in the goose meadow, and how he had to run after the hat in the wind.

147

Der alte König befahl ihm, den nächsten Tag wieder   24.1
hinauszutreiben, und er selbst, wie es Morgen war,
setzte sich hinter das finstere Thor und hörte da, wie
sie mit dem Haupt des Falada sprach, und dann ging
er ihr auch nach in das Feld, und barg sich in einem
Busch auf der Wiese.

The old king ordered him to go out again the next day, and
he himself, as it was morning, sat down behind the dark
gate, and there heard her talking to the head of Falada, and
then he also went after her into the field, and hid himself in
a bush in the meadow.

Da sah er nun bald mit seinen eigenen Augen, wie die   24.2
Gänsemagd und der Gänsejunge die Herde getrieben
brachten, und wie nach einer Weile sie sich setzte
und ihre Haare losflocht, die strahlten von Glanz.

There he soon saw with his own eyes how the goose-maid
and the goose-boy drove the flock, and how after a while
she sat down and unbraided her hair, which shone with
splendor.

Gleich sprach sie wieder: 24.3

In a moment she spoke again:

»Weh, weh, Windchen, faß Kürdchen sein Hütchen,	"Woe, woe, little wind, grab Kürdchen's little hat,
und laß'n sich mit jagen,	and let themselves be hunted,
bis daß ich mich geflochten und geschnatzt	until I am braided and laced
und wieder aufgesatzt.«	and put it back on again."

148

26.1 Da kam ein Windstoß und fuhr mit Kürdchens Hut weg, daß es weit zu laufen hatte, und die Magd kämmte und flocht ihre Locken still fort, welches der alte König alles beobachtete.

Then came a gust of wind, and carried off Kürdchen's hat, so that it had far to run, and the maid combed and plaited her curls in silence, which the old King observed.

26.2 Darauf ging er unbemerkt zurück, und als abends die Gänsemagd heim kam, rief er sie beiseite und fragte, warum sie das alles so thäte?

Then he went back unnoticed, and when the goose-maid came home in the evening, he called her aside and asked her why she was doing all this?

26.3 »Das darf ich Euch nicht sagen, und darf auch keinem Menschen mein Leid klagen, denn so hab ich mich unter freiem Himmel verschworen, weil ich sonst um mein Leben gekommen wäre.«

"I must not tell you that, nor must I tell anyone of my sorrow, because I have conspired to do so in the open air, otherwise I would have lost my life."

26.4 Er drang in sie und ließ ihr keinen Frieden,

He penetrated her and left her no peace,

26.5 aber er konnte nichts aus ihr herausbringen. Da sprach er,

but he could get nothing out of her. Then he said,

26.6 »Wenn du mir nicht sagen willst,

"If you will not tell me,

26.7 so klag dem Eisenofen da dein Leid.« und ging fort.

tell the iron furnace there your sorrow." and went away.

Da kroch sie in den Eisenofen, fing an zu jammern
und zu weinen, schüttete ihr Herz aus und sprach: 26.8

Then she crawled into the iron furnace, and began to wail
and weep, and poured out her heart, and said,

»Da sitze ich nun von aller Welt verlassen, und   26.9
bin doch eine Königstochter, und eine falsche
Kammerjungfer hat mich mit Gewalt dahin gebracht,
daß ich meine königlichen Kleider habe ablegen
müssen, und hat meinen Platz bei meinem Bräutigam
eingenommen, und ich muß als Gänsemagd gemeine
Dienste thun.

"There I sit forsaken by all the world, and yet I am a King's
daughter, and a false chambermaid has made me take
off my royal garments by force, and has taken my place
with my bridegroom, and I must do mean service as a
goose-maid.

Wenn das meine Mutter wüßte,   26.10

If my mother knew this,

das Herz im Leibe thät ihr zerspringen.«   26.11

her heart would burst within her."

Der alte König stand aber außen an der Ofenröhre,   26.12
lauerte ihr zu und hörte, was sie sprach.

But the old King stood outside by the stove-pipe, and
listened to what she said.

Da kam er wieder herein und hieß sie aus dem Ofen   26.13
gehen.

Then he came in again and ordered her out of the oven.

Da wurden ihr königliche Kleider angethan, und es   26.14
schien ein Wunder, wie sie so schön war.

Then royal clothes were put on her, and it seemed a wonder
how she was so beautiful.

26.15 Der alte König rief seinen Sohn und offenbarte ihm,
The old King called his son,

26.16 daß er die falsche Braut hätte:
and told him that he had the wrong bride:

26.17 die wäre bloß ein Kammermädchen,
she was only a chambermaid,

26.18 die wahre aber stände hier als die gewesene Gänsemagd.
but the real one was standing here as the former goose-maid.

26.19 Der junge König war herzensfroh, als er ihre Schönheit und Tugend erblickte, und ein großes Mahl wurde angestellt, zu dem alle Leute und guten Freunde gebeten wurden.
The young king was heartily rejoiced when he saw her beauty and virtue, and a great banquet was arranged, to which all the people and good friends were invited.

26.20 Obenan saß der Bräutigam, die Königstochter zur einen Seite und die Kammerjungfer zur anderen, aber die Kammerjungfer war verblendet und erkannte jene nicht mehr in dem glänzenden Schmuck.
Upstairs sat the bridegroom, the king's daughter on one side and the chambermaid on the other, but the chambermaid was blinded and no longer recognized her in the shining jewels.

Als sie nun gegessen und getrunken hatten und gutes   26.21
Muts waren, gab der alte König der Kammerfrau ein
Rätsel auf, was eine solche wert wäre, die den Herrn
so und so betrogen hätte, erzählte damit den ganzen
Verlauf und fragte,

Now when they had eaten and drunk and were in good
spirits, the old king gave the chambermaid a riddle as to the
worth of one who had deceived her master in such and such
a way, and told her the whole course of events, and asked,

»Welches Urteils ist diese würdig?«   26.22

"What judgment is she worthy of?"

Da sprach die falsche Braut: 26.23

Then the false bride said,

»Die ist nichts Besseres wert, als daß sie splitternackt   26.24
ausgezogen und in ein Faß gesteckt wird, das
inwendig mit spitzen Nägeln beschlagen ist, und
zwei weiße Pferde müssen vorgespannt werden, die
sie Gasse auf Gasse ab zu Tode schleifen.«

"She is worth nothing better than to be stripped stark
naked and put into a barrel, which is shod with sharp nails
on the inside, and two white horses must be harnessed to
drag her down alley after alley to her death."

»Das bist du.« sprach der alte König,   26.25

"That is you." said the old king,

»und hast dein eigen Urteil gefunden,   26.26

"and you have found your own judgment,

und danach soll dir widerfahren.«   26.27

and it shall be done to you."

26.28 Und als das Urteil vollzogen war, vermählte sich der junge König mit seiner rechten Gemahlin, und beide beherrschten ihr Reich in Frieden und Seligkeit.

And when the sentence had been carried out, the young king married his right hand wife, and both ruled their kingdom in peace and bliss.

Der junge Riese

The Young Giant

1.1 Ein Bauersmann hatte einen Sohn, der war so groß wie ein Daumen und ward gar nicht größer und wuchs in etlichen Jahren nicht ein Haarbreit.

A farmer had a son who was as big as a thumb and didn't grow a hair's breadth in several years.

1.2 Einmal wollte der Bauer ins Feld gehen und pflügen, da sagte der Kleine,

Once the farmer wanted to go out into the field to plow, and the little boy said,

1.3 »Vater, ich will mit hinaus.«

"Father, I want to go out with you."

1.4 »Du willst mit hinaus? «, sprach der Vater,

"You want to go out with me? ", said the father,

1.5 »bleib du hier, dort bist du zu nichts nutz:

"you stay here, you're no good there:

1.6 du könntest mir auch verloren gehen.«

you could get lost to me too."

Da fing der Däumling an zu weinen, und um Ruhe zu haben, steckte ihn der Vater in die Tasche und nahm ihn mit.

1.7

Then Thumbelina began to cry, and in order to have some peace, his father put him in his pocket and took him with him.

Draußen auf dem Felde holte er ihn wieder heraus und setzte ihn in eine frische Furche.

1.8

Out in the field he took him out again and put him in a fresh furrow.

Wie er da so saß, kam über den Berg ein großer Riese daher.

1.9

As he sat there, a great giant came over the hill.

»Siehst du dort den großen Butzemann?«

1.10

"Do you see the big bogeyman there?"

sagte der Vater, und wollte den Kleinen schrecken, damit er artig wäre,

1.11

said his father, trying to scare the little boy into being good,

»der kommt und holt dich.«

1.12

"he's coming to get you."

Der Riese aber hatte mit seinen langen Beinen kaum ein paar Schritte gethan, so war er bei der Furche.

1.13

But the giant had hardly taken a few steps with his long legs before he was at the furrow.

Er hob den kleinen Däumling mit zwei Fingern behutsam in die Höhe,

1.14

He gently lifted the little thumbelina up with two fingers,

1.15 betrachtete ihn und ging ohne ein Wort zu sprechen
mit ihm fort.
looked at him and walked away with him without saying a
word.

1.16 Der Vater stand dabei, konnte vor Schrecken keinen
Laut hervorbringen und dachte nicht anders, als sein
Kind für verloren, also daß er's sein, Lebtag nicht
wieder mit Augen sehen würde.
The father stood by, unable to utter a sound for terror, and
could not help thinking that his child was lost, and that he
would not see him again with his eyes for the rest of his life.

2.1 Der Riese aber trug es heim und ließ es an seiner
Brust saugen,
But the giant carried it home and let it suckle at his breast,

2.2 und der Däumling wuchs und ward groß und stark
nach Art der Riesen.
and the Thumbelina grew and became big and strong like a
giant.

2.3 Nach Verlauf von zwei Jahren ging der Alte mit ihm
in den Wald, wollte ihn versuchen und sprach,
After two years the old man took him into the forest,
wanted to try him and said,

2.4 »Zieh dir eine Gerte heraus.«
"Pull out a whip for yourself."

2.5 Da war der Knabe schon so stark, daß er einen jungen
Baum mit den Wurzeln aus der Erde riß.
By then the boy was so strong that he pulled a young tree
out of the ground by its roots.

2.6 Der Riese aber meinte: »Das muß besser kommen.«
But the giant said, "That had better come."

nahm ihn wieder mit und säugte ihn noch zwei Jahre.

2.7

He took him back with him and nursed him for another two years.

Als er ihn versuchte, hatte seine Kraft schon so zugenommen, daß er einen alten Baum aus der Erde brechen konnte.

2.8

When he tried him, his strength had already increased so much that he was able to break an old tree out of the ground.

Das war dem Riesen noch immer nicht genug, er säugte ihn abermals zwei Jahre, und als er dann mit ihm in den Wald ging und sprach,

2.9

This was still not enough for the giant, and he nursed him again for two years, and when he went with him into the forest and said,

»Nun reiß einmal eine ordentliche Gerte aus.«

2.10

"Now tear out a good crop."

so riß der Junge den dicksten Eichenbaum aus der Erde, daß er krachte, und war ihm nur ein Spaß.

2.11

the boy tore the thickest oak tree out of the ground so that it cracked, and it was only a joke to him.

»Nun ist's genug.« sprach der Riese,

2.12

"Now that's enough." said the giant,

»du hast ausgelernt.«

2.13

"you've finished learning."

und führte ihn zurück auf den Acker, wo er ihn geholt hatte.

2.14

and led him back to the field where he had fetched him.

2.15 Sein Vater stand da hinter dem Pflug, der junge Riese ging auf ihn zu und sprach:

His father stood there behind the plow, the young giant walked up to him and said,

2.16 »Sieht Er wohl, Vater, was sein Sohn für ein Mann geworden ist.«

"Can you see, father, what a man his son has become."

2.17 Der Bauer erschrak und sagte:

The farmer was startled and said,

2.18 »Nein, du bist mein Sohn nicht, ich will dich nicht, geh weg von mir.«

"No, you are not my son, I don't want you, go away from me."

2.19 »Freilich bin ich sein Sohn, laß Er mich an die Arbeit, ich kann pflügen so gut als Er und noch besser.«

"Of course I am his son, let him put me to work, I can plow as well as he can and even better."

2.20 »Nein, nein, du bist mein Sohn nicht, du kannst auch nicht pflügen, geh weg, von mir.«

"No, no, you are not my son, you can't plow either, go away from me."

2.21 Weil er sich aber vor dem großen Mann fürchtete, ließ er den Pflug los, trat zurück und setzte sich zur Seite ans Land.

But because he was afraid of the big man, he let go of the plow, stepped back and sat down on the land to one side.

Da nahm der Junge das Geschirr und drückte bloß   2.22
mit einer Hand darauf, aber der Druck war so
gewaltig, daß der Pflug tief in die Erde ging.
Then the boy took the harness and merely pressed on it
with one hand, but the pressure was so great that the plow
went deep into the ground.

Der Bauer konnte das nicht mit ansehen und   2.23
rief ihm zu:
The farmer could not stand to see this and called out to
him,

»Wenn du pflügen willst, mußt du nicht so gewaltig   2.24
drücken, das giebt schlechte Arbeit.«
"If you want to plow, you must not push so hard, it makes
for bad work."

Der Junge aber spannte die Pferde aus, zog selber den   2.25
Pflug und sagte:
But the boy unhitched the horses, pulled the plow himself,
and said,

»Geh Er nur nach Haus, Vater, und laß Er die Mutter   2.26
eine große Schüssel voll Essen kochen;
"Go home, father, and let your mother cook a big bowl of
food;

ich will derweil den Acker schon umreißen.«   2.27
I'll plow the field in the meantime."

Da ging der Bauer heim und bestellte das Essen bei   2.28
seiner Frau;
Then the farmer went home, and ordered the food to his
wife;

160

2.29 der Junge aber pflügte das Feld, zwei Morgen groß, ganz allein, und dann spannte er sich auch selber vor die Egge und eggte alles mit zwei Eggen zugleich.

but the boy plowed the field, two acres in extent, all by himself, and then he harnessed himself to the harrow, and harrowed it all with two harrows at once.

2.30 Wie er fertig war, ging er in den Wald und riß zwei Eichenbäume aus, legte sie auf die Schultern, und hinten und vorn eine Egge daraus, und hinten und vorn auch ein Pferd, und trug das alles, als wär es ein Bund Stroh, nach seiner Eltern Haus.

When he had finished, he went into the forest, and pulled up two oak-trees, laid them on his shoulders, and made a harrow of them behind and in front, and also a horse behind and in front, and carried them all, as if they were a bundle of straw, to his parents' house.

2.31 Wie er in den Hof kam, erkannte ihn seine Mutter nicht und fragte,

When he came into the yard, his mother did not recognize him and asked,

2.32 »Wer ist der entsetzliche große Mann?« Der Bauer sagte,

"Who is that horrible big man?" The farmer said,

2.33 »Das ist unser Sohn.« Sie sprach:

"That's our son." She said,

2.34 »Nein, unser Sohn ist das nimmermehr, so groß haben wir keinen gehabt, unser war ein kleines Ding.«

"No, it's never our son, we've never had one that big, ours was a little thing."

2.35 Sie rief ihm zu: »Geh fort, wir wollen dich nicht.«

She called out to him: "Go away, we don't want you."

Der Junge schwieg still, zog seine Pferde in den Stall, gab ihnen Hafer und Heu, alles wie sich's gehörte. 2.36
The boy remained silent, pulled his horses into the stable, gave them oats and hay, everything as it should be.

Als er fertig war, ging er in die Stube, setzte sich auf die Bank und sagte: 2.37
When he had finished, he went into the parlor, sat down on the bench and said,

»Mutter, nun hätte ich Lust zu essen, ist's bald fertig?« 2.38
"Mother, now I feel like eating, will it be ready soon?"

Da sagte sie: »Ja.« 2.39
She said, "Yes."

und brachte zwei große Schüsseln voll herein, 2.40
and brought in two large bowls,

daran hätte sie und ihr Mann acht Tage lang satt gehabt. 2.41
which would have fed her and her husband for eight days.

Der Junge aber aß sie allein aus und fragte, 2.42
But the boy ate them alone,

ob sie nicht mehr vorsetzen könnte? »Nein.« sagte sie, 2.43
and asked if she could not serve more? "No." she said,

»das ist alles, was wir haben.« 2.44
"that's all we have."

»Das war ja nur zum Schmecken, ich muß mehr haben.« 2.45
"That was only to taste, I must have more."

2.46 Sie getraute nicht ihm zu widerstehen, ging hin und setzte einen großen Schweinekessel voll übers Feuer, und wie es gar war, trug sie es herein.

Not daring to resist him, she went and put a large cauldron full of pork over the fire, and when it was cooked she carried it in.

2.47 »Endlich kommen noch ein paar Brocken.«

"At last there will be some more."

2.48 sagte er und aß alles hinein; es war aber doch nicht genug seinen Hunger zu stillen.

said he, and ate it all, but it was not enough to satisfy his hunger.

2.49 Da sprach er:

Then he said,

2.50 »Vater, ich sehe wohl, bei Ihm werde ich nicht satt, will Er mir einen Stab von Eisen verschaffen, der stark ist und den ich vor meinen Knien nicht zerbrechen kann, so will ich fort in die Welt gehen.«

"Father, I see that I shall not be satisfied with Him; if He will give me a rod of iron that is strong, and which I cannot break before my knees, I will go away into the world."

2.51 Der Bauer war froh, spannte seine zwei Pferde vor den Wagen und holte bei dem Schmied einen Stab so groß und dick, als ihn die zwei Pferde nur fortschaffen konnten.

The farmer was glad, harnessed his two horses to the cart and fetched a staff from the blacksmith as big and thick as the two horses could carry.

2.52 Der Junge nahm ihn vor die Knie und ratsch!

The boy took it in front of his knees and, snap!

brach er ihn wie eine Bohnenstange in der Mitte 2.53
entzwei und warf ihn weg.

he broke it in half like a beanstalk and threw it away.

Der Vater spannte vier Pferde vor und holte einen 2.54
Stab so groß und dick, als ihn die vier Pferde
fortschaffen konnten.

The father harnessed four horses and fetched a stick as big
and thick as the four horses could carry it away.

Der Sohn knickte auch diesen vor dem Knie entzwei, 2.55
warf ihn hin und sprach:

The son also bent it in two at the knee, threw it down and
said,

»Vater, der kann mir nicht helfen, Er muß besser 2.56
vorspannen und einen stärkeren Stab holen.«

"Father, he can't help me, he had better harness it and get a
stronger stick."

Da spannte der Vater acht Pferde vor und holte einen 2.57
so groß und dick,

Then the father harnessed eight horses,

als ihn die acht Pferde herbeifahren konnten. 2.58

and fetched one as big and thick as the eight horses could
bring.

Wie der Sohn den in die Hand nahm, brach er gleich 2.59
oben ein Stück davon ab und sagte:

As soon as the son took it in his hand, he broke off a piece at
the top and said,

2.60 »Vater, ich sehe, Er kann mir keinen Stab anschaffen wie ich ihn brauche, ich will nicht länger bei Ihm bleiben.«

"Father, I see He can't get me a staff like I need, I don't want to stay with Him any longer."

3.1 Da ging er fort und gab sich für einen Schmiedegesellen aus.

So he went away and pretended to be a journeyman blacksmith.

3.2 Er kam in ein Dorf, darin wohnte ein Schmied, der war ein Geizmann, gönnte keinem Menschen etwas und wollte alles allein haben;

He came to a village where a blacksmith lived, who was a miser, begrudged no one anything and wanted everything for himself;

3.3 zu dem trat er in die Schmiede und fragte, ob er keinen Gesellen brauchte.

he went into the smithy and asked him if he didn't need a journeyman.

3.4 »Ja.« sagte der Schmied, sah ihn an und dachte,

"Yes." said the blacksmith, looking at him and thinking,

3.5 »Das ist ein tüchtiger Kerl,

"That's a good fellow,

3.6 der wird gut vorschlagen und sein Brot verdienen.« Er fragte,

he'll make a good job and earn his bread." He asked,

3.7 »Wie viel willst du Lohn haben?«

"How much wages do you want?"

»Gar keinen will ich haben.« antwortete er,   3.8
"None at all." he replied,

»nur alle vierzehn Tage, wenn die anderen Gesellen   3.9
ihren Lohn bezahlt kriegen, will ich dir zwei Streiche
geben, die mußt du aushalten.«
"only every two weeks, when the other journeymen are
paid their wages, I'll give you two strokes, you'll have to
endure them."

Das war der Geizmann von Herzen zufrieden und   3.10
dachte damit viel Geld zu sparen.
The miser was heartily pleased with this and thought it
would save him a lot of money.

Am anderen Morgen sollte der fremde Geselle zuerst   3.11
vorschlagen, wie aber der Meister den glühenden
Stab brachte und jener den ersten Schlag that, so
flog das Eisen voneinander und der Amboß sank
in die Erde, so tief, daß sie ihn gar nicht wieder
herausbringen konnten.
The next morning the strange journeyman was to strike
first, but when the master brought the red-hot rod, and
the latter struck the first blow, the iron flew apart, and the
anvil sank into the ground so deep that they could not get it
out again.

Da ward der Geizmann bös und sagte: 3.12
Then the miser became angry and said,

»Ei was, dich kann ich nicht brauchen, du schlägst   3.13
gar zu grob, was willst du für den einen Zuschlag
haben?«
"Why, I can't use you, you strike too roughly, what do you
want for the one blow?"

Da sprach er,   3.14
Then he said,

3.15 »Ich will dir nur einen ganz kleinen Streich geben,
"I will only give you a very small stroke,

3.16 weiter nichts.«
nothing more."

3.17 Und hob seinen Fuß auf und gab ihm einen Tritt, daß er über vier Fuder Heu hinausflog.
And he lifted up his foot and gave it a kick that sent it flying over four cartloads of hay.

3.18 Darauf suchte er sich den dicksten Eisenstab aus, der in der Schmiede war, nahm ihn als einen Stock in die Hand und ging weiter.
Then he picked out the thickest iron bar that was in the smithy, took it in his hand as a stick, and went on his way.

4.1 Als er eine Weile gezogen war, kam er zu einem Vorwerk und fragte den Amtmann, ob er keinen Großknecht nötig hätte.
When he had traveled for a while, he came to a farm and asked the bailiff if he did not need a farmhand.

4.2 »Ja.« sagte der Amtmann, »ich kann einen brauchen;
"Yes." said the bailiff, "I can use one;

4.3 du siehst aus wie ein tüchtiger Kerl, der schon was vermag, wie viel willst du Jahreslohn haben?«
you look like a capable fellow who can already do something, how much do you want in annual wages?"

4.4 Er antwortete wiederum, er verlangte gar keinen Lohn, aber alle Jahre wollte er ihm drei Streiche geben, die müßte er aushalten.
He replied again that he did not want any wages at all, but that he would give him three strokes every year, which he would have to endure.

Das war der Amtmann zufrieden, denn er war auch ein Geizhals.

4.5

The bailiff was satisfied, for he was also a miser.

Am anderen Morgen, da sollten die Knechte ins Holz fahren, und die anderen Knechte waren schon auf, er aber lag noch im Bett.

4.6

The next morning the servants were to go to the wood, and the other servants were already up, but he was still in bed.

Da rief ihn einer an:

4.7

Then one of them called to him,

»Steh auf, es ist Zeit, wir wollen ins Holz, und du mußt mit.«

4.8

"Get up, it's time, we're going to the wood, and you must come with us."

»Ach.« sagte er ganz grob und trotzig, »geht ihr nur hin,

4.9

"Oh." he said rudely and defiantly, "you go along,

ich komme doch eher wieder als ihr alle miteinander.«

4.10

I'll be back sooner than all of you."

Da gingen die anderen zum Amtmann und erzählten ihm, der Großknecht läge noch im Bett und, wollte nicht mit ins Holz fahren.

4.11

Then the others went to the bailiff and told him that the great servant was still in bed and did not want to go to the wood.

Der Amtmann sagte, sie sollten ihn noch einmal wecken und ihn heißen die Pferde vorspannen.

4.12

The bailiff told them to wake him up again and harness him to the horses.

4.13 Der Großknecht aber sprach wie vorher: »Geht ihr nur hin,

But the farmhand said as before, "You go on,

4.14 ich komme doch eher wieder als ihr alle miteinander.«

I'll be back sooner than all of you."

4.15 Darauf blieb er noch zwei Stunden liegen, da stieg er endlich aus den Federn, holte sich aber erst zwei Scheffel voll Erbsen vom Boden, kochte sich einen Brei und aß den mit guter Ruhe, und wie das alles geschehen war, ging er hin, spannte die Pferde vor und fuhr ins Holz.

Thereupon he lay still for two hours, when at last he got out of bed, but first fetched two bushels of peas from the ground, cooked himself a porridge, and ate it with good rest, and when all this was done, he went, harnessed the horses, and drove into the wood.

4.16 Nicht weit vor dem Holz war ein Hohlweg, wo er durch mußte, da fuhr er den Wagen erst vorwärts, dann mußten die Pferde stille halten, und er ging hinter den Wagen, nahm Bäume und Reisig und machte da eine große Hucke (Verhack), sodaß kein Pferd durchkommen konnte.

Not far from the wood there was a hollow way through which he had to pass, so he first drove the cart forward, then the horses had to keep still, and he went behind the cart, took trees and brushwood and made a big hump so that no horse could get through.

4.17 Wie er nun vors Holz kam, fuhren die anderen eben mit ihren beladenen Wagen heraus und wollten heim, da sprach er zu ihnen,

When he came to the wood, the others were just coming out with their loaded wagons and wanted to go home, so he said to them,

»Fahrt nur hin, ich komme doch eher als ihr nach Haus.«   4.18

"Go on, I'll get home sooner than you."

Er fuhr gar nicht weit ins Holz, riß gleich zwei der allergrößten Bäume aus der Erde, warf sie auf den Wagen und drehte um.   4.19

He drove not far into the wood, pulled two of the biggest trees out of the ground, threw them onto the cart and turned around.

Als er vor der Hucke anlangte,   4.20

When he arrived in front of the hut,

standen die anderen noch da und konnten nicht durch.   4.21

the others were still standing there and couldn't get through.

»Seht ihr wohl.« sprach er,   4.22

"You see." he said,

»wärt ihr bei mir geblieben,   4.23

"if you had stayed with me,

so wärt ihr ebenso schnell nach Haus gekommen und hättet noch eine Stunde schlafen können.«   4.24

you would have gotten home just as quickly and could have slept for another hour."

4.25 Er wollte nun zufahren, aber seine Pferde konnten sich nicht durcharbeiten, da spannte er sie aus, legte sie oben auf den Wagen, nahm selber die Deichsel in die Hand, und hüf! zog er alles durch, und das ging so leicht als hätte er Federn geladen.

He now wanted to drive up, but his horses could not work their way through, so he unhitched them, put them on top of the cart, took the drawbar in his own hand, and pulled everything through, and that went as easily as if he had loaded feathers.

4.26 Wie er drüben war, sprach er zu den anderen: »Seht ihr wohl,

When he was over, he said to the others, "You see,

4.27 ich bin schneller hindurch als ihr.« fuhr weiter,

I am through faster than you." He drove on,

4.28 und die anderen mußten stehen bleiben.

and the others had to stop.

4.29 In dem Hof aber nahm er einen Baum in die Hand, zeigte ihn dem Amtmann und sagte,

But in the courtyard he took a tree in his hand, showed it to the bailiff, and said,

4.30 »Ist das nicht ein schönes Klafterstück?«

"Is not this a fine fathom?"

4.31 Da sprach der Amtmann, zu seiner Frau: »Der Knecht ist gut;

Then the bailiff said to his wife: "The servant is good;

4.32 wenn er auch lange schläft,

even if he sleeps a long time,

171

er ist doch eher wieder da als die anderen.« 4.33
he will be back sooner than the others."

Nun diente er dem Amtmann ein Jahr; 5.1
Now he served the bailiff for a year;

wie das herum war, und die anderen Knechte ihren 5.2
Lohn kriegten, sprach er es wäre Zeit, er wollte sich
auch seinen Lohn nehmen.
when that was over and the other servants had received
their wages, he said it was time for him to take his wages
too.

Dem Amtmann ward aber angst vor den Streichen, 5.3
die er kriegen sollte, und bat ihn inständig, er möchte
sie ihm schenken, lieber wollte er selbst Großknecht
werden, und er sollte Amtmann sein.
But the bailiff was afraid of the strokes he was to get, and
begged him imploringly to give them to him; he would
rather become a great servant himself, and be a bailiff.

»Nein.« sprach er, 5.4
"No." he said,

»ich will kein Amtmann werden, ich bin Großknecht 5.5
und will's bleiben, ich will aber austeilen was
bedungen ist.«
"I don't want to be a bailiff, I'm a great servant and I want
to stay that way, but I want to give out what is due."

Der Amtmann wollte ihm geben, was er nur 5.6
verlangte, aber es half nichts, der Großknecht sprach
zu allem:
The bailiff wanted to give him what he asked for, but it was
no use, the great servant said:

5.7 »Nein.«
"No."

5.8 Da wußte sich der Amtmann nicht zu helfen und bat ihn um vierzehn Tage Frist, er wollte sich auf etwas besinnen.
Then the bailiff did not know what to do and asked him for two weeks to think about something.

5.9 Der Großknecht sprach, die Frist sollte er haben.
The great servant said that he should have that time.

5.10 Der Amtmann berief alle seine Schreiber zusammen,
The bailiff called all his scribes together,

5.11 sie sollten sich bedenken und ihm einen Rat geben.
told them to think things over and give him some advice.

5.12 Die Schreiber besannen sich lange, endlich sagten sie, vor dem Großknecht wäre niemand seines Lebens sicher, der schlüge einen Menschen wie eine Mücke tot.
The scribes deliberated for a long time, and finally they said that no one's life was safe from the great servant, who would kill a man like a mosquito.

5.13 Er sollte ihn heißen, in den Brunnen steigen und ihn reinigen, wenn er unten wäre, wollten sie einen von den Mühlsteinen, die da lägen, herbeirollen und ihm auf den Kopf werfen, dann würde er nicht wieder an das Tageslicht kommen.
They told him to go down into the well and cleanse him, and when he was down they would roll up one of the millstones lying there and throw it on his head, then he would not come out into the light of day again.

Der Rat gefiel dem Amtmann, und der Großknecht war bereit in den Brunnen hinabzusteigen.   5.14

The bailiff liked the advice and the great servant was ready to descend into the well.

Als er unten auf dem Grund stand, rollten sie den größten Mühlstein hinab, und meinten der Kopf wäre ihm eingeschlagen, aber er rief: 5.15

When he stood at the bottom, they rolled down the largest millstone, and thought his head was smashed in, but he cried,

»Jagt, die Hühner vom Brunnen weg, die kratzen da oben im Sand und werfen mir die Körner in die Augen, daß ich nicht sehen kann.«   5.16

"Chase the hens away from the well, they are scratching in the sand up there, and throwing the grains into my eyes so that I cannot see."

Da rief der Amtmann: »Husch! husch!«   5.17

Then the bailiff cried, "Shoo! shoo!"

und that als scheuchte er die Hühner weg.   5.18

and pretended to shoo the hens away.

Als der Großknecht mit seiner Arbeit fertig war, stieg er herauf und sagte,   5.19

When the great servant had finished his work, he climbed up and said,

»Seht einmal, ich habe doch ein schönes Halsband um.«   5.20

"Look, I have a beautiful collar about my neck."

da war es der Mühlstein, den er um den Hals trug.   5.21

It was the millstone which he wore about his neck.

5.22 Der Großknecht wollte jetzt seinen Lohn nehmen,

The great servant now wanted to take his wages,

5.23 aber der Amtmann bat wieder um vierzehn Tage Bedenkzeit.

but the bailiff again asked for two weeks to think it over.

5.24 Die Schreiber kamen zusammen und gaben den Rat, er sollte den Großknecht in die verwünschte Mühle schicken, um dort in der Nacht Korn zu mahlen;

The scribes came together and advised him to send the great servant to the cursed mill to grind grain there during the night;

5.25 von da wäre noch kein Mensch morgens lebendig herausgekommen.

no one had ever come out of there alive in the morning.

5.26 Der Anschlag gefiel dem Amtmann,

The bailiff liked the plan,

5.27 er rief den Großknecht noch denselben Abend und hieß ihn acht Malter in die Mühle fahren und in der Nacht noch mahlen;

he called the great servant that very evening and ordered him to drive eight maltons to the mill and grind them that night;

5.28 sie hätten's nötig.

they needed it.

Da ging der Großknecht auf den Boden und that zwei
Malter in seine rechte Tasche, zwei in die linke, vier
nahm er in einem Quersack halb auf den Rücken,
halb auf die Brust, und ging also beladen nach der
verwünschten Mühle.

5.29

So the great servant went to the ground and put two malt
in his right pocket, two in his left, and took four in a cross-
body bag, half on his back, half on his chest, and went thus
laden to the cursed mill.

Der Müller sagte ihm, bei Tag könnte er recht gut da
mahlen, aber nicht in der Nacht, da wäre die Mühle
verwünscht, und wer da noch hinein gegangen wäre,
den hätte man am Morgen tot darin gefunden.

5.30

The miller told him that he could grind there quite well
by day, but not at night, because the mill was cursed, and
anyone who went in there would have been found dead in
the morning.

Er sprach: »Ich will schon durchkommen,

5.31

He said, "I will get through,

macht Euch nur fort und legt Euch aufs Ohr.«

5.32

just go away and lie down."

Darauf ging er in die Mühle und schüttete das Korn
auf.

5.33

Then he went into the mill and piled up the grain.

Gegen elf Uhr ging er in die Müllerstube und setzte
sich auf die Bank.

5.34

At about eleven o'clock he went into the miller's room and
sat down on the bench.

5.35 Als er ein Weilchen da gesessen hatte, that sich auf einmal die Thür auf und kam eine große große Tafel herein, und auf die Tafel stellte sich Wein und Braten und viel gutes Essen, alles von selber, denn es war niemand da, der's auftrug.

When he had sat there for a while, the door suddenly opened and a large table came in, and wine and roast meat and lots of good food were placed on the table, all by themselves, for there was no one there to serve it.

5.36 Und danach rückten sich die Stühle herbei, aber es kamen keine Leute, bis auf einmal sah er Finger, die hantierten mit den Messern und Gabeln und legten Speisen auf die Teller, aber sonst konnte er nichts sehen.

And then the chairs drew near, but no people came, until all at once he saw fingers handling the knives and forks and putting food on the plates, but otherwise he could see nothing.

5.37 Da er hungrig war und die Speisen sah, so setzte er sich auch an die Tafel, aß mit und ließ sich's gut schmecken.

Since he was hungry and saw the food, he sat down at the table, ate and enjoyed the meal.

5.38 Als er satt war und die anderen ihre Schüsseln auch ganz leer gemacht hatten, da wurden die Lichter auf einmal alle ausgeputzt, das hörte er deutlich, und wie's nun stockfinster war, so kriegte er so etwas wie eine Ohrfeige ins Gesicht.

When he had eaten his fill and the others had also emptied their bowls, the lights were all put out at once, he heard that clearly, and as it was now pitch dark, he got something like a slap in the face.

5.39 Da sprach er: »Wenn noch einmal so etwas kommt,

Then he said, "If anything like that happens again,

so teil ich auch wieder aus.« 5.40

I'll deal again."

Und wie er zum zweitenmale eine Ohrfeige kriegte, 5.41

And when he was slapped in the face a second time,

da schlug er gleichfalls mit hinein. 5.42

he slapped him again.

Und so ging das fort die ganze Nacht er nahm nichts 5.43
umsonst, sondern gab reichlich zurück und schlug
nicht faul um sich herum; bei Tagesanbruch aber
hörte alles auf.

And so it went on all night; he took nothing in vain, but
gave back plentifully, and did not lazily beat about; but at
daybreak everything ceased.

Wie der Müller aufgestanden war, wollte er nach ihm 5.44
sehen und verwunderte sich, daß er noch lebte.

When the miller got up, he went to look after him and was
surprised to see that he was still alive.

Da sprach er: 5.45

Then he said,

»Ich habe mich satt gegessen, habe Ohrfeigen 5.46
gekriegt, aber ich habe auch Ohrfeigen ausgeteilt.«

"I have eaten my fill, I have been slapped in the face, but I
have also dealt out slaps."

Der Müller freute sich und sagte, nun wäre die Mühle 5.47
erlöst, und wollte ihm gern zur Belohnung viel Geld
geben.

The miller rejoiced and said that now the mill was
redeemed, and wanted to give him a lot of money as a
reward.

5.48 Er sprach aber: »Geld will ich nicht, ich habe doch genug.«

But he said, "I don't want money, I have enough."

5.49 Dann nahm er sein Mehl auf den Rücken, ging nach Haus und sagte dem Amtmann, er hätte die Sache ausgerichtet und wollte nun seinen bedungenen Lohn haben.

Then he took his flour on his back, went home and told the bailiff that he had settled the matter and now wanted his due reward.

5.50 Wie der Amtmann das hörte, da ward ihm erst recht angst:

When the bailiff heard this, he was really frightened:

5.51 er wußte sich nicht zu lassen, ging in der Stube auf und ab, und die Schweißtropfen liefen ihm von der Stirn herunter.

he could not help himself, walked up and down the room, and the drops of sweat ran down his forehead.

5.52 Da machte er das Fenster auf nach frischer Luft, ehe er sich's aber versah, hatte ihm der Großknecht einen Tritt gegeben, daß er durchs Fenster in die Luft hineinflog, immer fort, bis ihn niemand mehr sehen konnte.

Then he opened the window for fresh air, but before he knew it, the great-servant had kicked him so that he flew through the window into the air, away and away until no one could see him any more.

5.53 Da sprach der Großknecht zur Frau des Amtmanns,

Then the great-servant said to the bailiff's wife,

5.54 »Kommt er nicht wieder,

"If he does not come back,

so müßt Ihr den anderen Streich hinnehmen.« Sie rief,   5.55

you must take the other blow." She cried,

»Nein, nein, ich kanns nicht aushalten.«   5.56

"No, no, I can't stand it."

und machte das andere Fenster auf,   5.57

and opened the other window,

weil ihr die Schweißtropfen die Stirn herunter liefen.   5.58

because drops of sweat were running down her forehead.

Da gab er ihr einen Tritt, daß sie gleichfalls hinausflog, und da sie leichter war, noch viel höher als ihr Mann.   5.59

Then he kicked her so that she flew out too, and as she was lighter, much higher than her husband.

Der Mann rief: »Komm doch zu mir.« sie aber rief,   5.60

The man cried, "Come to me." but she cried,

»Komm du zu mir, ich kann nicht zu dir.«   5.61

"You come to me, I cannot come to you."

Und sie schwebten da in der Luft, und konnte keins zum anderen kommen, und ob sie da noch schweben, das weiß ich nicht;   5.62

And they floated there in the air, and neither could come to the other, and whether they were still floating there, I do not know;

der junge Riese aber nahm seine Eisenstange und ging weiter.   5.63

but the young giant took his iron bar and went on.

Dat Erdmänneken

The Earthman

1.1 Et was mal en rik Künig west, de hadde drei Döchter had, de wören alle Dage in den Schlottgoren spazeren gaen, un de Künig, dat was so en Leivhawer von allerhand wackeren Bömen west:

There was once a rich king in the west, who had three daughters, who went for a walk in the Schlottgoren every day, and the king, who was the owner of all sorts of brave trees in the west:

1.2 un einen, den hadde he so leiv had, dat he denjenigen, de ümme en Appel dervon plückede, hunnerd Klafter unner de Eere verwünschede.

and one of them he had so much love for, that he would have cursed the one who came to him for an apple a hundred fathoms below the ground.

1.3 As et nu Hervest war,

When it was time for the harvest,

1.4 da worden de Appel an den einen Baume so raut ase Blaud.

the apples on the one tree became as rough as blue.

De drei Döchter gungen alle Dage unner den Baum un seihen to ov nig de Wind 'n Appel herunner schlagen hädde, awerst se fannen er Levedage kienen, un de Baum de satt so vull, dat he breken wull, un de Telgen (Zweige) hungen bis up de Eere. 1.5

The three daughters went under the tree every day to see if the wind could blow the apples down, but they could not find any leaves, and the tree was so full that it wanted to break, and the branches reached up to the ice.

Da gelustede den jungesten Künigskinne gewaldig un et segde to sinen Süstern: 1.6

Then the youngest child got angry and said to his sibling:

»Use Teite (Vater), det hett us viel to leiv, ase dat he us verwünschen deihe: 1.7

"Use Teite (father), that's too much fun for us, but he's cursing us:

ik glöve dat he dat nur wegen de frümden Lude dahen hat.« 1.8

I think he's only here because of the early kids."

Un indes plücked dat Kind en gans dicken Appel af un sprunk für sinen Süstern und segde: 1.9

Meanwhile, the child plucked up a big appetizer and spoke for his sweetie, saying:

»A, nu schmecket mal, mine lewen Süsterkes, nu hew ik doch min Levedage so wat schönes no nig schmecket.« 1.10

"A, now taste it, my dear sweeties, I've never tasted anything so nice in my life."

1.11 Da beeten de beiden annern Künigsdöchter auch mal in den Appel, un da versünken se alle drei deip unner de Eere, dat kien Haan mer danach krähete.

Then the two other daughters of the king prayed into the apples, and all three of them were so sweet under the egg that no one crowed for it.

2.1 As et da Middag is, da wull se de Künig do Diske roopen, do sind so nirgends to finnen:

When it was midday, the king wanted to open up the disks, but they were nowhere to be found:

2.2 he söket se so viel im Schlott un in Goren,

he saw them so much in the castle and in the gorges,

2.3 awerst he kun se nig finnen.

but he couldn't find them.

2.4 Da werd he so bedröwet un let dat ganse Land upbeien (aufbieten), un wer ünne sine Döchter wier brechte, de sull ene davon tor Fruen hewen.

He was so worried and let the whole country go up, and whoever broke his daughters should have one of them as a wife.

2.5 Da gahet so viele junge Lude uwer Feld un söket, dat is gans ut der Wiese (über alle Maßen), denn jeder hadde he drei Kinner geren had, wiil se wören gegen jedermann so fründlig un so schön von Angesichte west.

There were so many young people walking across the field and they said that it was all out of the meadow, because they each had three children, because they were so friendly and beautiful to everyone.

Un et togen auck drei Jägerburschen ut, un ase da wol
en acht Dage riefet hadden, da kümmet se up en grot
Schlott, da woren so hübsche Stoben inne west, un
in keinen Zimmer is en Disch decket, darup wören
so söte Spisen, de sied noch so warme dat se dampet,
awerst in den ganzen Schlott, is kien Minsk to hören
noch to seihen.

2.6

And then three hunter boys came out, and when they had
called for eight days, they came to a large chimney, there
were such pretty stools in the west, and in none of the
rooms was a table covered, there were such sweet spits,
which were still so warm that they steamed, but in the
whole chimney, there was no noise to be heard or seen.

Do wartet se noch en halwen Dag, un de Spisen
bliwet immer warme un dampet, bis up et lest, da
weret se so hungerig, dat se sik derbie settet un ettet,
un macket mit en anner ut, se wüllen up den Schlotte
wuhnen bliewen, un wüllen darümme loosen, dat
eine in Huse blev un de beiden annern de Döchter
söketen;

2.7

They waited half a day, and the spit remained warm and
steamy until it was time to leave, when they were so hungry
that they sat down and waited, and made out with another,
they wanted to stay in the barn, and wanted to solve the
problem that one of them was at home and the other two
were looking after their daughters;

dat doet se auck, un dat Los dreppet den ölesten.

2.8

they did so, and the lot went to the eldest.

Den annern Dag da gaet de twei jüngesten söken,

2.9

The next day,

un de öleste mot to Huse bliewen.

2.10

the two youngest went to school and the oldest stayed at
home.

2.11 Am Middoge kümmt der so en klein klein Männeken un hölt um 'n Stückesken Braud ane, da nümmt he von dem Braude, wat he da funnen hädde, un schnitt en Stücke rund umme den Braud weg un will ünne dat giewen, indes dat he et ünne reiket, lett et dat kleine Männeken fallen und segd, he sulle dok so gut sin un giewen ün dat Stücke wier.

In the middle of the day, a small little man comes and hangs around a piece of brew, then he takes from the brew what he has found there, and cuts away a piece around the brew and wants to give it to him, while he is cutting it, the little man drops it and says that he should be so good and give it to him.

2.12 Da will he dat auck doen und bucket sik, mit des nümmt, dat Männeken en Stock un packt ünne bie den Haaren un gift ünne düete Schläge.

Then he wants to do the same and, with that in mind, he bends the girl over a stick, grabs her by the hair and gives her a few thin blows.

2.13 Den anneren Dag, da is de tweide to Hus bliewen, den geit et nicks better.

The next day, when the two stayed at home, things went better.

2.14 Ase de beiden annern da den Awend nah Hus kümmet,

When the other two returned to the house,

2.15 da segt de öleste: »No, wie hätt et die dann gaen?«

the eldest said: "No, how would it have gone then?"

2.16 »O, et geit mit gans schlechte.«

"Oh, it's going so badly."

Da klaget se sik enanner ere Naud, awerst den
jungesten hadden se nicks davonne sagd, den hadden
se gar nig lien (leiden) mögt un hadden ünne jummer
den dummen Hans heiten, weil he nig recht van de
Weld was.

2.17

Then they complained to each other, but they didn't say
anything to the youngest, they didn't like him at all and
they had to treat the stupid Hans because he wasn't really
of the world.

Den dritten Dag, da blivt de jungeste to Hus, da
kümmet dat kleine Männeken wier und holt um
en Stücksken Braud an;

2.18

The third day, when the youngest stayed at home, the little
man came and asked for a piece of bread;

da he ünne dat giewen hätt,

2.19

when he had given it to him,

let he et wier fallen un segt he mügte dock so gut sien
un reicken ünne dat Stücksken wier.

2.20

he let it fall and said he wanted to be as good as he could be
and give him the piece of bread.

Da segd he to den kleinen Männeken: »Wat!

2.21

Then he said to the little man: "What!

kannst du dat Stücke nig sulwens wier up nümmen,
wenn du die de Möhe nig mal um dine dägliche
Narunge giewen wust, so bist du auck nich wert,
dat du et etest.«

2.22

Can't you just pick up the piece again, if you don't even
know how to give the cows your daily dose, then you're not
worth it."

Da word dat Männeken so bös und segde he möst et
doen:

2.23

Then the man became so angry and said he wanted to do it:

2.24 he awerst nig fuhl,

"He doesn't feel anything,

2.25 nam min lewe Männeken un drosch et duet dör (tüchtig durch).

name my dear man and push him through.

2.26 Da schriege dat Männeken so viel un rep:

Then the man shouted as much as he could and said:

2.27 »Hör up, hör up, un lat mie geweren, dann will ik die auck seggen, wo de Künigsdöchter sied.«

"Listen up, listen up, and let me win, then I'll tell you where the king's daughters are."

2.28 Wie he dat hörde, häll hei üp to slaen, un dat Männeken vertelde he wör en Erdmänneken, un sulke wären mehr ase dusend, he mögte man mit ünne gaen, dann wulle he ünne wiesen wo de Künigsdöchter weren.

As he listened to this, he began to talk, and the man told him he was an earthling, and if there were more than thou, he would like to go with him, then he would like to tell him where the king's daughters were.

2.29 Da wist he ünne en deipen Born,

Then he knew there was a small fountain,

2.30 da is awerst kien Water inne west.

but there was no water in the west.

Da segt dät Männeken, he wüste wohl dat et sine   2.31
Gesellen nig ehrlich mit ünne meinten, wenn he de
Künigskinner erlösen wulle, dann möste he et alleine
doen.

Then the man said that he probably knew that his
companions didn't mean anything by him, that if he
wanted to redeem the king's children, he would have to
do it alone.

De beiden annern Broer wullen wohl auck geren   2.32
de Künigsdöchter wier hewen, awerst se wullen
der kiene Möge un Gefahr umme doen, he möste so
en grauten Korv nümmen, un möste sik mit sinen
Hirschfänger un en Schelle darinne setten un sik
herunter winnen laten:

The two other brothers probably wanted to keep the king's
daughters, but they didn't want to put him in any danger,
so he had to take a gray basket, sit in it with his deerstalker
and a cuff and let himself be winched down:

unnen da wören drei Zimmer, in jeden sette ein   2.33
Künigskind un hädde en Drachen mit villen Köppen
to lusen, den möste he de Köppe afschlagen.

and there were three rooms, in each of which a king's child
sat and had a dragon with many heads to lure, which he
had to knock off the heads.

Ase dat Erdmänneken nu dat alle sagd hadde,   2.34
verschwand et.

When the earth girl had said all that, it disappeared.

Ase't Awend is, da kümmet de beiden annern un   2.35
fraget wie et ün gaen hädde, da segd he:

At the end of the day, the two others came and asked how it
had gone, then he said:

»O, so wit gut.«   2.36

"Oh, so good."

188

2.37 un hädde keinen Minsken sehen, ase des Middags, da wer so ein klein Männeken kummen, de hädde ün umme en Stücksken Braud biddit, do he et ünne giewen hädde, hädde dat Männeken et fallen laten un hädde segd, he mögtet ünne doch wier üp nümmen, wie he dat nig hadde doen wullt, da hädde et anfangen to puchen, dat hädde he awerst unrecht verstan un hädde dat Männeken prügelt, un da hädde et ünne vertellt wo de Künigsdöchter wären.

and didn't see a girl, but the other day, a little girl came and asked him for a piece of bread, when he had given it to him, the girl dropped it and said, He told them to take it again, as he had not wanted to do, then he started to pick on them, but he was wrong and beat the girl, and she told him where the king's daughters were.

2.38 Da ärgerten sik de beiden so viel, dat se gehl un grön wören.

The two of them were so angry that they grew tall and big.

2.39 Den annern Morgen da gungen se to haupe an den Born un mackten Lose, wer sik dat erste in den Korv setten sulle, da feel dat Los wier den öllesten to, he mot sik darin fetten un de Klingel mitnümmen.

The next morning, they went up to the fountain and drew lots to see who would be the first to sit down in the basket.

2.40 Da segd he: »Wenn ik klingele,

Then he says: "When I ring the bell,

2.41 so mutt gi mik nur geschwinne wier herupwinnen.«

I just have to win it."

2.42 Ase he en bitken herunner is, da klingelte wat, da winnen se ünne wier heruper;

When he came down a bit, something rang, they won five more;

da sett sik de tweide herinne, de maket ewen sau;

2.43

then the two women came down, they made a mess;

nu kümmet dann auck de Riege an den jungesten,

2.44

then the youngest of the group came down,

de lät sik awerst gans drinne runner winnen.

2.45

they let themselves be won completely inside.

Ase he ut den Korve stiegen is, da nümmet he sienen Hirschfänger un geit vor der ersten Doer staen un lustert, da hort he den Drachen gans lute schnarchen.

2.46

As he climbed out of the basket, he took his deerstalker and went to stand in front of the first dock, where he heard the dragon snoring loudly.

He macket langsam de Döre oppen,

2.47

He slowly opens the door,

da sitt da de eine Künigsdochter und häd op eren Schot niegene (neun) Drachenköppe ligen un luset de.

2.48

there sits one of the king's daughters and has no (nine) dragon heads lying on his sheet and is laughing.

Da nümmet he sinen Hirschfänger und hogge to, da siet de niegne Koppe awe.

2.49

Then he took his deerstalker and went to look at the nine heads.

De Künigsdochter sprang up un fäl ünne um den Hals un drucket un piepete (küßte) ünn so viel, un nümmet ihr Bruststücke, dat wor von rauen Golle west, un henget ünne dat umme.

2.50

The king's daughter jumped up and clasped her around the neck and squeezed and kissed her breast, which was made of rough wool, and put it around her neck.

2.51 **Da geit he auck nach der tweiden Künigsdochter, de häd en Drachen mit sieven Köppe to lusen un erlöset de auck, so de jungeste, de hadde en Drachen mit viere Köppen to lusen had, da geit he auck hinne.**

Then he went to the two king's daughters, who had a dragon with seven heads to louse and redeemed them, so the youngest, who had a dragon with four heads to louse, went back.

2.52 **Do froget se sich alle so viel,**

Then they all asked each other so much,

2.53 **un drucketen un piepeten ohne uphören.**

and squeaked and peeped without listening.

2.54 **Da klingelte he sau harde, bis dat se owen hört.**

He rang the bell so hard until he heard them.

2.55 **Da set he de Künigsdöchter ein nach der annern in den Korv un let se alle drei heruptrecken, wie nu an ünne de Riege kümmt, da fallet ün de Woore (Worte) von den Erdmänneken wier bie, dat et sine Gesellen mit ünne nig gut meinden.**

Then he put the king's daughters in the basket one after the other and let them all three come up, just as he was about to go to the bar, when he heard the words of the earthmen that his companions didn't mean well by him.

Da nümmet he en groten Stein de da ligt un legt ün
in den Korv, ase de Korv da ungefähr bis in de Midde
herup is, schnien de falsken Broer owen dat Strick
af, dat de Korv mit den Stein up den Grund füll, un
meinten he wäre nu daude, un laupet mit de drei
Künigsdöchter wege un lotet sik dervan verspreken
dat se an ehren Vater seggen willt dat se beiden se
erlöset hädden;

2.56

Then he takes a large stone that is lying there and puts it
in the basket, as the basket is about halfway up, the wrong
brothers cut off the rope that fills the basket with the stone
to the bottom, and think he is now dead, and leaves with
the three king's daughters, promising that they will tell
their father that they have both redeemed them;

da kümmet se tom Künig, un begert se tor Fruen.

2.57

Then they came to the king and begged him for wives.

Unnerdies geit de jungeste Jägerbursche gans
bedröwet in den drei Kammern herummer un denket
dat he nu wull sterwen möste, da süht he an der
Wand 'n Fleutenpiepe hangen, da segd he:

2.58

In addition, the youngest huntsman walks into the three
chambers in a daze and thinks that he now wants to die,
when he sees a bunting hanging on the wall and says:

»Worümme hengest du da wull,

2.59

"What are you doing there,

hier kann ja doch keiner lustig sin?«

2.60

no one can be happy here?"

He bekucket auck de Drachenköpp un segd:

2.61

He also looks at the dragon's head and says:

»Ju künnt mie nu auck nig helpen.«

2.62

"You can't help me now."

2.63 He geit so mannigmal up un af spatzeren, dat de Erdboden davon glatt werd.

He goes up and down so many times that the ground becomes smooth.

2.64 Un et lest, da kriegt he annere Gedanken, da nümmet he de Fleutenpiepen van der Wand un blest en Stücksken, up eenmahl kummet da so viele Erdmännekens, bie jeden Don, den he däht, kummt eint mehr;

And then he gets another thought, he takes the peepers from the wall and blows a piece of paper, at one point there are so many earthen masks, with every don he turns there is one more;

2.65 da blest he so lange dat Stücksken, bis det Zimmer stopte vull is.

he blows the piece of paper until the room is completely full.

2.66 De fraget alle wat sin Begeren wöre, da segd he he wull geren wier up de Eere an Dages Licht, da satten se ünne alle an, an jeden Spir (Faden) Haar, wat he up sinen Koppe hadde, un sau steiget se mit ünne herupper bis up de Eere.

They all asked him what his companion was, then he said he wanted to go back to his room at the light of day, they all looked at him, at every strand of hair he had on his head, and then they climbed up to his room with him.

2.67 Wie he owen is, geit he glick nach den Künigsschlott wo grade de Hochtit mit der einen Künigsdochter sin sulle, un geit up den Zimmer, wo de Künig mit sinen drei Döchtern is.

As he is gone, he goes to the king's castle where the king's daughter is, and goes to the room where the king is with his three daughters.

Wie ünne da de Kinner seihet,   2.68
When she sees the children there,

da wered se gans beschwämt (ohnmächtig).   2.69
she is completely stunned (faints).

Da werd de Künig so böse un let ünne glick in een   2.70
Gefängnisse setten, weil he meint he hädde den
Kinnern en Leid anne daen.
Then the king gets so angry and lets them go to prison
because he thinks he's doing the children a disservice.

Ase awer de Künigsdöchter wier to sik kummt,   2.71
But when the king's daughters came to him,

da biddet se so viel he mogte ünne doch wier lose   2.72
laten.
they begged him to let them go.

De Künig fraget sie worümme, da segd se dat se dat   2.73
nig vertellen dorften, awerst de Vaer de segd se füllen
et den Owen (Ofen) vertellen.
The king asked her why, and she told him that she couldn't
tell him, but the father told her to fill the oven.

Da geit he herut un lustert an de Döre ün hört alles.   2.74
He goes over and listens to the door and hears everything.

Da lät he de beiden an en Galgen hängen,   2.75
Then he lets the two of them hang on a gallows,

un den einen givt he de jungeste Dochter;   2.76
and he gives one of them to the youngest daughter;

2.77 un da trok ik en Paar gläserne Schohe an, un da stott ik an en Stein, da segd et

and then I hit a pair of glass shoes, and when I bumped into a stone, he said

2.78 »klink!« da wören se kaput.

"clink!" and they were broken.

Der König vom goldenen Berg
The King of the Golden Mountain

1.1 Ein Kaufmann, der hatte zwei Kinder, einen Buben und ein Mädchen, die waren beide noch klein und konnten noch nicht laufen.

There was a merchant who had two children, a boy and a girl, both of whom were still small and could not yet walk.

1.2 Es gingen aber zwei reichbeladene Schiffe von ihm auf dem Meere, und sein ganzes Vermögen war darin, und wie er meinte dadurch viel Geld zu gewinnen, kam die Nachricht, sie wären versunken.

But there were two richly laden ships of his on the sea, and his whole fortune was in them, and as he thought to gain much money by them, news came that they had sunk.

1.3 Da war er nun statt eines reichen Mannes ein armer Mann und hatte nichts mehr übrig als einen Acker vor der Stadt.

Instead of a rich man, he was now a poor man and had nothing left but a field outside the city.

Um sich sein Unglück ein wenig aus den Gedanken zu schlagen, ging er hinaus auf den Acker, und wie er da so auf - und abging, stand auf einmal ein kleines schwarzes Männchen neben ihm und fragte, warum er so traurig wäre, und was er sich so sehr zu Herzen nähme. *1.4*

To take his mind off his misfortune, he went out into the field, and as he was walking up and down, a little black man suddenly stood next to him and asked why he was so sad and what he was so worried about.

Da sprach der Kaufmann: »Wenn du mir helfen könntest, *1.5*

Then the merchant said, "If you could help me,

wollt ich dir es wohl sagen.« *1.6*

I would tell you."

»Wer weiß.« antwortete das schwarze Männchen, *1.7*

"Who knows." replied the little black man,

»vielleicht helf ich dir.« *1.8*

"perhaps I will help you."

Da erzählte der Kaufmann, daß ihm sein ganzer Reichtum auf dem Meer zu Grunde gegangen wäre, und hätte er nichts mehr übrig als diesen Acker. *1.9*

Then the merchant told him that all his wealth had been lost at sea and that he had nothing left but this field.

»Bekümmere dich nicht.« sagte das Männchen, *1.10*

"Don't worry." said the little man,

1.11 »wenn du mir versprichst das, was dir zu Haus am ersten widers Bein stößt, in zwölf Jahren hierher auf den Platz zu bringen, sollst du Geld haben so viel du willst.«

"if you promise me to bring what you have at home to this place in twelve years, you shall have as much money as you want."

1.12 Der Kaufmann dachte: »Was kann das anders sein als mein Hund?«

The merchant thought, "What can it be but my dog?"

1.13 aber an seinen kleinen Jungen dachte er nicht und sagte ja,

but he did not think of his little boy and said yes,

1.14 gab dem schwarzen Mann Handschrift und Siegel darüber und ging nach Haus.

gave the black man his signature and seal and went home.

2.1 Als er nach Haus kam, da freute sich sein kleiner Junge so sehr darüber, daß er sich an den Bänken hielt, zu ihm herbei wackelte und ihn an den Beinen fest packte.

When he came home, his little boy was so pleased that he held on to the benches, wobbled over to him and grabbed him by the legs.

2.2 Da erschrak der Vater, denn es fiel ihm sein Versprechen ein und er wußte nun, was er verschrieben hatte;

Then the father was frightened, for he remembered his promise, and now he knew what he had promised;

2.3 weil er aber immer noch kein Geld in seinen Kisten und Kasten fand,

but as he still found no money in his boxes and chests,

dachte er es wäre nur ein Spaß von dem Männchen gewesen.

2.4

he thought it was only a joke on the part of the little man.

Einen Monat nachher ging, er auf den Boden und wollte altes Zinn zusammen suchen, und verkaufen, da sah er einen großen Haufen Geld liegen.

2.5

A month later he went to the ground and wanted to collect some old pewter and sell it, when he saw a large pile of money lying there.

Nun war er wieder guter Dinge, kaufte ein, ward ein größerer Kaufmann als vorher und ließ Gott einen guten Mann sein.

2.6

Now he was in good spirits again, made his purchases, became a greater merchant than before, and let God be a good man.

Unterdessen ward der Junge groß und dabei klug und gescheit.

2.7

In the meantime, the boy grew up and became wise and clever.

Je näher aber die zwölf Jahre herbei kamen, je sorgenvoller ward der Kaufmann, sodaß man ihm die Angst im Gesicht sehen konnte.

2.8

But the closer the twelve years approached, the more worried the merchant became, so that you could see the fear in his face.

Da fragte ihn der Sohn einmal was ihm fehlte;

2.9

Once the son asked him what was wrong with him;

2.10 der Vater wollte es nicht sagen, aber jener hielt so lange an, bis er ihm endlich sagte, er hätte ihn, ohne es zu wissen was er verspräche, einem schwarzen Männchen zugesagt und vieles Geld dafür bekommen.

the father would not tell him, but he persisted until at last he told him that he had promised him, without knowing what he promised, to a little black man, and had received a great deal of money for it.

2.11 Er hätte seine Handschrift mit Siegel darüber gegeben, und nun müßte er ihn, wenn zwölf Jahre herum wären, ausliefern.

He had put his signature and seal on it, and now he would have to hand it over when twelve years had passed.

2.12 Da sprach der Sohn,

Then the son said,

2.13 »O Vater, laßt Euch nicht bang sein, das, soll schon gut werden;

"O father, don't be afraid, it will be all right;

2.14 der Schwarze hat doch keine Macht über mich.«

the black man has no power over me."

3.1 Der Sohn ließ sich von dem Geistlichen segnen, und als die Stunde kam, gingen sie zusammen hinaus auf den Acker, und der Sohn machte einen Kreis und stellte sich mit seinem Vater hinein.

The son had himself blessed by the priest, and when the hour came, they went out into the field together, and the son made a circle and stood in it with his father.

3.2 Da kam das schwarze Männchen und sprach zu dem Alten:

Then the little black man came and said to the old man:

»Hast du mitgebracht, was du mir versprochen hast?« 3.3
"Have you brought what you promised me?"

Er schwieg still, aber der Sohn fragte: 3.4
He remained silent, but the son asked:

»Was willst du hier?« Da sagte das schwarze 3.5
Männchen:
"What do you want here?" Then the little black man said:

»Ich habe mit deinem Vater zu sprechen und nicht 3.6
mit dir.«
"I have to talk to your father and not to you."

Der Sohn antwortete: 3.7
The son replied:

»Du hast meinen Vater betrogen und verführt, 3.8
"You have deceived and seduced my father,

gieb die Handschrift heraus.« 3.9
hand over the handwriting."

»Nein.« sagte das schwarze Männchen, 3.10
"No." said the black man,

»mein Recht geb ich nicht auf.« 3.11
"I will not give up my right."

3.12 Da redeten sie noch lange miteinander, endlich wurden sie einig, der Sohn, weil er nicht dem Erbfeind und nicht mehr seinem Vater zugehörte, sollte sich in ein Schiffchen setzen, das auf, einem hinabwärtsfließenden Wasser stände, und der Vater sollte es mit seinem eigenen Fuß fortstoßen, und, dann sollte der Sohn dem Wasser überlassen bleiben.

Then they talked together for a long time, and at last they agreed that the son, because he did not belong to the hereditary enemy and no longer to his father, should put himself into a little boat that stood on a downward-flowing stream, and the father should push it away with his own foot, and then the son should be left to the water.

3.13 Da nahm er Abschied von seinem Vater, setzte sich in ein Schiffchen, und der Vater mußte es mit seinem eigenen Fuß fortstoßen.

So he took leave of his father, sat down in a boat, and his father had to push it away with his own foot.

3.14 Das Schiffchen schlug um, sodaß der unterste Teil oben war, die Decke aber im Wasser;

The boat overturned, so that the lowest part was up, but the top was in the water;

3.15 und der Vater glaubte, sein Sohn wäre verloren, ging heim und trauerte um ihn.

and the father thought his son was lost, and went home and mourned for him.

4.1 Das Schiffchen aber versank nicht, sondern floß ruhig fort, und der Jüngling saß sicher darin;

But the little boat did not sink, but floated quietly away, and the youth sat safely in it;

4.2 und so floß es lange,

and so it floated for a long time,

bis es endlich an einem unbekannten Ufer festsitzen blieb.

4.3

until at last it came to rest on an unknown shore.

Da stieg er ans Land, sah ein schönes Schloß vor sich liegen und ging darauf los.

4.4

Then he stepped ashore, saw a beautiful castle lying before him, and went towards it.

Wie er aber hineintrat, war es verwünscht;

4.5

But when he entered it, it was cursed;

er ging durch alle Zimmer, aber sie waren leer, bis er in die letzte Kammer kam, da lag eine Schlange darin und ringelte sich.

4.6

he went through all the rooms, but they were empty, until he came to the last chamber, where a serpent lay writhing in it.

Die Schlange aber war eine verwünschte Jungfrau, die freute sich, wie sie ihn sah, und sprach zu ihm,

4.7

But the serpent was a cursed maiden, who rejoiced when she saw him, and said to him,

»Kommst du, mein Erlöser?

4.8

"Are you coming, my deliverer?

auf dich habe ich schon zwölf Jahre gewartet;

4.9

I have been waiting for you for twelve years;

dies Reich ist verwünscht, und du mußt es erlösen.«

4.10

this kingdom is cursed, and you must deliver it."

»Wie kann ich das?« fragte er.

4.11

"How can I do that?" he asked.

4.12 »Heute Nacht kommen zwölf schwarze Männer, die mit Ketten behangen sind, die werden dich fragen was du hier machst, da schweig aber still und gieb ihnen keine Antwort, und laß sie mit dir machen was sie wollen;

"Tonight twelve black men will come, hung with chains, they will ask you what you are doing here, but keep quiet and give them no answer, and let them do what they like with you;

4.13 sie werden dich quälen, schlagen und stechen, laß alles geschehen, nur rede nicht;

they will torture you, beat you and stab you, let everything happen, only do not speak;

4.14 um zwölf Uhr müssen sie wieder fort.

at twelve o'clock they must go away again.

4.15 Und in der zweiten Nacht werden wieder zwölf andere kommen, in der dritten vierundzwanzig, die werden dir den Kopf abhauen;

And on the second night twelve others will come again, on the third twenty-four, they will cut off your head;

4.16 aber um zwölf Uhr ist ihre Macht vorbei, und wenn du dann ausgehalten und kein Wörtchen gesprochen hast, so bin ich erlöst.

but at twelve o'clock their power is over, and if you have then endured and not spoken a word, I am delivered.

4.17 Ich komme zu dir, und habe in einer Flasche das Wasser des Lebens, damit bestreiche ich dich, und dann bist du wieder lebendig und gesund wie zuvor.«

I will come to you, and I have the water of life in a bottle, with which I will sprinkle you, and then you will be alive and well as before."

Da sprach er: »Gern will ich dich erlösen.«   4.18
Then he said: "I will gladly redeem you."

Es geschah nun alles so, wie sie gesagt hätte: 4.19
Everything happened just as she had said:

die schwarzen Männer konnten ihm kein Wort   4.20
abzwingen, und in der dritten Nacht ward die
Schlange zu einer schönen Königstochter, die kam
mit dem Wasser des Lebens und machte ihn wieder
lebendig.
the black men could not force a word out of him, and on the
third night the serpent became a beautiful princess, who
came with the water of life and brought him back to life.

Und dann fiel sie ihm um den Hals und küßte ihn,   4.21
And then she fell on his neck and kissed him,

und es war Jubel und Freude im ganzen Schloß.   4.22
and there was rejoicing and joy in the whole castle.

Da wurde ihre Hochzeit gehalten und er war König   4.23
vom goldenen Berg.
Then their wedding was held and he was king of the golden
mountain.

Also lebten sie vergnügt zusammen,   5.1
So they lived happily together,

und die Königin gebar einen schönen Knaben.   5.2
and the queen gave birth to a beautiful boy.

Acht Jahre waren schon herum, da fiel ihm sein Vater   5.3
ein und sein Herz ward bewegt, und er wünschte ihn
einmal heimzusuchen.
Eight years had passed, when he remembered his father,
and his heart was moved, and he wished to visit him once.

5.4 Die Königin wollte ihn aber nicht fortlassen und sagte,

But the queen would not let him go, and said,

5.5 »Ich weiß schon, daß es mein Unglück ist.«

"I already know that it is my misfortune."

5.6 er ließ ihr aber keine Ruhe bis sie einwilligte.

But he gave her no peace until she consented.

5.7 Beim Abschied gab sie ihm noch einen Wünschring und sprach:

At parting she gave him a wishing ring and said,

5.8 »Nimm diesen Ring und steck ihn an deinen Finger, so wirst du alsbald dahin versetzt, wo du dich hinwünschest, nur mußt du mir versprechen, daß du ihn nicht gebrauchst, mich von hier weg zu deinem Vater zu wünschen.«

"Take this ring and put it on your finger, and you will soon be transferred to wherever you wish to go, only you must promise me that you will not use it to wish me away from here to your father."

5.9 Er versprach ihr das, steckte den Ring an seinen Finger und wünschte sich heim vor die Stadt, wo sein Vater lebte.

He promised her this, put the ring on his finger and wished himself home to the town where his father lived.

5.10 Im Augenblick befand er sich auch dort und wollte in die Stadt; wie er aber vors Thor kam, wollten ihn die Schildwachen nicht einlassen, weil er seltsame und doch so reiche und prächtige Kleider anhatte.

At the moment he was there too and wanted to go into the city, but when he came to the gate, the guards would not let him in because he was wearing strange and yet so rich and splendid clothes.

Da ging er auf einen Berg, wo ein Schäfer hütete, 5.11
tauschte mit diesem die Kleider und zog den alten
Schäferrock an und ging also ungestört in die Stadt
ein.
So he went to a mountain where a shepherd was herding,
exchanged clothes with him and put on the old shepherd's
coat, and so entered the city undisturbed.

Als er zu seinem Vater kam, gab er sich zu erkennen, 5.12
der aber glaubte nimmermehr, daß es sein Sohn wäre
und sagte, er hätte zwar einen Sohn gehabt, der wäre
aber längst tot;
When he came to his father, he made himself known, but
he never believed that it was his son, and said that he had
had a son, but that he had died long ago;

doch weil er sähe, daß er ein armer dürftiger Schäfer 5.13
wäre, so wollte er ihm einen Teller voll zu essen
geben.
but because he saw that he was a poor, poor shepherd, he
wanted to give him a plateful to eat.

Da sprach der Schäfer zu seinen Eltern: 5.14
Then the shepherd said to his parents,

»Ich bin wahrhaftig euer Sohn, wißt ihr kein Mal an 5.15
meinem Leibe, woran ihr mich erkennen könnt?«
"I am truly your son, do you not know any mark on my
body by which you can recognize me?"

»Ja.« sagte die Mutter, 5.16
"Yes." said the mother,

»unser Sohn hatte eine Himbeere unter dem rechten 5.17
Arm.«
"our son had a raspberry under his right arm."

5.18 Er streifte das Hemd zurück, da sahen sie die Himbeere unter seinem rechten Arm und zweifelten nicht mehr, daß es ihr Sohn wäre.

He pulled back his shirt, and they saw the raspberry under his right arm, and no longer doubted that it was their son.

5.19 Darauf erzählte er ihnen, er wäre König vom goldenen Berg und eine Königstochter wäre seine Gemahlin, und sie hätten einen schönen Sohn von sieben Jahren.

Then he told them that he was king of the golden mountain, and that a king's daughter was his wife, and that they had a beautiful son of seven years of age.

5.20 Da sprach der Vater: »Nun und nimmermehr ist das wahr:

Then the father said, "Now and never again is this true:

5.21 das ist mir ein schöner König,

this is a handsome king to me,

5.22 der in einem zerlumpten Schäferrock hergeht.«

who walks about in a ragged shepherd's coat."

5.23 Da ward der Sohn zornig und drehte, ohne an sein Versprechen zu denken, den Ring herum und wünschte beide, seine Gemahlin und sein Kind, zu sich.

Then the son was angry and, without thinking of his promise, turned the ring round and wished both his wife and his child to come to him.

5.24 In dem Augenblick waren sie auch da, aber die Königin klagte und weinte, und sagte er hätte sein Wort gebrochen und hätte sie unglücklich gemacht.

At that moment they were there, but the queen wailed and wept, and said he had broken his word and made her unhappy.

Er sagte,

He said,

»Ich habe es unachtsam gethan und nicht mit bösem
Willen.«

"I did it carelessly, and not with evil intent."

und redete ihr zu; sie stellte sich auch als gäbe sie
nach,

and spoke to her; she also pretended to yield,

aber sie hatte Böses im Sinn.

but she had evil in mind.

Da führte er sie hinaus vor die Stadt auf den Acker
und zeigte ihr das Wasser, wo das Schiffchen war
abgestoßen worden, und sprach dann:

Then he led her out into the field outside the town and
showed her the water where the little boat had been
launched, and then said,

»Ich bin müde, setze dich nieder, ich will ein wenig
auf deinem Schoß schlafen.«

"I am tired, sit down, I want to sleep a little on your lap."

Da legte er seinen Kopf auf ihren Schoß und sie lauste
ihn ein wenig, bis er einschlief.

So he laid his head on her lap and she listened to him for a
while until he fell aslcep.

Als er eingeschlafen war, zog sie erst den Ring von
seinem Finger, dann zog sie den Fuß unter ihm weg
und ließ nur den Toffel zurück;

When he had fallen asleep, she first took the ring off his
finger, then pulled his foot out from under him, leaving
only the towel;

6.5 hierauf nahm sie ihr Kind in den Arm und wünschte sich wieder in ihr Königreich.

then she took her child in her arms and wished herself back into her kingdom.

6.6 Als er aufwachte, lag er da ganz verlassen, und seine Gemahlin und das Kind waren fort und der Ring vom Finger auch, nur der Toffel stand noch da zum Wahrzeichen.

When he awoke, he lay there quite deserted, and his wife and child were gone, and so was the ring from his finger, only the toff was still there as a symbol.

6.7 »Nach Haus zu deinen Eltern kannst du nicht wieder gehen.«

"You can't go home to your parents again."

6.8 dachte er,

he thought,

6.9 »die würden sagen, du wärst ein Hexenmeister, du willst aufpacken und gehen, bis du in dein Königreich kommst.«

"they would say you were a sorcerer, you want to pack up and leave until you get to your kingdom."

6.10 Also ging er fort und kam endlich zu einem Berg, vor dem drei Riesen standen und mit einander stritten, weil sie nicht wußten, wie sie ihres Vaters Erbe teilen sollten.

So he went away and finally came to a mountain where three giants were standing and arguing with each other because they did not know how to divide their father's inheritance.

Als sie ihn vorbeigehen sahen, riefen sie ihn an und sagten, kleine Menschen hätten klugen Sinn, er sollte ihnen die Erbschaft verteilen.

6.11

When they saw him passing by, they called to him and said that little men had clever minds and that he should distribute the inheritance to them.

Die Erbschaft aber bestand aus einem Degen, wenn einer den in die Hand nahm und sprach,

6.12

But the inheritance consisted of a sword, if one took it in his hand and said,

»Köpf alle runter, nur meiner nicht.«

6.13

"All heads down, except mine."

so lagen alle Köpfe auf der Erde;

6.14

all the heads lay on the ground;

zweitens aus einem Mantel, wer den anzog, war unsichtbar;

6.15

secondly, of a cloak, whoever put it on was invisible;

drittens aus ein paar Stiefeln, wenn man die angezogen hatte und sich wohin wünschte, so war man im Augenblick da.

6.16

thirdly, of a pair of boots, if one had put them on and wished to go somewhere, one was there in an instant.

Er sagte:

6.17

He said,

»Gebt mir die drei Stücke, damit ich probieren kann, ob sie noch in gutem Stande sind.«

6.18

"Give me the three pieces so that I can try them to see if they are still in good condition."

6.19 Da gaben sie ihm den Mantel, und als er ihn umgehängt hatte, war er unsichtbar und war in eine Fliege verwandelt.

So they gave him the cloak, and when he had put it on, he was invisible and turned into a fly.

6.20 Dann nahm er wieder seine Gestalt an und sprach:

Then he took on his form again and said

6.21 »Der Mantel ist gut, nun gebt mir das Schwert.« Sie sagten:

"The cloak is good, now give me the sword." They said:

6.22 »Nein, das geben wir nicht! Wenn du sprächst,

"No, we won't give it to you! If you said,

6.23 »Köpf alle runter, nur meiner nicht!«

"All heads down but mine!"

6.24 so wären unsere Köpfe alle herab und du allein hättest den deinigen noch.«

our heads would all be down and you alone would still have yours."

6.25 Doch gaben sie es ihm unter der Bedingung, daß er's an einem Baum probieren sollte.

But they gave it to him on condition that he should try it on a tree.

6.26 Das that er und das Schwert zerschnitt den Stamm eines Baumes wie einen Strohhalm.

He did so, and the sword cut the trunk of a tree like a straw.

6.27 Nun wollte er noch die Stiefeln haben, sie sprachen aber:

Now he wanted the boots, but they said,

»Nein, die geben wir nicht weg, wenn du sie angezogen hättest und wünschtest dich oben auf den Berg, so stünden wir da unten und hätten nichts.«

6.28

"No, we will not give them away, if you had put them on and wished yourself up the mountain, we would be down there and have nothing."

»Nein.« sprach er, »das will ich nicht thun.«

6.29

"No." he said, "I will not do that."

Da gaben sie ihm auch die Stiefeln.

6.30

So they gave him the boots also.

Wie er nun alle drei Stücke hatte, so dachte er an nichts als an seine Frau und sein Kind und sprach so vor sich hin,

6.31

As he now had all three pieces, he thought of nothing but his wife and his child, and said to himself,

»Ach wäre ich auf dem goldenen Berg.«

6.32

"Oh, if I were on the golden mountain."

und alsbald verschwand er vor den Augen der Riesen,

6.33

and immediately he disappeared before the eyes of the giants,

und war also ihr Erbe geteilt.

6.34

and so their inheritance was divided.

Als er nahe beim Schloß war, hörte er Freudengeschrei, Geigen und Flöten, und die Leute sagten, ihm, seine Gemahlin feierte ihre Hochzeit mit einem andern.

6.35

When he was near the castle, he heard shouts of joy, violins and flutes, and the people told him that his wife was celebrating her wedding with another.

6.36 **Da ward er zornig und sprach:**
Then he was angry and said,

6.37 **»Die Falsche, sie hat mich betrogen und mich verlassen, als ich eingeschlafen war.«**
"The false one, she has deceived me and left me when I was asleep."

6.38 **Da hing er seinen Mantel um und ging unsichtbar ins Schloß hinein.**
So he put on his cloak and went into the castle out of sight.

6.39 **Als er in den Saal eintrat, war da eine große Tafel mit köstlichen Speisen besetzt, und die Gäste aßen und tranken, lachten und scherzten.**
When he entered the hall, there was a large table set with delicious food, and the guests were eating and drinking, laughing and joking.

6.40 **Sie aber saß in der Mitte in prächtigen Kleidern auf einem königlichen Sessel und hatte die Krone auf dem Haupt.**
But she was sitting in the middle on a royal armchair in splendid clothes with a crown on her head.

6.41 **Er stellte sich hinter sie und niemand sah ihn.**
He stood behind her and no one saw him.

6.42 **Wenn sie ihr ein Stück Fleisch auf den Teller legten,**
When they put a piece of meat on her plate,

6.43 **nahm er ihn weg und aß es;**
he took it away and ate it;

6.44 **und wenn sie ihr ein Glas Wein einschenkten,**
and when they poured her a glass of wine,

nahm er's weg und trank's aus;   6.45
he took it away and drank it;

sie gaben ihr immer und sie hatte doch immer nichts,   6.46
denn Teller und Glas verschwanden augenblicklich.
they always gave it to her, and yet she always had nothing,
for plate and glass disappeared at once.

Da ward sie bestürzt und schämte sie sich, stand auf   6.47
und ging in ihre Kammer und weinte, er aber ging
hinter ihr her.
Then she was distressed and ashamed, and got up and went
into her chamber and wept, but he went after her.

Da sprach sie: »Ist denn der Teufel über mir,   6.48
Then she said, "Is the devil upon me,

oder kam mein Erlöser nie?«   6.49
or did my Savior never come?"

Da schlug er ihr ins Angesicht und sagte: 6.50
Then he struck her in the face and said,

»Kam dein Erlöser nie? Er ist über dir, du Betrügerin.   6.51
"Did your Savior never come? He is above you, you
deceiver.

Habe ich das an dir verdient?« Da machte er sich   6.52
sichtbar,
Did I deserve this from you?" Then he made himself visible,

ging in den Saal und rief: »Die Hochzeit ist aus,   6.53
went into the hall and shouted: "The wedding is over,

der wahre König ist gekommen!«   6.54
the true king has come!"

6.55 Die Könige, Fürsten und Räte, die da versammelt wären, höhnten und verlachten ihn; er aber gab kurze Worte und sprach,

The kings, princes and councillors who were gathered there jeered and ridiculed him, but he spoke briefly and said,

6.56 »Wollt ihr hinaus oder nicht?«

"Do you want to go out or not?"

6.57 Da wollten sie ihn fangen und drangen auf ihn ein, aber er zog sein Schwert und sprach,

Then they wanted to catch him and came at him, but he drew his sword and said,

6.58 »Köpf alle runter, nur meiner nicht.«

"All heads down, except mine."

6.59 Da rollten alle Köpfe zur Erde,

Then all the heads rolled to the ground,

6.60 und er war allein der Herr und der König vom goldenen Berg.

and he alone was the lord and king of the golden mountain.

Der alte Hildebrand

The Old Hildebrand

1.1 Es war amahl a Baur und a Bäurin, und dö Bäurin, dö hat der Pfarra im Dorf gern gesegn, und da hat er alleweil gwunschen, wann er nur amahl an ganzen Tag mit der Bäurin allan recht vergnügt zubringa kunnt, und der Bäurin der wars halt a recht gewesn.

There was once a farmer and a farmer's wife, and the farmer's wife, the parish priest in the village liked to bless her, and he always wished that he could spend a whole day with the farmer's wife, and the farmer's wife liked it.

1.2 No, da hat er amahl zu der Bäurin gsagt:

No, then he said to the baker:

1.3 »Hanz, mei liebi Bäurin, hietzt, hab i was ausstudiert, wie wir halt amahl an ganzen Tag recht vergnügt mitanander zubringa kunnten.

"Hey, my dear baker, now I've worked out how we could have fun together all day long.

Wißts was, ös legts eng aufm Mittwoch ins Bett und   1.4
sagts engern Mon ös seits kräng, und lamatierts
und übelts nur recht, und das treibts fort bis aufm
Sunta, wann i die Predi halt, und da wir (werde) i
predigen, daß wer z'Haus a krangs Kind, an krängen
Mon, a krangs Weib, an krangen Vader, a krange
Muader, a krange Schwester, Bruader, oda wers
sunst nacha is, hat, und der thut a Wollfart aufm
Göckerliberg in Wälischland, wo ma um an Kreuzer
an Metzen Lorberbladen kriegt, dem wirds krange
Kind, der krange Mon, 's krange Weib, der krange
Vader, d'krange Muader, d'krange Schwester, oda
wers sunst nacha is, auf der Stell gsund.«

You know, I'll lie down in bed on Wednesday and tell my
close friend Mon that I'm sick, and I'll lambast her and
make her sick, and that'll go on until Sunday, when I'll
preach, and then I'll preach that whoever has a sick child,
a sick husband, a sick wife, a sick father, a sick mother at
home, a sick sister, brother, or whoever else is next, and
who does a wool farm on the Göckerliberg in Wälischland,
where you can get a packet of Lorberbladen for a kreuzer,
the sick child, the sick mon, the sick wife, the sick father,
the sick mother, the sick sister, or whoever else is next, will
be healthy on the spot."

»Dös wir i schon machen.« hat die Bäurin drauf gsagt.   2.1

"We're already doing that." the farmer's wife said.

No, drauf, aufm Mittwoch hat sie halt d'Bäurin ins   2.2
Bett glegt und hat glamatiert und gübelt als wie, und
ihr Mon hat ihr alles brucht, was er nur gwißt hat, 's
hat aber halt nix gholfn.

Well, on Wednesday, the farmer's wife went to bed and was
tossing and turning and moaning, and her husband tried
everything he knew, but it didn't help.

2.3 Wie denn der Sunta kuma is, hat d'Bäurin gsagt:

When Sunday came, the farmer's wife said:

2.4 »Mir is zwar so miserabel als ob i glei verschaden sollt, aber ans möcht i do no vor mei End, i möcht halt in Herrn Pfarra sei Predi hörn, dö er heund halten wird.«

"I feel so miserable that I feel like dying, but before I go I want to hear the sermon the parson will preach today."

2.5 »A, mei Kind.« sagt der Baur drauf,

"Oh, my child." the farmer says,

2.6 »thu du dös nit, du kunntst schlechter wern, wann aufstundst.

"don't do that, you could get worse if you get up.

2.7 Schau, es wir i in d'Predi gehn und wir recht acht gebe und wir dir alles wieder derzöhln, was der Herr Pfarra gsagt hat.«

Look, I will go to the sermon and we will pay close attention and we will tell you everything the parson said."

2.8 »No.« hat d'Bäurin gsagt,

'No.' said the farmer's wife,

2.9 »so geh halt und gib recht acht und derzöhl mir alles, was d'ghört hast.«

"so just go and pay close attention and tell me everything you heard."

No, und da is der Baur halt in d'Predi ganga, und da hat der Herr Pfarra also angfangt zun predigen und hat halt gsagt, wann ans a krangs Kind, an krangen Mon, a krangs Weib, an krangen Vader, a krange Muader, a krange Schwester, Bruader, oda wers sunst nacha war, z'Haus hat, und der wollt a Wollfart machen aufm Göckerliberg in Wälischland, wo der Metzen Lorberbladen an Kreuzer kost, dem wirds krange Kind, der krange Mon, 's krange Weib, der krange Vader, d'krange Muader, d'krange Schwester, Bruader, oda wers sunst nacha war, auf der Stell gsund wern, und wer also dö Ras unternehma wollt, der soll nach der Meß zu ihm kuma, da wird er ihm den Lorbersack gebn und den Kreuzer.

So the farmer went to church, and the pastor began to preach and said, if a sick child, a sick mother, a sick wife, a sick father, a sick mother, a sick sister, a brother or whatever else, has at home, and he also wanted to make a pilgrimage to Göckerliberg in Wälischland, where a leaf of the meadows costs a Kreuzer, the child will be sick, the sick man, the sick woman, the sick father, the sick mother, the sick sister, brother, or whatever else was needed, to be healthy on the spot, and whoever wanted to undertake this madness should come to him after mass, and he would give him the laurel bag and the cruiser.

2.10

Da war niembd fröher als der Bauer, und nach der Meß is er gleich zum Pfarra ganga, und der hat ihm also den Lorbersack gebn und den Kreuzer.

There was no one there earlier than the farmer, and after mass he went straight to the parish, and so he gave him the laurel bag and the cruiser.

2.11

Drauf is er nach Haus kuma und hat schon bei der Hausthür eini geschrien:

Then he came home and shouted at the front door:

2.12

2.13 »Juchesha, liebes Weib, hietzt is so viel als obs gsund warst.

"Juchesha, dear wife, today is as good as you were healthy.

2.14 Der Herr Pfarra hat heunt predigt, daß wer a krangs Kind, a krangen Mon, a kranges Weib, an krangen Vader, a krange Muader, a krange Schwester, Bruader, oda wers sunst nacha war, z'Haus hat, und der macht a Wollfart aufm Göckerliberg in Wälischland, wo der Metzen Lorberbladen an Kreuzer kost, dem wirds 's krange Kind, der krange Mon, 's krange Weib, der krange Vader, d'krange Muader, d'krange Schwester, Bruader, oda wers sunst nacha war, auf der Stell gsund;

The pastor preached today that whoever has a sick child, a sick husband, a sick wife, a sick father, a sick mother, a sick sister, brother, or whatever else is wrong, has a sick child, a sick husband, a sick wife, a sick father, a sick mother, a sick sister, brother, or whatever else is wrong, has a sick child, a sick husband, a sick wife, a sick father, a sick mother, a sick sister, brother, or whatever else is wrong, has a sick child, a sick husband, a sick wife, a sick father, a sick mother, a sick sister, brother, or whatever else is wrong, has a sick child, a sick husband, a sick wife, a sick father, a sick mother, a sick sister, brother, or whatever else is wrong, has a sick child, a sick husband, a sick wife, a sick father, a sick mother, a sick sister, brother, or whatever else is wrong, has a sick child, a sick husband, a sick wife, a sick father, a sick mother, a sick sister, brother, or whatever else is wrong, has a sick child, a sick husband, a sick wife on the Göckerliberg in Wälischland, where a metzen bay leaf costs a kreuzer, the 's krane child, the krane man, the krane father, the krane mother, the krane sister, brother, or whatever else it was, would be healthy on the spot;

und hietzt hab i mir schon den Lorbersack gholt vom
Herrn Pfarra und den Kreuzer, und wir glei mein
Wanderschaft antreten, daß d' desto ehender gsund
wirst.«

2.15

and now I have already got the laurel bag from the pastor
and the cruiser, and we will start my journey immediately,
so that you will be healthy sooner."

und drauf is er fort ganga.

2.16

And then he left.

Er war aber kam fort, so is die Bäurin schon auf
gwesn, und der Pfarra war a glei do.

2.17

But he had left, so the farmer's wife had already woken up,
and the pastor was there right away.

Hietzt lassen wir aber dö zwa indessen auf der Seiten
und gänga mir mit'n Baur.

2.18

But now we leave them on the page for a while and move on
to the farmer.

Der is halt alleweil drauf los ganga, damit er desto
ehender aufm Göckerliberg kummt, und wie halt so
geht, begegnt ihm sein Gvatter.

2.19

He just set off, so that he would arrive at the Göckerliberg
all the sooner, and as luck would have it, he met his
godfather.

Sein Gvatter dös war an Armon (Eiermann), und der
is just von Mark kuma, wo er seine Ar verkauft hat.

2.20

His godfather was an egg seller and had just come from
Mark, where he had sold his eggs.

»Gelobt seist.« sagt sein Gvatter,

2.21

"Praise be." says his godfather,

»wo gehst denn so trabi hin, Gvatter?«

2.22

'where are you going, Godfather?'

2.23 »In Ewigkeit, Gvatter.«

'In eternity, Godfather.'

2.24 sagt der Baur, »mein Weib is krang worn, und da hob i heund in Herrn Pfarra sein Predi ghört, und da hat er predigt, daß wann aner z'Haus an krangs Kind, an krangen Mon, a krangs Weib, an krangen Vader, a krange Muader, a krange Schwester, Bruader, oda wers sunst nacha war, hat, und er macht a Wollfart aufm Göckerliberg in Wälischland, wo der Metzen Lorberbladen an Kreuzer kost, dem wird's krange Kind, der krange Mon, 's krange Weib, der krange Vader, d'krange Muader, d'krange Schwester, Bruader, oda wers sunst nacha war, auf der Stell gsund, und da hab i mir von Herrn Pfarra den Lorbersack und den Kreuzer gholt, und hietzt trit i halt mein Wanderschaft an.«

says the farmer, "my wife has become ill, and so I heard his sermon in the pastor's house, and he preached that when someone at home has a sick child, a sick mother, a sick wife, a sick father, a sick mother, sister, brother, or whoever it was, and he goes on a pilgrimage to the Göckerliberg in Wälischland, where a leaf of the mezzanin costs a cruiser, the sick child, the sick man, the wife, the sick father, the sick mother, the sick sister, brother, or whatever else it was, was healthy on the spot, and so I got the Lorber sack and the cruiser from Mr. Pfarra, and now I'm just starting my journey."

2.25 »Aber hanz, Gvatter.« hat der Gvatter zum Baur gsagt:

"But, grandfather." said the farmer's grandfather,

2.26 »Seids denn gar so backet (einfältig), daß so was glauben könts?

'are you so simple that you can believe such a thing?

225

Wißts, was is?   2.27
Do you know what it is?

der Pfarra möcht gern mit engern Weib an ganzen   2.28
Tag allan recht vergnügt zubringa, drum habn's eng
den Bärn anbunden, daß ihr'en aus'n Füßen kumts.«
The parson would like to spend the whole day alone with
his wife, so he tied the bear to her so that you can't get out
of your feet.'

»Mein.« hat der Baur gsagt,   2.29
"My." said the farmer,

»so möcht i do wissen, ob das wahr is.«   2.30
"I should like to know if that is true."

»No.« hat der Gvatter gsagt,   2.31
"Well." said the grandfather,

»wast was, setz di in mein Arkorb eini, so will i di   2.32
nach Haus tragn, und da wirst es selber segn.«
"if it is, sit down in my basket, and I will carry thee home,
and there thou shalt be blessed thyself."

No, das is also geschegn, und den Baur hat sein   2.33
Gvatter in sein Arkorb eini gsetzt, und der hat'n
nach Haus tragn.
Well, that is what happened, and the farmer was put in his
grandfather's basket, and he carried him home.

Wie's nach Haus kuma san, holla, da is schon lusti   2.34
zuganga.
As soon as they arrived home, there was already a merry
atmosphere.

2.35 Da hat die Bäurin schon fast alles, was nur in ihrem Hof war, abgstochen ghabt, und Krapfen hats bachen, und der Pfarra war a schon da und hat a sein Geige mitbracht ghabt.

The farmer's wife had already cut up almost everything that was in her yard, and she was baking doughnuts, and the pastor was already there and had brought his violin.

2.36 Und da hat halt der Gvatter anklopft, und d'Bäurin hat gfragt, wer draussen war.

And then the godfather knocked, and the farmer's wife asked who was outside.

2.37 »I bins, Gvatterin.« hat der Gvatter gsagt,

"It's me, godmother." said the father-in-law,

2.38 »mei, gebts mir heund nacht a Herberg, i hab meini Ar aufm Mark nit verkauft, und hietzt muß i's wieder nach Haus trage, und sö san gar z'schwar, i bring's nit fort, es is a schon finster.«

"oh, give me shelter tonight too, I did not sell my load at the market, and now I have to carry it home again, and they are so very heavy, I can't carry them, it is already getting dark."

2.39 »Ja, mein Gvatter.« sagt d' Bäurin drauf,

"Yes, my father-in-law." said the farmer's wife,

2.40 »ös kumts mir recht zur unglegna Zeit.

"you are very welcome.

2.41 No, weils halt her nit anders is, so kömts eina und setzt's eng dort auf d'Ofenbank.«

Well, because it is not otherwise here, come in and sit down there on the stove bench."

No hat sie der Gvatter also mit sein Buckelkorb auf d'Ofenbank gsetzt.
2.42

So her grandfather sat down on the stove bench with his pannier.

Der Pfarra aber und d'Bäurin dö warn halt recht lusti.
2.43

But the parson and the farmer's wife were quite amused.

Endli fangt der Pfarra an und sagt:
2.44

Finally the parson begins and says:

»Hanz, mein liebi Bäurin, ös könnts ja so schön singa, singts mir do ans.«
2.45

"Hans, my dear farmer, you sing so beautifully, sing this to me."

»A.« sagt die Bäurin,
2.46

"A." Says the farmer's wife,

»hietzt kann i nix mehr singa, ja, in mein junge Jahren, da hab i's wohl könna, aber hietzt is schon vorbei.«
2.47

"I can't sing anything now, yes, in my younger years I could, but now it's all over."

»Ei.« sagt wieder der Pfarra, »singts do nur a bißl.«
2.48

"No." says the parson again, 'just sing a little.'

No, da fangt die Bäurin an und singt:
2.49

So the farmer's wife begins and sings:

»I hab mein Mon wohl ausgesandt	"I have probably sent out my mon
aufm Göckerliberg in Wälischland.«	on the Göckerliberg in Wälischland."

4.1 Drauf singt der Pfarra:
Then the parish priest sings:

»I wollt, er blieb da a ganzes Jahr,	"I wanted him to stay there for a whole year,
was fragt i nach dem Lorbersack.	what do I ask about the Lorber bag.
Halleluja!«	Hallelujah! "

6.1 Hietzt fangt der Gvatter hinten an und singt (da muß i aber derzöhln, daß der Baur Hildebrand ghassen hat) also der Gvatter:
Now the father starts at the back and sings (but I have to tell you that the farmer hated Hildebrand):

»Ei du, mein lieber Hildebrand,	"Oh you, my dear Hildebrand,
was machst du auf der Ofenbank?	what are you doing on the stove bench?
Halleluja!«	Hallelujah! "

8.1 Und hietzt singt der Baur in Korb drinna a:
And now the baur in the basket sings:

8.2 »Hietzt kann i das Singa nimmermehr leiden,
"Now I can't stand the singing anymore,

8.3 hietzt muß i aus mein Buckelkorb steigen.«
now I have to get out of my humpback basket."

Und steigt aus'n Korb und prügelt den Pfaffen beim Haus hinaus. 9.1

And gets out of the basket and beats the priest out of the house.

De drei Vügelkens

The Three Little Pigeons

1.1 **Et is wul dusent un meere Jaare hen, da wören hier im Lanne luter kleine Künige, da hed auck einer up den Keuterberge wünt (gewohnt), de gink san geren up de Jagd.**

There were a lot of little kings here in the country, one of them lived (lived) on the Keuterberg, who liked to go hunting.

1.2 **Ase nu mal mit sinen Jägern vom Schlotte heruttrok, höen (hüteten) unner den Berge drei Mäkens ire Köge (Kühe), un wie sei den Künig mit den vielen Lüen (Leuten) seien, so reip de ölleste den annern beden Mäkens to, un weis up den Künig:**

When he and his hunters came back from the castle, three men were herding their cows under the mountain, and as they approached the king with all the people, the oldest one called out to the other two men and said to the king:

1.3 **»Helo! helo! wenn ik den nig kriege, so will ik keinen.«**

"Hello! Hello! If I don't get any, I don't want any."

Da antworde de zweide up de annere Side vom Berge, un weis up den, de dem Künige rechter Hand gink:

1.4

Then the two answered on the other side of the mountain, and pointed to the one on the king's right hand:

»Helo! helo! wenn ik den nig kriege, so will ik keinen.«

1.5

"Hello! Hello! If I don't get him, I don't want one."

Da reip de jüngeste, un weis up den, de linker Hand gink:

1.6

Then the youngest one reaches out and points to the one on his left hand:

»Helo! helo! wenn ik den nig kriege, so will ik keinen.«

1.7

"Hello! Hello! If I don't get it, I don't want it."

Dat wören awerst de beden Ministers.

1.8

These were the two ministers.

Dat hörte de Künig alles, und ase von der Jagd heime kummen was, leit he de drei Mäkens to sik kummen un fragete se, wat se da gistern am Berge segd heddeu.

1.9

The king heard all this, and when he came home from the hunt, he led the three men to him and asked them what they had heard on the mountain.

Dat wullen se nig seggen, de Künig frog awerst de ölleste, ob se ün wol tom Manne hewen wulle?

1.10

They didn't want to say, but the king asked the oldest if they wanted to have her as their husband?

1.11 Da segde se ja, un ere beiden Süstern friggeten de beiden Ministers, denn se wören alle drei scheun un schier (klar, schön) von Angesicht, besunners de Königin, de hadde Hare ase Flass.

So they said yes, and our two sweethearts welcomed the two ministers, for they were all three beautiful and fair of face, especially the queen, who had hair like a river.

2.1 De beiden Süstern awerst kregen keine Kinner, un ase de Künig mal verreisen moste, let he se tor Künigin kummen, um se up to munnern, denn se was grae (gerad) swanger.

The two sweethearts, however, had no children, and when the king had to go on a trip, he let them come to the queen to munner her, because she was just pregnant.

2.2 Se kreg en keinen Jungen,

She didn't have a boy,

2.3 de hadde 'n ritsch roen (roten) Stern mit up de Weld.

she had a bright red star with her.

2.4 Da sehden de beiden Süstern, eine tör annern, se wullen den hübsken Jungen in't Water werpen.

Then the two sisters, one for the other, saw that they wanted to throw the pretty boy into the water.

2.5 Wie se'n darin worpen hadden (ick glöwe, et is de Weser West), da flügt 'n Vügelken in de Högte, dat sank:

As they had thrown him in (I think it was the Weser West), a bird flew into the water and sank:

»Tom Daude bereit, "Tom Daude ready,

up wietern Bescheid up wietern Bescheid

233

tom Lilienstrus:

tom Lilienstrus:

wacker Junge, bist du's?«

brave boy, is that you?"

Da dat de beiden hörten, kregen se de Angst up'n
Lieve, un makten, dat se fort keimen.

4.1

When the two of them heard this, they became afraid and
went away.

Wie de Künig na Hus kam, sehden se to üm, de
Königin hedde 'n Hund kregen.

4.2

When the king came home, they saw that the queen had
been given a dog.

Da segde de Künig: »Wat Gott deiet,

4.3

Then the king said: "What God has given,

dat is wole dahn.«

4.4

that's what I want."

Et wunde awerst 'n Fisker an den Water, de fiskede
den kleinen Jungen wier herut, ase noch ewen
lebennig was, un da sine Fru kene Kinner hadde,
foerden (fütterten) s'en up.

5.1

First a fisker came to the water, which brought the little
boy back when he was still only a few years old, and since
his wife had no children, she fed him.

Na'n Jaar was de Künig wier verreist, da krig de
Königin wier'n Jungen, den namen de beiden falsken
Süstern un warpen 'n auck in't Water, da flügt dat
Vügelken wier in de Högte un sank:

5.2

After a year, the king had gone away, the queen gave birth
to a baby boy, who was named by the two false southsiders
and dropped into the water, where the bird flew into the
hollow and sank:

»Tom Daude bereit,   "Tom Daude ready,

up wietern Bescheid   up wietern Bescheid

tom Lilienstrus: tom Lilienstrus:

wacker Junge, bist du's?« brave boy, is that you?"

7.1 **Un wie de Künig torügge kam, sehden se to üm, de Königin hedde wier 'n Hund bekummen, un he segde wier:**
And when the king came back, they saw that the queen had been given a dog, and he said:

7.2 **»Wat Gott deit, dat is wole dahn.«**
"What God says, that's what it is."

7.3 **Awerst de Fisker trok dösen auck ut den Water un foerd 'n up.**
However, the fisker trotted out of the water and fished up.

8.1 **Da verreisede de Künig wier, und de Königin kreg 'n klein Mäken, dat Warpen de falsken Süstern auck in't Water.**
Then the king went away, and the queen got a little girl, who threw the false south star into the water.

8.2 **Da flügt dat Vügelken wier in de Högte und sank:**
Then the bird flew into the hollow and sank:

»Tom Daude bereit,   "Tom Daude ready,

up wietern Bescheid   up wietern Bescheid

tom Lilienstrus:

tom Lilienstrus:

wacker Mäken, bist du's?«

Wacker Mäken, is that
you?"

Un wie de König na Hus kam, sehden se to üm, de
Königin hedde ne Katte kregt.
And when the king came home, they saw that the queen
had been given a cat.

10.1

Da worde de Künig beuse un leit sine Fru in't
Gefängnis smieten,
Then the king went to bed and led his wife to prison,

10.2

da hed se lange Jaare in setten.
where she spent many years.

10.3

De Kinner wören unnerdes angewassen, da gink de
ölleste mal mit annern Jungens herut to fisken, da
wüllt ün de annern Jungens nig twisken sik hewen
un segget:
The children were being touched all the time, so the oldest
boy came over to fish with the other boys, and the other
boys wanted to have a little talk with him and said:

11.1

»Du Fündling, gaa du diner Wege.«
"You youngster, go your own way."

11.2

Da ward he gans bedröwet und fräggt den olen Fisker,
ob dat war wöre?
Then he gets all misty-eyed and asks the old fisker if that
was true?

11.3

De verteilt ün, dat he mal fisked hedde, un hedde ün
ut den Water troken (gezogen).
He told him that he had once fished and pulled him out of
the water.

11.4

11.5 Da segd he, he wulle fürt un sinen Teilen (Vater) söken.

Then he said that he wanted to go and see his father.

11.6 De Fisker de biddet 'n, he mögde doch bliven, awerst he let sik gar nich hallen, bis de Fisker et tolest to givt.

The skipper begged him to stay, but he didn't let himself go until the skipper gave up.

11.7 Da givt he sik up den Weg un geit meere Dage hinnern anner, endlich kömmt he vor 'n graut allmächtig Water, davor steit 'ne ole Fru un fiskede.

Then he goes on his way and walks for several days, finally he arrives in front of a gray almighty water, in front of it stands an old woman and speaks.

11.8 »Guden Dag, Moer.« segde de Junge.

"Have a good day, Moer." said the boy.

11.9 »Groten Dank.«

"Thank you very much."

11.10 »Du süst da wol lange fisken, e du 'n Fisk fängest.«

"You'll be fishing for a long time before you catch a fish."

11.11 »Un du wol lange söken, e du dinen Teiten findst.

"And you'll have to look for a long time before you find your day.

11.12 Wie wust du der denn da över't Water kummen?« sehde de Fru.

How did you come across the water?" the woman asked.

11.13 »Ja, dat mag Gott witten.«

"Yes, God may know that."

Da nümmt de ole Fru ün up den Rüggen un dragt 'n derdörch,

11.14

Then the old woman takes one up on the bridge and drags him down,

un he söcht lange Tiid un kann sinen Teiten nig finnen.

11.15

and he looks for a long time and can't find his door.

Ase nu wol 'n Jaar veröwer is,

11.16

Now that a year has passed,

da trekt de tweide auck ut un will sinen Broer söken.

11.17

the young woman comes out and wants to see her brother.

He kümmt an dat Water, un da geit et ün ewen so, ase sinen Broer.

11.18

He comes to the water, and that's how it goes, just like his brother.

Nu was nur noch de Dochter allein to Hus, de jammerde so viel na eren Broern, dat se upt lest auck den Fisker bad, he mögte se treken laten, se wulle ere Broerkes söken.

11.19

Now there was only the daughter left at home, she was whining so much for her own bread that she asked the fisherman to let her go, she wanted to eat her bread.

Da kam se auck bie den grauten Water, da sehde se tor olen Fru:

11.20

Then she came to the gray water and saw her old wife:

»Guden Dag, Moer.«

11.21

"Good day, Moer."

»Groten Dank.«

11.22

"Thank you very much."

11.23 »Gott helpe ju bie juen fisken.«

"God help me to be happy."

11.24 Ase de ole Fru dat hörde, da word se gans fründlich un drog se över't Water un gab er 'n Roe (Ruthe), un sehde to er:

When the old woman heard this, she became very kind and carried her over the water and gave her a rod, and said to her:

11.25 »Nu gah man jummer up düsen Wege to, mine Dochter, un wenn du bie einen groten swarten Hund vorbeikümmst, so must du still un drist un one to lachen un one ün antokicken, vorbie gaan.

"Now go quietly on your way, my daughter, and when you pass a large, alert dog, you must be quiet and silent and laugh and kick one in the face.

11.26 Dann kümmest du an 'n grot open Schlott, up'n Süll (Schwelle) most du de Roe fallen laten un stracks dörch dat Schlott an den annern Side wier herutgahen;

Then you come to a large, open chimney, on the threshold you must drop the door and walk straight through the chimney to the other side;

11.27 da is 'n olen Brunnen, darut is 'n groten Boom wassen, daran hänget 'n Vugel im Buer, den nümm af, dann nümm noch 'n Glas Water ut den Brunnen un gaa mit düsen beiden den sülvigen Weg wier torügge;

there is an old fountain, underneath is a large boom, with a bird hanging from it in the brush, which you take down, then take another glass of water from the fountain and walk with the two of you along the southern path;

up den Süll nümm de Roe auck wier mit, un wenn du 11.28
dann wier bie den Hund vorbiekummst, so schlah ün
in't Gesicht, awerst sü to, dat du ün treppest, un dann
kumm nur wier to me torügge.«

Take the roe with you up the hill, and when you come to
the dog, sleep on your face, but make sure you step on it,
and then just come back to me."

Da fand se et grade so, ase de Fru et sagd hadde, un up 11.29
den Rückwege da fand se de beiden Broer, de sik de
halve Welt durchsöcht hadden.

She found it just as the woman had said, and on the way
back she found the two brothers who had traveled halfway
around the world.

Se gink tosammen bis wo de swarte Hund an den Weg 11.30
lag, den schlag se in't Gesicht, da word et 'n schönen
Prinz, de geit mit ünnen bis an dat Water.

They walked together until they came to where the old dog
lay on the path, she hit him in the face, and there was a
beautiful prince, who walked with her to the water's edge.

Da stand da noch de ole Fru, de frögede sik ser, da se 11.31
alle wier da wören, un drog se alle över't Water, un
dann gink se auck weg, denn se was nu erlöst.

The old woman was still standing there, happy that they
were all still there, and she pushed them all over the water,
and then she walked away, for she was now redeemed.

De annern awerst gingen alle na den olen Fisker, un 11.32
alle wören froh, dat se sik wier funnen hadden, den
Vugel awerst hüngen se an der Wand.

The others, on the other hand, all went to the old fisker,
and everyone was glad that they had found each other
again, but they hung the bird on the wall.

De tweide Suhn kunne awerst nig to Huse rasten, 12.1

The two sons could only rest a little at home,

240

12.2 un nam 'n Flitzebogen un gink up de Jagd.

and took a bow and went hunting.

12.3 Wie he möe was, nam he sine Flötepipen, un mackte 'n Stücksken.

As he did, he named his flute pipes and made a piece of music.

12.4 De Künig awerst wör auck up de Jagd un hörde dat, da gink he hin, un wie he den Jungen drap, so sehde he:

The king, on the other hand, was also out hunting and heard that, so he went there, and as he looked at the boy, he saw:

12.5 »We hett die verlöwt hier to jagen?«

"Who has chosen to hunt here?"

12.6 »O, neimes (niemand).«

"Oh, nobody (nobody)."

12.7 »Wen hörst du dann to?«

"Then who are you listening to?"

12.8 »Ik bin den Fisker sin Suhn.«

"I am the skipper's son."

12.9 »De hett ja keine Kinner.«

"He doesn't have any children."

12.10 »Wenn du't nig glöwen wust, so kum mit.«

"If you don't know anything, come with me."

12.11 Dat dehe de Künig un frog den Fisker, de vertälle ün alles, un dat Vügelken an der Wand fing an to singen:

The king said this and asked the fisherman, who told him everything, and the bird on the wall began to sing:

»De Möhme (Mutter) sitt allein,

"De Möhme (mother) sits alone,

wol in dat Kerkerlein.

wol in dat dungeon.

O Künig, edeles Blod,

O Künig, noble blood,

dat sind dine Kinner god.

dat sind dine Kinner god.

De falsken Süstern beide

De falsken Süstern both

de dehen de Kinnerkes Leide,

de dehen de Kinnerkes Leide,

wol in des Waters Grund,

wol in the bottom of the water,

wo se de Fisker fund.«

where they found the Fisker."

Da erschraken se alle un de Künig nahm den Vugel, den Fisker un de drei Kinner mit sik na dem Schlotte un leit dat Gefänknis upschluten un nam sine Fru wier herut, de was awerst gans kränksch un elennig woren.

14.1

Then they were all frightened and the king took the bird, the fisker and the three children with him to the castle and led the prison up the slope and called his wife back, who was very sickly and elderly.

Da gav er de Dochter von den Water ut den Brunnen to drinken, da war se frisk un gesund.

14.2

Then he gave her daughter a drink of water from the well and she was fresh and healthy.

De beiden falsken Süstern wören awerst verbrennt,

14.3

The two false sweethearts were burnt to death,

242

14.4 **un de Dochter friggede den Prinzen.**
and the daughter ate the prince.

Das Wasser des Lebens

The Water of Life

1.1 **Es war einmal ein König, der war krank, und niemand glaubte, daß er mit dem Leben davonkäme.**
Once upon a time there was a king who was ill, and no one believed that he would escape with his life.

1.2 **Er hatte aber drei Söhne, die waren darüber betrübt, gingen hinunter in den Schloßgarten und weinten.**
But he had three sons who were saddened by this and went down into the castle garden and wept.

1.3 **Da begegnete ihnen ein alter Mann, der fragte sie nach ihrem Kummer.**
Then they met an old man who asked them about their grief.

1.4 **Sie sagten ihm, ihr Vater wäre so krank, daß er wohl sterben würde, denn es wollte ihm nichts helfen.**
They told him that their father was so ill that he would probably die, for nothing would help him.

1.5 **Da sprach der Alte:**
Then the old man said,

»Ich weiß noch ein Mittel, das ist das Wasser des Lebens, wenn er davon trinkt, so wird er wieder gesund; es ist aber schwer zu finden.«.

1.6

"I know another remedy, that is the water of life, if he drinks it he will get well again, but it is hard to find.".

Der älteste sagte: »Ich will es schon finden.«

1.7

The eldest said, "I will find it."

ging zum kranken König und bat ihn, er möchte ihm erlauben auszuziehen, um das Wasser des Lebens zu suchen, denn das könnte ihn allein heilen.

1.8

The eldest went to the sick king and asked him to allow him to go out in search of the water of life, for that alone could cure him.

»Nein.« sprach der König,

1.9

"No." said the king,

»die Gefahr dabei ist zu groß, lieber will ich sterben.«

1.10

"the danger is too great, I would rather die."

Er bat aber so lange, bis der König einwilligte.

1.11

But he begged until the king agreed.

Der Prinz dachte in seinem Herzen: Bringe ich das Wasser,

1.12

The prince thought in his heart: "If I bring the water,

so bin ich meinem Vater der liebste und erbe das Reich.«

1.13

I will be my father's favorite and inherit the kingdom."

2.1 Also machte er sich auf, und als er eine Zeitlang fortgeritten war, stand da ein Zwerg auf dem Wege, der rief ihn an und sprach,

So he set off, and when he had ridden on for a while, a dwarf stood on the path, who called to him and said,

2.2 »Wo hinaus so geschwind?«

"Where are you going so quickly?"

2.3 »Dummer Knirps.« sagte der Prinz ganz stolz,

"Silly little fellow." said the prince proudly,

2.4 »das brauchst du nicht zu wissen.« und ritt weiter.

"you don't need to know that." and rode on.

2.5 Das kleine Männchen aber war zornig geworden und hatte einen bösen Wunsch gethan.

But the little man had become angry and had made a bad wish.

2.6 Der Prinz geriet bald hernach in eine Bergschlucht, und je weiter er ritt, je enger thaten sich die Berge zusammen, und endlich ward der Weg so eng, daß er keinen Schritt weiter konnte;

The prince soon found himself in a mountain gorge, and the farther he rode the closer the mountains came together, and at last the path became so narrow that he could not go a step farther;

2.7 es war nicht möglich das Pferd zu wenden oder aus dem Sattel zu steigen,

it was impossible to turn the horse or get out of the saddle,

2.8 und er saß da wie eingesperrt.

and he sat there as if shut in.

Der kranke König wartete lange Zeit auf ihn, aber er kam nicht. 2.9

The sick king waited a long time for him, but he did not come.

Da sagte der zweite Sohn: »Vater, 2.10

Then the second son said, "Father,

laß mich ausziehen und das Wasser suchen.« und dachte bei sich, 2.11

let me go out and seek the water." and thought to himself,

»Ist mein Bruder tot, so fällt das Reich mir zu.« 2.12

"If my brother is dead, the kingdom will fall to me."

Der König wollte ihn anfangs auch nicht ziehenlassen, 2.13

At first the king did not want to let him go either,

endlich gab er nach. 2.14

but finally he gave in.

Der Prinz zog also auf demselben Weg fort, den sein Bruder eingeschlagen hatte, und begegnete auch dem Zwerg, der ihn anhielt und fragte wohin er so eilig wollte. 2.15

So the prince set off along the same path his brother had taken and met the dwarf, who stopped him and asked where he was going in such a hurry.

»Kleiner Knirps.« sagte der Prinz, 2.16

"Little gnome." said the prince,

»das brauchst du nicht zu wissen.« 2.17

"you don't need to know."

2.18 und ritt fort ohne sich weiter umzusehen.

and rode off without looking back.

2.19 Aber der Zwerg verwünschte ihn, und er geriet wie der andere in eine Bergschlucht und konnte nicht vorwärts und rückwärts.

But the dwarf cursed him, and he, like the other, got into a mountain gorge and could not go forwards or backwards.

2.20 So geht's aber den Hochmütigen.

But so it is with the proud.

3.1 Als auch der zweite Sohn ausblieb, so erbot sich der jüngste auszuziehen und das Wasser zu holen, und der König mußte ihn endlich ziehen lassen.

When the second son also failed to appear, the youngest offered to go out and fetch the water, and the king finally had to let him go.

3.2 Als er dem Zwerg begegnete und dieser fragte, wohin er so eilig wolle, so hielt er an, gab ihm Rede und Antwort und sagte,

When he met the dwarf and asked him where he was going in such a hurry, he stopped and answered him, saying,

3.3 »Ich suche das Wasser des Lebens,

"I am looking for the water of life,

3.4 denn mein Vater ist sterbenskrank.«

for my father is dying of illness."

3.5 »Weißt du auch, wo das zu finden ist?«

"Do you know where to find it?"

3.6 »Nein.« sagte der Prinz.

"No." said the prince.

»Weil du dich betragen hast wie sich's geziemt, nicht   3.7
übermütig wie deine falschen Brüder, so will ich dir
Auskunft geben und dir sagen, wie du zu dem Wasser
des Lebens gelangst.

"Because you have behaved as you should, not
overconfidently like your false brothers, I will give you
information and tell you how to get to the water of life.

Es quillt aus einem Brunnen in dem Hofe eines   3.8
verwünschten Schlosses, aber du dringst nicht
hinein, wenn ich dir nicht eine eiserne Rute gebe
und zwei Laiberchen Brot.

It springs from a well in the courtyard of a cursed castle,
but you will not enter it unless I give you an iron rod and
two loaves of bread.

Mit der Rute schlag dreimal an das eiserne Thor des   3.9
Schlosses,

Strike the iron gate of the castle three times with the rod,

so wird es aufspringen;   3.10

and it will burst open;

inwendig liegen zwei Löwen, die den Rachen   3.11
aufsperren, wenn du aber jedem ein Brot
hineinwirfst, so werden sie still und dann eile dich
und hol' von dem Wasser des Lebens bevor es zwölf
schlägt, sonst schlägt das Thor wieder zu und du bist
eingesperrt.«

inside there are two lions who will open their mouths, but
if you throw them each a loaf of bread, they will be quiet,
and then hurry and get some of the water of life before it
strikes twelve, otherwise the gate will slam shut again and
you will be locked in."

Der Prinz dankte ihm,   3.12

The prince thanked him,

250

3.13 **nahm die Rute und das Brot und machte sich auf den Weg.**

took the rod and the bread and set off.

3.14 **Und als er anlangte, war alles so, wie der Zwerg gesagt hatte.**

And when he arrived, everything was just as the dwarf had said.

3.15 **Das Thor sprang beim dritten Rutenschlag auf, und als er die Löwen mit dem Brot gesänftigt hatte, trat er in das Schloß und kam in einen großen schönen Saal, darin saßen verwünschte Prinzen, denen zog er die Ringe vom Finger, dann lag da ein Schwert und ein Brot, das nahm er weg.**

The gate burst open at the third stroke of the rod, and when he had appeased the lions with the bread, he entered the castle and came into a large beautiful hall, in which sat cursed princes, from whose fingers he took off the rings, and then there lay a sword and a loaf of bread, which he took away.

3.16 **Und weiter kam er in ein Zimmer, darin stand eine schöne Jungfrau, die freute sich als sie ihn sah, küßte ihn und sagte, er hätte sie erlöst, und sollte ihr ganzes Reich haben, und wenn er in einem Jahre wiederkäme, so sollte ihre Hochzeit gefeiert werden.**

And then he came into a room where stood a beautiful maiden, who rejoiced when she saw him, kissed him, and said that he had redeemed her, and should have her whole kingdom, and if he came again in a year's time their wedding should be celebrated.

Dann sagte sie ihm auch, wo der Brunnen wäre mit dem Lebenswasser, er müßte sich aber eilen und daraus schöpfen eh es zwölf schlüge.

3.17

Then she also told him where the well of water of life was, but that he must hasten and draw from it before it struck twelve.

Da ging er weiter und kam endlich in ein Zimmer, wo ein schönes frischgedecktes Bett stand, und weil er müde war, wollte er erst ein wenig ausruhen.

3.18

So he went on and at last came to a room where there was a beautiful freshly-covered bed, and because he was tired he wanted to rest a little first.

Also legte er sich und schlief ein;

3.19

So he lay down and fell asleep;

als er erwachte, schlug es drei Viertel auf zwölf.

3.20

when he awoke it was three-quarters to twelve.

Da sprang er ganz erschrocken auf, lief zu dem Brunnen und schöpfte daraus mit einem Becher, der daneben stand, und eilte, daß er fortkam.

3.21

Then he jumped up, quite frightened, ran to the well and drew from it with a cup that stood beside it, and hurried away.

Wie er eben zum eisernen Thor hinaus ging, da schlug's zwölf, und das Thor schlug so heftig zu, daß es ihm noch ein Stück von der Ferse wegnahm.

3.22

Just as he was going out to the iron gate, the clock struck twelve, and the gate slammed so violently that it took a piece off his heel.

4.1 Er aber war froh, daß er das Wasser des Lebens erlangt hatte, ging heimwärts und kam wieder an dem Zwerg vorbei.

But he was glad that he had obtained the water of life, went home and passed the dwarf again.

4.2 Als dieser das Schwert und das Brot sah, sprach er,

When the dwarf saw the sword and the bread, he said,

4.3 »Damit hast du großes Gut gewonnen:

"You have gained great wealth with this:

4.4 mit dem Schwert kannst du ganze Heere schlagen,

with the sword you can defeat whole armies,

4.5 das Brot aber wird niemals all.«

but the bread will never be enough."

4.6 Der Prinz wollte ohne seine Brüder nicht zu dem Vater nach Haus kommen und sprach,

The prince did not want to come home to his father without his brothers and said,

4.7 »Lieber Zwerg,

"Dear dwarf,

4.8 kannst du mir nicht sagen wo meine zwei Brüder sind?

can't you tell me where my two brothers are?

4.9 Sie sind früher als ich nach dem Wasser des Lebens ausgezogen und sind nicht wiedergekommen.«

They left for the water of life earlier than I did and have not returned."

4.10 »Zwischen zwei Bergen stecken sie eingeschlossen.«

"They are trapped between two mountains."

sprach der Zwerg, 4.11

said the dwarf,

»dahin habe ich sie verwünscht, weil sie so 4.12
übermütig waren.«

"I cursed them there because they were so boisterous."

Da bat der Prinz so lange, bis der Zwerg sie wieder los 4.13
ließ, aber er warnte ihn und sprach,

The prince begged until the dwarf let them go again, but he
warned him and said,

»Hüte dich vor ihnen, sie haben ein böses Herz.« 4.14

"Beware of them, they have an evil heart."

Als seine Brüder kamen, freute er sich und erzählte 5.1
ihnen wie es ihm ergangen wäre, daß er das
Wasser des Lebens gefunden und einen Becher voll
mitgenommen, und eine schöne Prinzessin erlöst
hätte, die wollte ein Jahr lang auf ihn warten, dann
sollte die Hochzeit gehalten werden, und er bekäme
ein großes Reich.

When his brothers came, he rejoiced and told them how he
had fared, that he had found the water of life and had taken
a cupful with him, and had redeemed a beautiful princess,
who would wait for him for a year, then the wedding would
be held, and he would have a great kingdom.

Danach ritten sie zusammen fort und gerieten in 5.2
ein Land, wo Hunger und Krieg war, und der König
glaubte schon er müßte verderben, so groß war die
Not.

Then they rode away together and came to a land where
there was famine and war, and the king thought he would
perish, so great was the need.

254

5.3 Da ging der Prinz zu ihm und gab ihm das Brot,

Then the prince went to him and gave him bread,

5.4 womit er sein ganzes Reich speiste und sättigte;

with which he fed and satisfied his whole kingdom;

5.5 und dann gab ihm der Prinz auch das Schwert,

and then the prince also gave him the sword,

5.6 damit schlug er die Heere seiner Feinde und konnte nun in Ruhe und Frieden leben.

with which he defeated the armies of his enemies and was now able to live in peace and quiet.

5.7 Da nahm der Prinz sein Brot und das Schwert wieder zurück,

Then the prince took back his bread and his sword,

5.8 und die drei Brüder ritten weiter.

and the three brothers rode on.

5.9 Sie kamen aber noch in zwei Länder, wo Hunger und Krieg herrschten, und da gab der Prinz den Königen jedesmal sein Brot und Schwert, und hatte nun drei Reiche gerettet.

But they came to two more countries where there was famine and war, and there the prince gave the kings his bread and sword each time, and had now saved three kingdoms.

5.10 Und danach setzten sie sich auf ein Schiff und fuhren übers Meer.

And then they got on a ship and sailed across the sea.

5.11 Während der Fahrt sprachen die beiden ältesten unter sich:

During the voyage, the two eldest said among themselves,

»Der jüngste hat das Wasser des Lebens gefunden und wir nicht, dafür wird ihm unser Vater das Reich geben, das uns gebührt, und er wird unser Glück wegnehmen.« 5.12

"The youngest has found the water of life and we have not, but our father will give him the kingdom that is due to us and he will take away our happiness."

Da wurden sie rachsüchtig und verabredeten miteinander, daß sie ihn verderben wollten. 5.13

Then they became vengeful and agreed among themselves that they would destroy him.

Sie warteten bis er einmal fest eingeschlafen war, da gossen sie das Wasser des Lebens aus dem Becher und nahmen es für sich, ihm aber gossen sie bitteres Meerwasser hinein. 5.14

They waited until he was fast asleep, then they poured out the water of life from the cup and took it for themselves, but for him they poured in bitter sea water.

Als sie nun daheim ankamen, brachte der jüngste dem kranken König seinen Becher, damit er daraus trinken und gesund werden sollte. 6.1

When they arrived home, the youngest brought his cup to the sick king so that he could drink from it and get well.

Kaum aber hatte er ein wenig von dem bittern Meerwasser getrunken, so ward er noch kränker als zuvor. 6.2

But no sooner had he drunk a little of the bitter sea water than he became even sicker than before.

6.3 Und wie er darüber jammerte, kamen die beiden
ältesten Söhne und klagten den jüngsten an, er hätte
ihn vergiften wollen, sie brächten ihm das rechte
Wasser des Lebens, und reichten es ihm.

And as he lamented this, the two eldest sons came and
accused the youngest of trying to poison him, saying that
they had brought him the right water of life and handed it
to him.

6.4 Kaum hatte er davon getrunken, so fühlte er seine
Krankheit verschwinden, und war stark und gesund
wie in seinen jungen Tagen.

As soon as he had drunk it, he felt his illness disappear and
was as strong and healthy as in his younger days.

6.5 Danach gingen die beiden zu dem jüngsten,
verspotteten ihn und sagten,

Then the two went to the youngest and mocked him,
saying,

6.6 »Du hast zwar das Wasser des Lebens gefunden,

"You have found the water of life,

6.7 aber du hast die Mühe gehabt und wir den Lohn;

but you have had the trouble and we the reward;

6.8 du hättest klüger sein und die Augen aufbehalten
sollen, wir haben dir's genommen während du auf
dem Meere eingeschlafen warst, und übers Jahr da
holt sich einer von uns die schöne Königstochter.

you should have been wiser and kept your eyes open, we
took it from you while you were asleep on the sea, and one
of us is going to get the beautiful king's daughter every
year.

Aber hüte dich, daß du nichts davon verrätst, der Vater glaubt dir doch nicht, und wenn du ein einziges Wort sagst, so sollst du noch obendrein dein Leben verlieren, schweigst du aber, so soll dir's geschenkt sein.«   6.9

But beware that thou tell nothing of it, for the father will not believe thee, and if thou say a single word, thou shalt lose thy life on top of it, but if thou keep silence, it shall be given thee."

Der alte König war zornig über seinen jüngsten Sohn und glaubte, er hätte ihm nach dem Leben getrachtet.   7.1

The old king was angry with his youngest son and believed that he had tried to kill him.

Also ließ er den Hof versammeln und das Urteil über ihn sprechen, daß er heimlich sollte erschossen werden.   7.2

So he had the court assembled and pronounced sentence on him that he should be shot in secret.

Als der Prinz nun einmal auf die Jagd ritt und nichts Böses vermutete,   7.3

When the prince rode out to hunt and suspected no evil,

mußte des Königs Jäger mitgehen.   7.4

the king's huntsman had to go with him.

Draußen, als sie ganz allein im Wald waren, und der Jäger so traurig, aussah, sagte der Prinz zu ihm,   7.5

Outside, when they were all alone in the forest, and the huntsman looked so sad, the prince said to him,

»Lieber Jäger, was fehlt dir?«   7.6

"Dear huntsman, what is the matter with you?"

7.7 Der Jäger sprach: »Ich kann's nicht, sagen und soll es doch.«
The huntsman said, "I can't tell you, but I should."

7.8 Da sprach der Prinz: »Sage es heraus was es ist,
Then the prince said, "Tell me what it is,

7.9 ich will dir's verzeihen.«
and I will forgive you."

7.10 »Ach.« sagte der Jäger, »ich soll Euch totschießen,
"Alas." said the huntsman, "I am to shoot you dead,

7.11 der König hat mir's befohlen.«
the king has commanded me."

7.12 Da erschrak der Prinz, und sprach:
Then the prince was frightened, and said,

7.13 »Lieber Jäger, laß mich leben, da gebe ich dir mein königliches Kleid, gieb mir dafür dein schlechtes.«
"Dear huntsman, let me live, and I will give you my royal dress, and in return give me your bad one."

7.14 Der Jäger sagte: »Das will ich gern thun, ich hätte doch nicht nach Euch schießen können.«
The huntsman said, "I will gladly do so, for I could not have shot at you."

7.15 Da tauschten sie die Kleider, und der Jäger ging heim, der Prinz aber ging weiter in den Wald hinein.
So they exchanged clothes, and the huntsman went home, but the prince went on into the forest.

Über eine Zeit, da kamen zu dem alten König drei
Wagen mit Gold und Edelsteinen, für seinen jüngsten
Sohn;

8.1

About a time there came to the old king three carts with
gold and precious stones for his youngest son;

sie waren von den drei Königen geschickt,

8.2

they were sent by the three kings who had slain the
enemies with the prince's sword and fed their country
with his bread,

die mit des Prinzen Schwert die Feinde geschlagen
und mit seinem Brot ihr Land ernährt hatten und die
sich dankbar bezeigen wollten.

8.3

and who wished to show their gratitude.

Da dachte der alte König,

8.4

Then the old king thought,

»Sollte mein Sohn unschuldig gewesen sein?«

8.5

"Should my son have been innocent?"

und sprach zu seinen Leuten:

8.6

and said to his people,

»Wäre er noch am Leben, wie thut mir's so leid, daß
ich ihn habe töten lassen.«

8.7

"If he were still alive, how sorry I am that I had him killed."

»Er lebt noch.« sprach der Jäger,

8.8

"He is still alive." said the huntsman,

»ich konnte es nicht übers Herz bringen Euern Befehl
auszuführen.«

8.9

"I could not bring myself to carry out your order."

8.10 und sagte dem König wie es zugegangen war.

and told the king what had happened.

8.11 Da fiel dem König ein Stein von dem Herzen, und er ließ in allen Reichen verkündigen, sein Sohn dürfte wiederkommen und sollte in Gnaden aufgenommen werden.

Then a stone fell from the king's heart, and he had it proclaimed in all the kingdoms that his son might return and should be received into mercy.

9.1 Die Königstochter aber ließ eine Straße vor ihrem Schloß machen, die war ganz golden und glänzend, und sagte ihren Leuten, wer darauf geradeswegs zu ihr geritten käme, das wäre der rechte, und den sollten sie einlassen; wer aber danebenkäme, der wäre der rechte nicht; und den sollten sie auch nicht einlassen.

But the king's daughter had a road made in front of her castle, which was all golden and shining, and told her people that whoever rode straight to her on it was the right one, and they should let him in; but whoever came beside it was not the right one, and they should not let him in either.

9.2 Als nun die Zeit bald herum war, dachte der älteste er wollte sich eilen, zur Königstochter gehen und sich für ihren Erlöser ausgeben, da bekäme er sie zur Gemahlin und das Reich daneben.

Now when the time was almost up, the eldest thought he would hasten to go to the king's daughter and pretend to be her deliverer, so that he could have her as his wife and the kingdom besides.

9.3 Also ritt er fort, und als er vor das Schloß kam und die schöne goldene Straße sah, dachte er:

So he rode off, and when he came to the castle and saw the beautiful golden road, he thought:

»Das wäre jammerschade, wenn du darauf rittest.« 9.4
"It would be a pity if you rode on it."

lenkte ab und ritt rechts nebenher. 9.5
So he turned off and rode to the right.

Wie er aber vor das Thor kam, sagten die Leute 9.6
zu ihm, er wäre der rechte nicht, er sollte wieder
fortgehen.
But when he came to the gate, the people said to him that
he was not the right one, and that he should go away again.

Bald darauf machte sich der zweite Prinz auf, und wie 9.7
der zur goldenen Straße kam und das Pferd den einen
Fuß darauf gesetzt hatte, dachte er,
Soon afterward the second prince set out, and when he
came to the golden road and the horse had set one foot on it,
he thought,

»Es wäre jammerschade, das könnte etwas abtreten.« 9.8
"It would be a pity, it might be a bit out of place."

lenkte ab und ritt links nebenher. 9.9
He turned off and rode alongside on the left.

Wie er aber vor das Thor kam, sagten die Leute, er 9.10
wäre der rechte nicht, er sollte wieder fortgehen.
But when he came to the gate, the people said that he was
not the right one and that he should go away again.

Als nun das Jahr ganz herum war, 9.11
When the year was completely over,

wollte der dritte aus dem Wald fort zu seiner Liebsten 9.12
reiten und bei ihr sein Leid vergessen.
the third wanted to ride away from the forest to his beloved
and forget his sorrow with her.

9.13 Also machte er sich auf und dachte immer an sie und wäre gern schon bei ihr gewesen, und sah die goldene Straße gar nicht.

So he set out, always thinking of her, and would have liked to have been with her already, and did not see the golden road at all.

9.14 Da ritt sein Pferd mitten darüber hin, und als er vor das Thor kam, ward es aufgethan, und die Königstochter empfing ihn mit Freuden und sagte, er wäre ihr Erlöser und der Herr des Königreichs, und ward die Hochzeit gehalten mit größer Glückseligkeit.

Then his horse rode right across it, and when he came to the gate, it was opened, and the king's daughter received him with joy, and said that he was her deliverer and the lord of the kingdom, and the wedding was held with great happiness.

9.15 Und als sie vorbei war, erzählte sie ihm, daß sein Vater ihn zu sich entboten und ihm verziehen hätte.

And when it was over she told him that his father had sent for him and forgiven him.

9.16 Da ritt er hin und sagte ihm alles,

So he rode up and told him everything,

9.17 wie seine Brüder ihn betrogen und er doch dazu geschwiegen hätte.

how his brothers had deceived him and yet he had kept silent about it.

9.18 Der alte König wollte sie strafen, aber sie hatten sich aufs Meer gesetzt und waren fortgeschifft, und kamen ihr Lebtag nicht wieder.

The old king wanted to punish them, but they had set out to sea and sailed away, and never came back for the rest of their lives.

Doktor Allwissend

Doctor Omniscient

1.1 Es war einmal ein armer Bauer Namens Krebs, der fuhr mit zwei Ochsen ein Fuder Holz in die Stadt und verkaufte es für zwei Thaler an einen Doktor.

Once upon a time there was a poor farmer named Krebs who drove a cartload of wood into town with two oxen and sold it to a doctor for two thalers.

1.2 Wie ihm nun das Geld ausbezahlt wurde, saß der Doktor gerade zu Tisch; da sah der Bauer wie er schön aß und trank, und das Herz ging ihm danach auf und er wäre auch gern ein Doktor gewesen.

When the money was paid to him, the doctor was sitting at table, and the farmer saw how well he ate and drank, and his heart sank, and he would have liked to be a doctor too.

1.3 Also blieb er noch ein Weilchen stehen und fragte endlich, ob er nicht auch könnte ein Doktor werden.

So he stood there for a while and finally asked if he could become a doctor too.

1.4 »O ja.« sagte der Doktor, »das ist bald geschehen.«

"Oh, yes." said the doctor, "that will soon be done."

»Was muß ich thun?« fragte der Bauer. 1.5

"What must I do?" asked the farmer.

»Erstlich kauf dir ein ABC-Buch, so ist eins, wo vorn 1.6
ein Göckelhahn drin ist;

"First of all, buy yourself an ABC book, one with a cock of
the walk in the front;

zweitens mache deinen Wagen und deine zwei 1.7
Ochsen zu Geld und schaff dir damit Kleider an und
was sonst zur Dokterei gehört;

secondly, turn your cart and your two oxen into money,
and buy some clothes with them, and whatever else belongs
to the doctor's trade;

drittens laß dir ein Schild malen mit den Worten, 1.8

thirdly, have a sign painted with the words,

›Ich bin der Doktor Allwissend‹ 1.9

'I am the Doctor All- knowing,'

und laß das oben über deine Hausthür nageln.« 1.10

and have it nailed over the door of your house."

Der Bauer that alles, wie's ihm geheißen war. 1.11

The farmer did as he was told.

Als er nun ein wenig gedoktert hatte, aber noch 1.12
nicht viel, ward einem reichen großen Herrn Geld
gestohlen.

When he had done a little, but not much, money was stolen
from a rich, great gentleman.

1.13 Da ward ihm von dem Doktor Allwissend gesagt,
der in dem und dem Dorfe wohnte und auch wissen
müßte wo das Geld hingekommen wäre.

Then he was told of the doctor Allwissend, who lived in this
and that village, and who ought to know where the money
had gone.

1.14 Also ließ der Herr seinen Wagen anspannen, fuhr
hinaus ins Dorf und fragte bei ihm an, ob er der
Doktor Allwissend wäre?

So the gentleman had his wagon hitched up, drove out to
the village and asked him if he was the doctor Allwissend?

1.15 »Ja, der wäre er.«

"Yes, he would be."

1.16 »So sollte er mitgehen und das gestohlene Geld
wieder schaffen.«

"So he should go with me and get the stolen money back."

1.17 »O ja, aber die Grete, seine Frau, müßte auch mit.«

"Oh yes, but Grete, his wife, would have to go too."

1.18 Der Herr war das zufrieden, und ließ sie beide in den
Wagen sitzen, und sie fuhren zusammen fort.

The master was satisfied with this, and let them both sit in
the carriage, and they drove away together.

1.19 Als sie auf den adligen Hof kamen, war der Tisch
gedeckt, da sollte er erst mitessen.

When they came to the nobleman's court, the table was
laid, and he was to dine with them.

1.20 »Ja, aber seine Frau, die Grete, auch.«

"Yes, but his wife, Grete, too."

1.21 sagte er und setzte sich mit ihr hinter den Tisch.

he said, and sat down with her behind the table.

Wie nun der erste Bediente mit einer Schüssel
schönem Essen kam, stieß der Bauer seine Frau an
und sagte,

1.22

When the first servant came with a bowl of delicious food,
the farmer nudged his wife and said,

»Grete, das war der erste.«

1.23

"Grete, that was the first one."

und meinte es wäre derjenige, welcher das erste
Essen brächte.

1.24

and said it was the one who brought the first meal.

Der Bediente aber meinte er hätte damit sagen
wollen,

1.25

But the servant thought he meant to say,

»Das ist der erste Dieb.«

1.26

"That's the first thief."

und weil er's nun wirklich war, ward ihm angst, und
er sagte draußen zu seinen Kameraden,

1.27

And because it really was him, he was frightened and said
to his companions outside,

»Der Doktor weiß alles, wir kommen übel an:

1.28

"The doctor knows everything, we're getting into trouble:

er hat gesagt, ich wäre der erste.«

1.29

he said I was the first."

Der zweite wollte gar nicht herein, er mußte aber
doch.

1.30

The second didn't want to come in, but he had to.

Wie er nun mit seiner Schüssel herein kam,

1.31

As he came in with his bowl,

1.32 stieß der Bauer seine Frau an: »Grete, das ist der zweite.«

the farmer nudged his wife: "Grete, that's the second one."

1.33 Dem Bedienten ward ebenfalls angst und er machte, daß er hinaus kam.

The servant was also frightened and made him come out.

1.34 Dem dritten ging's nicht besser, der Bauer sagte wieder:

The third was no better, the farmer said again:

1.35 »Grete, das ist der dritte.«

"Grete, that's the third."

1.36 Der vierte mußte eine verdeckte Schüssel hereintragen, und der Herr sprach zum Doktor, er sollte seine Kunst zeigen und raten was darunter läge; es waren aber Krebse.

The fourth had to carry in a covered bowl, and the master said to the doctor that he should show his skill and guess what was underneath, but it was crabs.

1.37 Der Bauer sah die Schüssel an, wußte nicht wie er sich helfen sollte und sprach:

The farmer looked at the bowl, did not know how to help himself and said,

1.38 »Ach, ich armer Krebs!« Wie der Herr das hörte, rief er:

"Oh, poor crab!" When the master heard this, he shouted:

1.39 »Da, er weiß es, nun weiß er auch wer das Geld hat.«

"There, he knows, now he knows who has the money."

Dem Bedienten aber ward gewaltig angst und er blinzelte den Doktor an, er möchte einmal heraus kommen.

2.1

The servant, however, was terrified and blinked at the doctor, asking him to come out.

Wie er nun hinaus kam, gestanden sie ihm alle viere, sie hätten das Geld gestohlen;

2.2

When he came out, all four of them confessed to him that they had stolen the money;

sie wollten's ja gern herausgeben und ihm eine schwere Summe dazu, wenn er sie nicht verraten wollte, es ginge ihnen sonst an den Hals.

2.3

they would gladly give it back to him and a large sum as well, if he would not betray them, otherwise it would be on their necks.

Sie führten ihn auch hin: wo das Geld versteckt lag.

2.4

They led him to where the money was hidden.

Damit war der Doktor zufrieden, ging wieder hinein, setzte sich an den Tisch und sprach:

2.5

The doctor was satisfied with that, went back inside, sat down at the table and said,

»Herr, nun will ich in meinem Buch suchen, wo das Geld steckt.«

2.6

"Sir, now I will look in my book to find out where the money is."

Der fünfte Bediente aber kroch in den Ofen und wollte hören, ob der Doktor noch mehr wüßte.

2.7

The fifth servant crawled into the oven and wanted to hear if the doctor knew anything else.

Der saß aber und schlug sein ABC-Buch auf,

2.8

But the doctor sat and opened his ABC book,

2.9 blätterte hin und her und suchte den Göckelhahn.

leafing back and forth and looking for the cockerel.

2.10 Weil er ihn nicht gleich finden konnte, sprach er:

Because he couldn't find it straight away, he said:

2.11 »Du bist doch darin und mußt auch heraus.«

"You're in there and you have to come out too."

2.12 Da glaubte der im Ofen, er wäre gemeint, sprang voller Schrecken heraus und rief:

The one in the oven thought he was meant, jumped out in horror and shouted:

2.13 »Der Mann weiß alles.«

"The man knows everything."

2.14 Nun zeigte der Doktor Allwissend dem Herrn, wo das Geld lag, sagte aber nicht wer's gestohlen hatte, bekam von beiden Seiten viel Geld zur Belohnung und ward ein berühmter Mann.

Now the Doctor All-Knowing showed the master where the money was, but did not say who had stolen it, received a lot of money as a reward from both sides and became a famous man.

Der Geist im Glas

The Ghost in the Glass

1.1 Es war einmal ein armer Holzhacker, der arbeitete vom Morgen bis in die späte Nacht.

Once upon a time there was a poor woodcutter who worked from morning till late at night.

1.2 Als er sich endlich etwas Geld zusammengespart hatte, sprach er zu seinem Jungen:

When he had at last saved up some money, he said to his boy,

1.3 »Du bist mein einziges Kind, ich will das Geld, das ich mit saurem Schweiß erworben habe, zu deinem Unterricht anwenden;

"You are my only child, I will use the money I have earned with sour sweat to teach you;

1.4 lernst du etwas Rechtschaffenes, so kannst du mich im Alter ernähren, wenn meine Glieder steif geworden sind und ich daheim sitzen muß.«

if you learn something righteous, you can feed me in my old age when my limbs have grown stiff and I have to sit at home."

Da ging der Junge auf eine hohe Schule und lernte fleißig, sodaß ihn seine Lehrer rühmten, und blieb eine Zeitlang dort.

1.5

So the boy went to a high school and studied hard, so that his teachers praised him, and he stayed there for a while.

Als er ein paar Schulen durchgelernt hatte, doch aber noch nicht in allem vollkommen war, so war das bißchen Armut, das der Vater erworben hatte, draufgegangen und er mußte wieder zu ihm heimkehren.

1.6

When he had gone through a few schools, but was not yet perfect in everything, the little poverty which his father had acquired was gone, and he had to return home to him.

»Ach.«

1.7

"Alas."

sprach der Vater betrübt, ich kann dir nichts mehr geben und kann in der teuren Zeit auch keinen Heller mehr verdienen als das tägliche Brot.«

1.8

said his father sadly, "I can give you nothing more, and in these dear times I cannot earn a penny more than my daily bread."

»Lieber Vater.« antwortete der Sohn,

1.9

"Dear father." replied the son,

»macht Euch darüber keine Gedanken, wenn's Gottes Wille also ist, so wird's zu meinem Besten ausschlagen;

1.10

"don't worry about that, if it is God's will, it will work out for my good;

ich will mich schon dreinschicken.«

1.11

I will send myself in."

1.12 Als der Vater hinaus in den Wald wollte, um etwas am Malterholz (am Zuhauen und Aufrichten) zu verdienen, so sprach der Sohn,

When the father wanted to go out into the forest to earn some money by cutting and raising wood, the son said,

1.13 »Ich will mit Euch gehen und Euch helfen.«

"I will go with you and help you."

1.14 »Ja, mein Sohn.« sagte der Vater,

"Yes, my son." said the father,

1.15 »das sollte dir beschwerlich ankommen, du bist an harte Arbeit nicht gewöhnt, du hältst das nicht aus;

"that should be difficult for you, you're not used to hard work, you can't stand it;

1.16 ich habe auch nur eine Axt und kein Geld übrig um noch eine zu kaufen.«

I only have one axe and no money left to buy another."

1.17 »Geht nur zum Nachbar.« antwortete der Sohn,

"Just go to your neighbor." replied the son,

1.18 »der leiht Euch seine Axt so lange bis ich mir selbst eine verdient habe.«

"he'll lend you his axe until I've earned one myself."

2.1 Da borgte der Vater beim Nachbar eine Axt, und am anderen Morgen, bei Anbruch des Tages, gingen sie zusammen hinaus in den Wald.

So the father borrowed an axe from the neighbor, and the next morning, at dawn, they went out into the forest together.

Der Sohn half dem Vater und war ganz munter und frisch dabei.   2.2

The son helped his father and was very lively and fresh.

Als nun die Sonne über ihnen stand, sprach der Vater: 2.3

When the sun was high above them, the father said:

»Wir wollen rasten und Mittag halten,   2.4

"Let's rest and have lunch,

hernach geht's noch einmal so gut.«   2.5

then we'll do just as well again."

Der Sohn nahm sein Brot in die Hand und sprach: »Ruht Euch nur aus, Vater, ich bin nicht müde, ich will in dem Wald ein wenig auf und ab gehen und Vogelnester suchen.«   2.6

The son took his bread in his hand and said, "Have a rest, father, I'm not tired, I want to walk up and down the forest a little and look for birds' nests."

»O du Geck.« sprach der Vater,   2.7

"Oh, you fop." said the father,

»was willst du da herumlaufen,   2.8

"what do you want to run about for,

hernach bist du müde und kannst den Arm nicht mehr aufheben;   2.9

you'll be tired afterwards and won't be able to lift your arm;

bleib hier und setze dich zu mir.«   2.10

stay here and sit with me."

3.1 Der Sohn aber ging in den Wald, aß sein Brot, war ganz fröhlich und sah in die grünen Zweige hinein, ob er etwa ein Nest entdeckte.

But the son went into the forest, ate his bread, was quite happy and looked into the green branches to see if he could discover a nest.

3.2 So ging er hin und her, bis er endlich zu einer großen gefährlichen Eiche kam, die gewiß schon viele hundert Jahre alt war und die keine fünf Menschen umspannt hätten.

So he walked to and fro, until at last he came to a great dangerous oak, which was certainly many hundred years old, and which no five men could have spanned.

3.3 Er blieb stehen und sah sie an und dachte,

He stopped and looked at it and thought,

3.4 »Es muß doch mancher Vogel sein Nest hineingebaut haben.«

"Some bird must have built its nest in it."

3.5 Da deuchte ihn auf einmal als hörte er eine Stimme.

Then he suddenly thought he heard a voice.

3.6 Er horchte und vernahm wie es mit so einem recht dumpfen Ton rief:

He listened and heard it call out in a rather muffled tone:

3.7 »Laß mich heraus, laß mich heraus.«

"Let me out, let me out."

3.8 Er sah sich rings um, konnte aber nichts entdecken, doch es war ihm als ob die Stimme unten aus der Erde hervor käme.

He looked around but couldn't see anything, but it seemed to him as if the voice was coming out of the ground below.

Da rief er: »Wo bist du?« Die Stimme antwortete: 3.9

Then he called out, "Where are you?" The voice replied:

»Ich stecke da unten bei den Eichwurzeln. Laß mich   3.10
heraus,

"I'm down there by the oak roots. Let me out,

laß mich heraus.«   3.11

let me out."

Der Schüler fing an unter dem Baum aufzuräumen   3.12
und bei den Wurzeln zu suchen, bis er endlich en
einer kleinen Höhlung eine Glasflasche entdeckte.

The pupil began to tidy up under the tree and search among
the roots until he finally discovered a glass bottle in a small
hollow.

Er hob sie in die Höhe und hielt sie gegen das Licht,   3.13
da sah er ein Ding, gleich einem Frosch gestaltet, das
sprang darin auf und nieder.

He lifted it up and held it up to the light, when he saw a
thing shaped like a frog jumping up and down in it.

»Laß mich heraus, laß mich heraus.«   3.14

"Let me out, let me out."

rief's von neuem, und der Schüler, der an nichts   3.15
Böses dachte, nahm den Pfropfen von der Flasche ab.

it cried again, and the pupil, thinking of no harm, took the
stopper off the bottle.

Alsbald stieg ein Geist heraus und fing an zu   3.16
wachsen, und wuchs so schnell, daß er in, wenigen
Augenblicken als ein entsetzlicher Kerl, so groß wie
der halbe Baum, vor dem Schüler stand.

Immediately a spirit came out and began to grow, and grew
so fast that in a few moments it stood before the pupil as a
horrible fellow as big as half the tree.

3.17 »Weißt du.« rief er mit einer fürchterlichen Stimme,
"You know." he cried in a terrible voice,

3.18 »was dein Lohn dafür ist, daß du mich herausgelassen hast?«
"what is your reward for letting me out?"

3.19 »Nein.« antwortete der Schüler ohne Furcht,
"No." answered the pupil without fear,

3.20 »Wie soll ich das wissen?«
"how should I know?"

3.21 »So will ich dir's sagen.« rief der Geist,
"So I will tell you." cried the ghost,

3.22 »den Hals muß ich dir dafür brechen.«
"I must break your neck for it."

3.23 »Das hättest du mir früher sagen sollen.«
"You should have told me sooner."

3.24 antwortete der Schüler, »so hätte ich dich stecken lassen;
replied the pupil, "so I would have let you get stuck;

3.25 mein Kopf aber soll vor dir wohl feststehen,
but my head must be fixed before you,

3.26 da müssen mehr Leute gefragt werden.«
more people must be asked."

3.27 »Mehr Leute hin, mehr Leute her.« rief der Geist,
"More people here, more people here." cried the ghost,

3.28 »deinen verdienten Lohn sollst du haben.
"you shall have your deserved reward.

Denkst du, ich wäre aus Gnade da so lange Zeit eingeschlossen worden, nein, es war zu meiner Strafe: 3.29

Do you think I was shut up there for so long out of mercy, no, it was for my punishment:

ich bin der großmächtige Merkurius, wer mich losläßt, dem muß ich den Hals brechen.« 3.30

I am the mighty Mercury, whoever lets me go must have his neck broken."

»Sachte.« antwortete der Schüler, 3.31

"Easy." replied the pupil,

»so geschwind geht das nicht, erst muß ich auch wissen, daß du wirklich in der kleinen Flasche gesessen hast und daß du der rechte Geist bist; 3.32

"it can't be done so quickly, first I must know that you have really been in the little bottle and that you are the right spirit;

kannst du auch wieder hinein, so will ich's glauben, und dann magst du mit mir anfangen was du willst.« 3.33

if you can get back in, I will believe it, and then you may do what you like with me."

Der Geist sprach voll Hochmut: »Das ist eine geringe Kunst.« 3.34

The spirit said, full of pride, "That is a small art."

zog sich zusammen und machte sich so dünn und klein wie er anfangs gewesen war, also daß er durch dieselbe Öffnung und durch den Hals der Flasche wieder hineinkroch. 3.35

contracted itself, and made itself as thin and small as it had been at first, so that it crept in again through the same opening and through the neck of the bottle.

3.36 Kaum aber war er darin, so drückte der Schüler den abgezogenen Pfropfen wieder auf und warf die Flasche unter die Eichwurzeln an ihren alten Platz, und der Geist war betrogen.

But as soon as it was in, the pupil pushed the plug back on and threw the bottle under the oak roots into its old place, and the spirit was deceived.

4.1 Nun wollte der Schüler zu seinem Vater zurückgehen, aber der Geist rief ganz kläglich,

Now the pupil wanted to go back to his father, but the spirit called out pitifully,

4.2 »Ach, laß mich doch heraus, laß mich doch heraus.«

"Oh, let me out, let me out."

4.3 »Nein.« antwortete der Schüler, »zum zweitenmal nicht;

"No." replied the pupil, "not for the second time;

4.4 wer mir einmal nach dem Leben gestrebt hat, den laß ich nicht los, wenn ich ihn wieder eingefangen habe.«

I won't let go of anyone who has tried to kill me once when I have caught him again."

4.5 »Wenn du mich frei machst.« rief der Geist,

"If you set me free." cried the spirit,

4.6 »so will ich dir so viel geben, daß du dein Lebtag genug hast.«

"I will give you so much that you will have enough for the rest of your life."

4.7 »Nein.« antwortete der Schüler,

"No." replied the disciple,

»du würdest mich betrügen wie das erste Mal.« 4.8
"you would deceive me as you did the first time."

»Du verscherzest dein Glück.« sprach der Geist, 4.9
"You are making a mistake." said the spirit,

»ich will dir nichts thun, sondern dich reichlich 4.10
belohnen.«
"I will do you no harm, but will reward you richly."

Der Schüler dachte: 4.11
The student thought,

»Ich will's wagen, vielleicht hält er Wort, und 4.12
anhaben soll er mir doch nichts.«
"I'll take a chance, maybe he'll keep his word, and he won't
hurt me."

Da nahm er den Pfropfen ab und der Geist stieg wie 4.13
das vorige Mal heraus,
So he took off the plug and the spirit came out as before,

dehnte sich auseinander und ward groß wie ein 4.14
Riese.
stretched out and became as big as a giant.

»Nun sollst du deinen Lohn haben.« 4.15
"Now you shall have your reward."

sprach er, und reichte dem Schüler einen kleinen 4.16
Lappen, ganz wie ein Pflaster, und sagte,
said he, and handed the disciple a small cloth, like a plaster,
and said,

»Wenn du mit dem einen Ende eine Wunde 4.17
bestreichst,
"If you apply one end to a wound,

4.18 so heilt sie;
it will heal it;

4.19 und wenn du mit dem anderen Ende Stahl und Eisen bestreichst,
and if you apply the other end to steel and iron,

4.20 so wird es in Silber verwandelt.«
it will be turned into silver."

4.21 »Das muß ich erst versuchen.«
"I must try that first."

4.22 sprach der Schüler, ging an einen Baum, ritzte die Rinde mit seiner Axt und bestrich sie mit dem einen Ende des Pflasters:
said the pupil, went to a tree, scratched the bark with his axe, and applied one end of the plaster to it:

4.23 alsbald schloß sie sich wieder zusammen und war geheilt.
it immediately closed up again and was healed.

4.24 »Nun, es hat seine Richtigkeit.« sprach er zum Geist,
"Well, it's all right." he said to the spirit,

4.25 »jetzt können wir uns trennen.«
"now we can part."

4.26 Der Geist dankte ihm für seine Erlösung,
The spirit thanked him for his salvation,

4.27 und der Schüler dankte dem Geist für sein Geschenk und ging zurück zu seinem Vater.
and the pupil thanked the spirit for his gift and went back to his father.

»Wo bist du herumgelaufen?« sprach der Vater,   5.1
"Where have you been running around?" said the father,

»warum hast du die Arbeit vergessen?   5.2
"why have you forgotten to work?

Ich habe es ja gleich gesagt, daß du nichts zustande   5.3
bringen würdest.«
I told you at once that you wouldn't get anything done."

»Gebt Euch zufrieden, Vater, ich will's nachholen.«   5.4
"Be content, father, I will make up for it."

»Ja nachholen.« sprach der Vater zornig,   5.5
"Yes, catch up." said the father angrily,

»das hat keine Art.«   5.6
"it's no good."

»Habt acht, Vater, den Baum da will ich gleich   5.7
umhauen, daß er krachen soll.«
"Take care, father, I will cut down that tree right away so
that it cracks."

Da nahm er sein Pflaster, bestrich die Axt damit und   5.8
that einen gewaltigen Hieb: aber weil das Eisen in
Silber verwandelt war, so legte sich die Schneide um.
Then he took his plaster, coated the axe with it, and struck a
mighty blow, but as the iron was turned to silver, the edge
fell over.

»Ei, Vater, seht einmal, was habt Ihr mir für eine   5.9
schlechte Axt gegeben, die ist ganz schief geworden.«
"Well, father, look what a bad axe you have given me, it is
all crooked."

Da erschrak der Vater und sprach: »Ach,   5.10
Then the father was frightened and said, "Oh,

5.11 **was hast du gemacht!**
what have you done!

5.12 **Nun muß ich die Axt bezahlen und weiß nicht womit;**
Now I have to pay for the axe and I don't know how;

5.13 **das ist der Nutzen, den ich von deiner Arbeit habe.«**
that's the benefit I get from your work."

5.14 **»Werdet nicht bös.« antwortete der Sohn,**
"Don't be angry." answered the son,

5.15 **»die Axt will ich schon bezahlen.«**
"I will pay for the axe."

5.16 **»O, du Dummbart.« rief der Vater,**
"Oh, you fool." cried the father,

5.17 **»wovon willst du sie bezahlen?**
"how will you pay for it?

5.18 **Du hast nichts als was ich dir gebe;**
You have nothing but what I give you;

5.19 **das sind Studentenkniffe, die dir im Kopf stecken, aber zum Holzhacken hast du keinen Verstand.«**
these are student tricks that are stuck in your head, but you have no sense enough to chop wood."

6.1 **Über ein Weilchen sprach der Schüler:**
After a while, the pupil said:

6.2 **»Vater, ich kann doch nichts mehr arbeiten, wir wollen lieber Feierabend machen.«**
"Father, I can't do any more work, we'd better call it a day."

»Ei was.« antwortete er,   6.3
"Well." he replied,

»meinst du, ich wollte die Hände in den Schoß   6.4
legen wie du?
"do you think I want to put my hands in my lap like you?

Ich muß noch schaffen, du kannst dich aber heim   6.5
packen.«
I still have to work, but you can go home."

»Vater, ich bin zum erstenmal hier in dem Walde, ich   6.6
weiß den Weg nicht allein, geht doch mit mir.«
"Father, this is my first time in the forest, I don't know the
way alone, why don't you go with me."

Weil sich der Zorn gelegt hatte,   6.7
When the anger had subsided,

so ließ der Vater sich endlich bereden und ging mit   6.8
ihm heim.
the father finally allowed himself to be persuaded and went
home with him.

Da sprach er zum Sohn: »Geh und verkauf' die   6.9
verschändete Axt und sieh zu, was du, dafür kriegst;
Then he said to his son, "Go and sell the axe, which you
have spoiled, and see what you can get for it;

das übrige muß ich verdienen, um sie dem Nachbar   6.10
zu bezahlen.«
I must earn the rest to pay my neighbor for it."

6.11 Der Sohn nahm die Axt und trug sie in die Stadt zu einem Goldschmied, der probierte sie, legte sie auf die Wage und sprach:
The son took the axe and carried it into the town to a goldsmith, who tried it, put it on the scales and said,

6.12 »Sie ist vierhundert Thaler wert, soviel habe ich nicht bar.«
"It is worth four hundred thalers, I have not that much cash."

6.13 Der Schüler sprach: »Gebt mir was Ihr habt,
The student said: "Give me what you have,

6.14 das übrige will ich Euch borgen.«
I will lend you the rest."

6.15 Der Goldschmied gab ihm dreihundert Thaler und blieb einhundert schuldig.
The goldsmith gave him three hundred thalers and owed him one hundred.

6.16 Darauf ging der Schüler heim und sprach:
The student then went home and said,

6.17 »Vater, ich habe Geld, geht und fragt, was der Nachbar für die Axt haben will.«
"Father, I have money, go and ask what the neighbor wants for the axe."

6.18 »Das weiß ich schon.« antwortete der Alte,
"I already know." replied the old man,

6.19 »einen Thaler sechs Groschen.«
"one thaler and six pennies."

»So gebt ihm zwei Thaler zwölf Groschen, das ist das Doppelte und ist genug; 6.20

"Then give him two thalers twelve groschen, that is double, and is enough;

seht Ihr, ich habe Geld in Überfluß.« 6.21

you see, I have money in abundance."

und gab dem Vater einhundert Thaler und sprach, 6.22

and gave the father one hundred thalers, saying,

»Es soll Euch niemals fehlen, lebt nach Eurer Bequemlichkeit.« 6.23

"You shall never want for it, live at your ease."

»Mein Gott.« sprach der Alte, 6.24

"My God." said the old man,

»wie bist du zu dem Reichtum gekommen?« 6.25

"how did you get so rich?"

Da erzählte er ihm wie alles zugegangen wäre und wie er im Vertrauen auf sein Glück einen so reichen Fang gethan hätte. 6.26

Then he told him how everything had happened and how he had made such a rich catch, trusting in his luck.

Mit dem übrigen Geld aber zog er wieder hin auf die hohe Schule und lernte weiter, und weil er mit seinem Pflaster alle Wunden heilen konnte, ward er der berühmteste Doktor auf der ganzen Welt. 6.27

But with the rest of his money he went back to the high school and continued to study, and because he could heal all wounds with his plaster, he became the most famous doctor in the whole world.

Des Teufels rußiger Bruder

The Devil's Sooty Brother

1.1 Ein abgedankter Soldat hatte nichts zu leben und wußte sich nicht mehr zu helfen.

A soldier who had resigned had nothing to live for and no longer knew how to help himself.

1.2 Da ging er hinaus in den Wald und als er ein Weilchen gegangen war, begegnete ihm ein kleines Männchen, das war aber der Teufel.

So he went out into the forest and when he had walked for a while, he met a little man, but he was the devil.

1.3 Das Männchen sagte zu ihm: »Was fehlt dir?

The little man said to him: "What's wrong with you?

1.4 Du siehst ja so trübselig aus.« Da sprach der Soldat:

You look so gloomy." The soldier said:

1.5 »Ich habe Hunger, aber kein Geld.« Der Teufel sagte:

"I'm hungry, but I have no money." The devil said,

1.6 »Willst du dich bei mir vermieten und mein Knecht sein,

"If you want to hire yourself out to me and be my servant,

so sollst du für dein Lebtag genug haben;   1.7
you shall have enough for the rest of your life;

sieben Jahre sollst du mir dienen,   1.8
you shall serve me for seven years,

hernach bist du wieder frei.   1.9
after which you will be free again.

Aber eins sag ich dir, du darfst dich nicht waschen,   1.10
nicht kämmen, nicht schnippen, keine Nägel und
Haare abschneiden und kein Wasser aus den Augen
wischen.«
But I tell you one thing, you must not wash yourself, comb
your hair or cut your nails, or wipe water from your eyes."

Der Soldat sprach: »Frisch dran,   1.11
The soldier said, "Fresh off,

wenn's nicht anders sein kann.« und ging mit dem   1.12
Männchen fort,
if it can't be helped." and went away with the little man,

das führte ihn geradeswegs in die Hölle hinein.   1.13
who led him straight into hell.

Dann sagte es ihm, was er zu thun hätte: 1.14
Then he told him what he had to do:

er müßte das Feuer schüren unter den Kesseln, wo   1.15
die Höllenbraten drin säßen, das Haus rein halten,
den Kehrdreck hinter die Thür tragen und überall auf
Ordnung sehen;
he must stir up the fire under the cauldrons where the hell-
fry were sitting, keep the house clean, carry the sweepings
behind the door, and see that everything was in order;

1.16 aber guckte er ein einziges Mal in die Kessel hinein,
but if he looked into the cauldrons once,

1.17 so würde es ihm schlimm ergehen. Der Soldat sprach,
he would have a bad time. The soldier said,

1.18 »Es ist gut, ich will's schon besorgen.«
"It's all right, I'll see to it."

1.19 Da ging nun der alte Teufel wieder hinaus auf seine
Wanderung und der Soldat trat seinen Dienst an,
legte Feuer zu, kehrte und trug den Kehrdreck hinter
die Thür, alles wie es befohlen war.
So the old devil went out again on his wanderings, and the
soldier went to his duty, lit the fire, swept up, and carried
the sweepings behind the door, all as ordered.

1.20 Wie der alte Teufel wieder kam, sah er nach, ob alles
geschehen war, zeigte sich zufrieden und ging zum
zweitenmal fort.
When the old devil returned, he checked that everything
had been done, was satisfied and went away for the second
time.

1.21 Der Soldat schaute sich nun einmal recht um da
standen die Kessel ringsherum in der Hölle und war
ein gewaltiges Feuer darunter,
The soldier took a good look around and there were
cauldrons all around him in hell and a huge fire
underneath,

1.22 und es kochte und brutzelte darin.
boiling and sizzling.

1.23 Er hätte für sein Leben gern hineingeschaut, wenn es
ihm der Teufel nicht so streng verboten hätte:
He would have liked to look inside for the life of him if the
devil had not forbidden it so strictly:

endlich konnte er sich nicht mehr anhalten, 1.24
at last he could stop himself no longer,

hob vom ersten Kessel ein klein bißchen den Deckel 1.25
auf und guckte hinein.
lifted the lid of the first cauldron a little and peered inside.

Da sah er seinen ehemaligen Unteroffizier darin 1.26
sitzen:
Then he saw his former sergeant sitting in it:

»Aha, Vogel.« sprach er, »treff' ich dich hier? 1.27
"Aha, bird." he said, "am I meeting you here?

Du hast mich gehabt, jetzt hab' ich dich.« 1.28
You had me, now I've got you."

ließ geschwind den Deckel fallen, 1.29
He quickly dropped the lid,

schürte das Feuer und legte noch frisch zu. 1.30
stoked the fire and added fresh fuel.

Danach ging er zum zweiten Kessel, hob den Deckel 1.31
auch ein wenig auf und guckte, da saß sein Fähnrich
darin:
Then he went to the second cauldron, lifted the lid a little
and looked to see his ensign sitting in it:

»Aha, Vogel, treff' ich dich hier? Du hast mich 1.32
gehabt,
"Aha, bird, will I meet you here? You've had me,

jetzt hab' ich dich.« 1.33
now I've got you."

1.34 machte den Deckel wieder zu und trug noch einen Klotz herbei, der sollte ihm erst recht heiß machen.

He closed the lid again and carried another log over to make him even hotter.

1.35 Nun wollte er auch sehen, wer im dritten Kessel säße, da war's gar ein General:

Now he wanted to see who was sitting in the third cauldron, and it was a general:

1.36 »Aha, Vogel, treff' ich dich hier? Du hast mich gehabt,

"Aha, bird, do I meet you here? You had me,

1.37 jetzt hab ich dich.«

now I've got you."

1.38 holte den Blasbalg und ließ das Höllenfeuer recht unter ihm flackern.

He fetched the bellows and let the hellfire flicker beneath him.

1.39 Also that er sieben Jahre seinen Dienst in der Hölle, wusch sich nicht, kämmte sich nicht, schnippte sich nicht, schnitt sich die Nägel und Haare nicht und wischte sich kein Wasser aus den Augen;

So he did his service in hell for seven years, did not wash himself, did not comb his hair, did not flick his hair, did not cut his nails and hair, and did not wipe the water out of his eyes;

1.40 und die sieben Jahre waren ihm so kurz, daß er meinte, es wäre nur ein halbes Jahr gewesen.

and the seven years were so short to him that he thought it had only been half a year.

Als nun die Zeit vollends herum war, kam der Teufel und sagte,

When the time was quite over, the devil came and said,

1.41

»Nun, Hans, was hast du gemacht?«

"Well, Hans, what have you done?"

1.42

»Ich habe das Feuer unter den Kesseln geschürt,

"I have stoked the fire under the boilers,

1.43

ich habe gekehrt und den Kehrdreck hinter die Thür getragen.«

I have swept and carried the sweepings behind the door."

1.44

»Aber du hast auch in die Kessel geguckt:

"But you also looked into the boilers:

1.45

dein Glück ist, daß du noch Holz zugelegt hast, sonst war dein Leben verloren;

your luck is that you added wood, otherwise your life would have been lost;

1.46

jetzt ist deine Zeit herum, willst du wieder heim?«

now your time is up, do you want to go home again?"

1.47

»Ja.« sagte der Soldat,

"Yes." said the soldier,

1.48

»ich wollt auch gern sehen, was mein Vater daheim macht.«

"I would also like to see what my father is doing at home."

1.49

Sprach der Teufel:

Said the devil:

1.50

»Damit du deinen verdienten Lohn kriegst,

"So that you can get your well-deserved pay,

1.51

1.52 geh und raffe dir deinen Ranzen voll Kehrdreck und nimm's mit nach Haus.

go and grab your satchel full of dirt and take it home with you.

1.53 Du sollst auch gehen ungewaschen und ungekämmt, mit langen Haaren am Kopf und am Bart, mit ungeschnittenen Nägeln und mit trüben Augen, und wenn du gefragt wirst, woher du kämst, sollst du sagen,

You shall also go unwashed and unkempt, with long hair on your head and beard, with untrimmed nails and dull eyes, and when you are asked where you come from, you shall say,

1.54 ›Aus der Hölle,‹

'From hell,'

1.55 und wenn du gefragt wirst, wer du wärst, sollst du sagen,

and when you are asked who you are, you shall say,

1.56 ›Des Teufels rußiger Bruder und mein König auch.

'The devil's sooty brother and my king too.

1.57 «« Der Soldat schwieg still und that, was der Teufel sagte, aber er war mit seinem Lohn gar nicht zufrieden.

The soldier remained silent and did as the devil said, but he was not at all satisfied with his reward.

Sobald er nun wieder oben im Walde war, hob
er seinen Ranzen vom Rücken und wollte ihn
ausschütten; wie er ihn aber öffnete, so war der
Kehrdreck pures Gold geworden.

2.1

As soon as he was back up in the forest, he took his satchel
off his back and wanted to empty it out, but when he
opened it, the dirt had turned to pure gold.

»Das hätte ich mir nicht gedacht.«

2.2

"I would never have imagined it."

sprach er, war vergnügt und ging in die Stadt hinein.

2.3

he said, delighted, and went into the town.

Vor dem Wirtshause stand der Wirt, und wie ihn
der herankommen sah, erschrak er, weil Hans so
entsetzlich aussah, ärger als eine Vogelscheuche.

2.4

The innkeeper was standing in front of the inn, and when
he saw him approaching, he was frightened because Hans
looked so horrible, worse than a scarecrow.

Er rief ihn an und fragte: »Woher kommst du?«

2.5

He called to him and asked: "Where are you from?"

»Aus der Hölle.«

2.6

"From hell."

»Wer bist du?«

2.7

"Who are you?"

»Dem Teufel sein rußiger Bruder und mein König
auch.«

2.8

"The devil's sooty brother and my king too."

296

2.9 Nun wollte der Wirt ihn nicht einlassen, wie er ihm aber das Gold zeigte, ging er und klinkte selber die Thür auf.

Now the innkeeper would not let him in, but when he showed him the gold, he went and unlocked the door himself.

2.10 Da ließ sich Hans die beste Stube geben und köstlich aufwarten, aß und trank sich satt, wusch sich aber nicht und kämmte sich nicht, wie ihm der Teufel geheißen hatte und legte sich endlich schlafen.

Then Hans was given the best parlor and served delicious food, ate and drank his fill, but did not wash or comb his hair as the devil had told him, and finally went to bed.

2.11 Dem Wirt aber stand der Ranzen voll Gold vor Augen und ließ ihm keine Ruhe, bis er in der Nacht hinschlich und ihn wegstahl.

The innkeeper, however, saw the satchel full of gold before his eyes and gave him no rest until he crept out in the night and stole it away.

3.1 Wie nun Hans am anderen Morgen aufstand, den Wirt, bezahlen und weitergehen wollte, da war sein Ranzen weg.

When Hans got up the next morning, paid the innkeeper and wanted to go on his way, his satchel was gone.

3.2 Er faßte sich aber kurz, dachte,

But he made himself short, thought,

3.3 »Du bist ohne Schuld unglücklich gewesen.«

"You have been unhappy through no fault of your own."

und kehrte wieder um, geradezu in die Hölle, da klagte er dem alten Teufel seine Not und bat ihn um Hilfe.

3.4

and turned back, straight to hell, where he complained to the old devil of his misery and asked him for help.

Der Teufel sagte:

3.5

The devil said,

»Setze dich, ich will dich waschen, kämmen, schnippen, die Haare und Nägel schneiden und die Augen auswischen.«

3.6

"Sit down, I will wash you, comb you, flick you, cut your hair and nails and wipe your eyes."

und als er mit ihm fertig war, gab er ihm den Ranzen wieder voll Kehrdreck und sprach:

3.7

And when he had finished with him, he gave him his satchel full of dirt again and said,

»Geh hin und sage dem Wirt, er sollte dir dein Gold wieder herausgeben, sonst wollt ich kommen und ihn abholen, und er sollte an deinem Platz das Feuer schüren.«

3.8

"Go and tell the innkeeper to give you back your gold, otherwise I will come and fetch it, and he should stoke the fire in your place."

Hans ging hinauf und sprach zum Wirt:

3.9

Hans went up and said to the innkeeper,

»Du hast mein Gold gestohlen, giebst du's nicht wieder, so kommst du in die Hölle an meinen Platz, und sollst aussehen so greulich wie ich.«

3.10

"You have stolen my gold, if you do not give it back, you will go to hell in my place, and shall look as hideous as I do."

3.11 Da gab ihm der Wirt das Gold und noch mehr dazu,
Then the innkeeper gave him the gold and more besides,

3.12 und bat ihn nur still davon zu sein;
and only asked him to be quiet about it;

3.13 und Hans war nun ein reicher Mann.
and Hans was now a rich man.

4.1 Hans machte sich auf den Weg heim zu seinem Vater, kaufte sich einen schlechten Linnenkittel auf den Leib, ging herum und machte Musik, denn das hatte er beim Teufel in der Hölle gelernt.
Hans made his way home to his father, bought himself a bad linen smock, went about and made music, for he had learned that from the devil in hell.

4.2 Es war aber ein alter König im Land, vor dem mußte er spielen, und der geriet darüber in solche Freude, daß er dem Hans seine älteste Tochter zur Ehe versprach.
But there was an old king in the country before whom he had to play, and he was so pleased that he promised Hans his eldest daughter in marriage.

4.3 Als die aber hörte, daß sie so einen gemeinen Kerl im weißen Kittel heiraten sollte, sprach sie:
But when she heard that she was to marry such a mean fellow in a white coat, she said,

4.4 »Ehe ich das thät, wollt ich lieber ins tiefste Wasser gehen.«
"Before I do that, I would rather go into the deepest water."

4.5 Da gab ihm der König die jüngste,
Then the king gave him the youngest,

die wollt's ihrem Vater zuliebe gern thun; 4.6

who was glad to do it for her father's sake;

und also bekam des Teufels rußiger Bruder die 4.7
Königstochter, und als der alte König gestorben
war, auch das ganze Reich.

and so the devil's sooty brother got the king's daughter, and
when the old king had died, the whole kingdom as well.

Möwenstein Books

www.mowenstein.com

Renowned Authors

H. G. Wells · Ernest Hemingway
H. P. Lovecraft · Lewis Carroll
Franz Kafka · Friedrich Nietzsche
Albert Einstein · Oscar Wilde
Hans Christian Andersen

Notable Works

Frankenstein · *Alice in Wonderland*
Heart of Darkness · *The Great Gatsby*
Siddhartha · *The Metamorphosis*
Thus Spoke Zarathustra

Translation Services

We offer translation services in various languages, including German, Spanish, Chinese, Korean, Arabic, and more. For custom translations or revisions, please contact us at:

Email: translation@mowenstein.com

Our Collections

Franz Kafka Collection

- The Metamorphosis / Die Verwandlung
- The Trial / Der Prozess
- The Castle / Das Schloss
- and many more...

Pakt mit dem Teufel

- Faust Parts I & II by Johann Wolfgang von Goethe
- Doctor Faustus by Christopher Marlowe

Portraits of Irishmen

- The Picture of Dorian Gray by Oscar Wilde
- A Portrait of the Artist as a Young Man by James Joyce

Children's Classics

- Winnie-the-Pooh / Pu der Bär
- Brothers Grimm Fairy Tales
- Fairy Tales Told for Children
    - Author: Hans Christian Andersen

Visit Us

At Möwenstein Books, we are committed to providing high-quality bilingual editions of classic works. Explore our collections and discover more titles across various genres and languages.

Website: www.mowenstein.com

www.ingramcontent.com/pod-product-compliance
Lightning Source LLC
Chambersburg PA
CBHW030402130626
46549CB00004B/1601